Chinese Regions in Change

This book offers extensive and quality research on and original insights into China's internal regional dynamics. It provides a focused analysis of the internal dynamics and regional economic diversity of China covering the eastern, central and western regions through case study, data analysis and review of state-initiated policy measures.

The book also identifies and analyses existing and potential challenges facing China's regions in their pursuit of sustainable development. Different regions in China have attempted to achieve fast economic growth and move up the industrial value chain through industrial restructuring and upgrading, inter-regional industrial transfer, urbanization or seeking central government's endorsement of new regional policies. The book examines the difference and similarities among local government policies to boost regional industrial and economic growth and assesses their implications and effectiveness. The author had conducted detailed studies in this field in order to bridge the existing research gap and the book will help to give rise to useful and illuminating discussion.

Hong Yu is a research fellow at the East Asian Institute, National University of Singapore. He obtained his PhD from the University of Sheffield. His research interests lie in the field of regional economic development in China. He also has a parallel interest in the areas of industrial development and political economy of China. Dr Yu's research articles have appeared in international journals such as *Journal of Contemporary China*; *East Asia: An International Quarterly*; *China: An International Journal*; *Asian Politics & Policy* and *East Asian Policy*. He is the single author of the book *Economic Development and Inequality in China: the Case of Guangdong* (Routledge, London and New York: 2011).

Chinese Regions in Change

Industrial upgrading and regional
development strategies

Hong Yu

Routledge
Taylor & Francis Group

LONDON AND NEW YORK

First published 2015
by Routledge
2 Park Square, Milton Park, Abingdon, Oxfordshire OX14 4RN

and by Routledge
711 Third Avenue, New York, NY 10017

First issued in paperback 2017

Routledge is an imprint of the Taylor & Francis Group, an informa business

British Library Cataloguing in Publication Data
A catalogue record for this book is available from the British Library

Library of Congress Cataloging-in-Publication Data
Yu, Hong, 1980-
    Chinese regions in change : industrial upgrading and regional development strategies / by Hong Yu.
        pages cm
    1. Economic development—China.   2. Industrial policy—China.
    3. Regional planning—China.   4. Rural development—China.
    5. China—Economic policy.   6. China—Economic conditions.   I. Title.
        HC427.95.Y822 2015
        338.951—dc 3
        2014036581

ISBN 13: 978-1-138-06691-5 (pbk)
ISBN 13: 978-1-138-79275-3 (hbk)

Typeset in Times
by Apex CoVantage, LLC

Contents

Figures

Tables

Appendices

Author biography

Dr Hong Yu is a research fellow at the East Asian Institute, National University of Singapore. He obtained his PhD from the University of Sheffield. His research interests lie in the field of regional economic development in China. He also has a parallel interest in the areas of state-owned enterprises, the railway sector, industrial development and the political economy of China. Dr Yu's research articles have appeared in international journals such as *Journal of Contemporary China; China: An International Journal; East Asia: An International Quarterly; The Copenhagen Journal of Asian Studies; Asian Politics & Policy* and *East Asian Policy*. He is the single author of the book *Economic Development and Inequality in China: the Case of Guangdong* (Routledge, London and New York: 2011). He co-edited the book *China's Industrial Development in the 21st Century* (World Scientific, Singapore: 2011). He is also the author of several book chapters. He has written a number of policy-oriented reports for the reference of the Singapore government on various subjects related to the regional political economy of China.

Preface

China's rapid economic growth over the past three decades has been truly spectacular at all levels, whether domestic, historical or international. China has now become the world's second largest economy after the United States. China's economic miracle since 1978 has been largely driven by investment and foreign trade. Export-oriented and labour-intensive manufacturing industries have boosted China's exports and have been an important force for China's industrial and economic development since the early 1980s. China has now become an important manufacturing factory for the world.

Nevertheless, China's economy is now reaching a critical turning point; its hyper growth era is ending, and economic growth has slowed to a "new normal" growth rate of about 7 per cent per year. China urgently needs to change its economic development model by driving more on its domestic consumption and pursuing a path of green and sustainable development. China's vast geographical and population size, rich regional diversity and internal dynamics are important sources to transfer the current investment and export-driven development model to one more dependent on domestic consumption.

The reality of the rise of China becoming a major power in the world system is coming to fruition. Taking into account the significance of the Chinese economy to the world, this nation's regional development and internal dynamics will generate both domestic and international implications.

The book intends to provide a focused analysis of the internal dynamics and regional economic diversity of China, covering the eastern, central and western regions through case study, data analysis and review of state-initiated policy measures. I have three main objectives in writing this book. First, I intend to illustrate an overall picture of China's regions in change, from industrial upgrading and economic restructuring in the eastern region, to industrial catching up in the central and western regions mainly through inter-regional industrial transfer. Second, by analysing central and local government regional development policies and strategies in China, I intend to offer a scholarly study on the effectiveness of these state-initiated strategies, and make an assessment on the latest regional developments in China. Third, I intend to present and examine the major problems and challenges faced by China's regions in pursuing regional economic development, covering the issues of regional competition and uncoordinated regional development, land-centred urbanization, local GDPism and the emergence of ghost cities.

This book, *Chinese Regions in Change: Industrial Upgrading and Regional Development Strategies*, addresses a relatively uncovered topic in the study of contemporary China, namely regional industrial upgrading and economic restructuring, and development strategies of Chinese regions. What are the latest developments in China's regions? What major changes are happening in China's regions? How well are industrial upgrading and economic restructuring performing in the eastern region? How far can Hainan go to develop itself into an international tourism destination? How to evaluate the effectiveness of inter-regional industrial transfer within China? How effective has the Chinese government's "western development strategy" been in achieving more balanced regional development in the 10 years of its implementation? What are the causes of the emergence of ghost cities in China? What are the problems and challenges faced by China in the urbanization and regional development processes? This book intends to address these issues.

China's regional dynamics could provide the foundation for greater domestic economic growth and a more sustainable growth model in the future. This book, by examining "Chinese regions in change", will offer extensive and high quality research and original insights. The author has conducted detailed studies in this field in seeking to bridge this research gap. I hope this book will give rise to useful and illuminating discussion. The author anticipates that this book will enhance understanding of recent developments in China's various regions and factors underlying their growth and economic problems, and will thus become an essential resource and reference for scholars, policy-makers and business people concerned with China's regional economic development.

This book is not intended to be a research monograph overloaded with academic jargon. I aim to provide an outstanding work of policy research for the reference of policymakers and the business community as well as researchers. In terms of the primary market, it is intended as a prestige and enlightened reference work for policymakers and for businesspersons seeking to enter the Chinese market, either to expand their business presence or explore business opportunities in a different locality in China. In terms of the secondary market, although this book is dedicated to policy-oriented research, it could be valuable supplementary reading for undergraduate and postgraduate students of contemporary Chinese politics and economics.

Some omissions and mistakes may have occurred. I accept full responsibility for any errors in this book's contents.

Acknowledgements

This book derives from policy-oriented research projects at the East Asian Institute (EAI), National University of Singapore. It is a summarization work of my research on the regional development of China over the past several years. Some chapters have been submitted to the Singapore government as internal reference reports.

I acknowledge the financial support from the EAI for my field research trips to Guangdong, Guangxi and Yunnan, China. I would like to express my thanks to the Guangdong, Guangxi and Yunnan governments for permitting me to conduct field research and field interviews with senior officials and other assistance given during my field research. The field research trips allowed me to develop a real sense of the latest developments in cities within Guangdong, Guangxi Beibu Gulf Economic Zone and the city of Kunming individually. It was a rewarding personal experience in terms of writing this book.

Regarding the publication of this book, I dedicate my sincere thanks to many experts, colleagues and close friends. In particular, Professor Zheng Yongnian, Director of the EAI, has read the manuscripts and provided me with many valuable comments in further manuscript revision. He is a brilliant scholar. The intellectual insight that he has shown will remain an enduring inspiration to me.

I would like to express my thanks to the following scholars, I have benefited from their wisdom and constructive comments: Professor Wu Yanrui, Professor Brantly Womack, Dr Gordon Cheung, Dr Michael Heng, Professor Li Chenyang, Dr Liang Bin and Dr Forrest Tan Qingshan. My gratitude also goes to my colleagues at the EAI for their helpful comments and criticisms: Professor John Wong, Professor Lu Ding, Dr Yang Mu, Dr Sarah Tong, Dr Bo Zhiyue, Mr Lye Liang Fook, Ms. Yao Jielu, Ms Catherine Chong and Ms Lim Wen Xin. I am very fortunate to have the support of many prominent scholars at the Institute.

An earlier form of some ideas presented in Chapter 7 was published in the *Asian Politics & Policy* journal. Chapter 2 was published in *China: An International Journal*; Chapter 6 was published in *East Asia: An International Quarterly* journal. I am grateful to these three publishers for giving permission for material and article republication. In addition, many thanks are due for the constructive comments and criticisms provided by the anonymous referees.

I want to take this opportunity to acknowledge my appreciation to Ms Lam Yong Ling of Routledge for welcoming this book and other assistance she provided during the book editing process. As usual, Routledge has served me well. I also want to thank Ms Rachel Grantham, Ms Jessica Loon and Ms Ho Wei Ling for providing efficient and valuable proofreading assistance. They are excellent proofreaders who have served me well. Without them, this book publication would not be possible at this time.

Last but not least, I want to express my heartfelt thanks to my parents, my wife Danlu and my lovely son Jianpeng Alvin for their unconditional love and sacrifice. Writing this book has taken up numerous weekends and much family time. Without their understanding and patience, I could not have started writing this book, let alone have completed it. I dedicate this book to them.

List of abbreviations

AIIB	Asian Infrastructure Investment Bank
ASEAN	Association of Southeast Asian Nations
BGEZ	Beibu Gulf Economic Zone
CCP	Chinese Communist Party
CEPA	Closer Economic Partnership Arrangements
CMQIP	China–Malaysia Qinzhou Industrial Park
CURD	coordinated urban-rural development
FDI	foreign direct investment
FIEs	foreign-invested enterprises
GDP	gross domestic product
GPN	global production network
GRP	gross regional product
GWD	great western development
HSR	high-speed railway
HYEDZ	Hainan Yangpu Economic Development Zone
ICTs	information and communication technologies
IMF	International Monetary Fund
IRIT	inter-regional industrial transfer
JING-JIN-JI	Beijing–Tianjin–Hebei Economic Region
LGFVs	local government-run financing vehicles
MNCs	multinational corporations
MSR	maritime silk road
MVAO	manufactured value-added output
NAO	National Audit Office
NDRC	National Development and Reform Commission
OECD	Organization for Economic Co-operation and Development
PRD	Pearl River Delta
R&D	research and development
S&T	scientific and technology
SEZ	Special Economic Zone
SSHIP	Singapore–Sichuan Hi-Tech Innovation Park
TBNA	Tianjin Binhai New Area
TNCs	transnational corporations
YRD	Yangtze River Delta

1 Introduction

China's double-digit economic growth over the past three decades has been truly spectacular at all levels of comparison, whether domestic, historical or international. China has now become the world's second largest economy, after only the United States. China's economic miracle since the early 1980s has been largely driven by investment and foreign trade. Export-oriented and labour-intensive industries have boosted China's exports and have been an important force for China's rapid industrialization and economic development during the reform and opening up period; essentially, China has now become a major global manufacturing factory.

Nevertheless, China's economy is now reaching a critical turning point; its double-digit growth era is ending. China's economic growth is slowing to about 7 per cent per year, as the "new normal" rate of growth. China's economic growth model, based on over-investment, over-export and under-consumption, is not sustainable.

Industries located in the eastern coastal region of China have faced increasing pressure to deal with fast rising labour and production costs, as well as appreciation of China's currency, the yuan, over the past several years. These factors have pushed up the prices of Chinese-manufactured labour-intensive products and affected the competitiveness of Chinese industrial goods in the foreign market. Even worse, China's exports to Western developed nations have dropped substantially since 2008 due to weak consumption demands for Chinese products, brought about by the Western economic crisis. In addition, as the European debt crisis is far from being resolved and in the wake of the slow US economic recovery, it is estimated that China's export-oriented industries, for example, the thousands of manufacturing concerns in its coastal eastern region, are likely to further feel the chill. Against this backdrop, the central and local governments have pumped in huge amounts of capital investment to further stimulate the gross domestic product (GDP) growth rate; this is especially true since the outbreak of global economic crisis in 2008.

What is more, China's economic development has heavily relied on the consumption of fossil fuel energy and other mineral resources. This development model has caused severe and worsening environmental pollution that poses a direct and unacceptable threat to human well-being.

Taking these factors into account, China urgently needs to change its economic development model by driving more on its domestic consumption and pursuing a path of green and sustainable development. Its vast geographical and population size, rich regional diversity and enormous regional development disparity are the keys to its transformation from the current investment and export-driven development model to one more dependent on domestic consumption.

The Chinese government has acknowledged the urgent need to transform China's economic development model and has adopted various policy measures to stimulate domestic consumption over the past several years. China's long-term sustainable development is irrevocably tied up with its internal dynamics and regional diversity. The new Chinese government, led by President Xi Jinping (习近平) and Prime Minster Li Keqiang (李克强), has identified urbanization and regional diversity as new engines to boost domestic economic growth in China. Rapid high-quality urbanization and balanced regional development will not only help to boost construction of urban transport, housing and other infrastructure, but could also unleash the huge potential of domestic consumption through steadily increasing income of the enormous rural population. According to the National New-type of Urbanization Plan (2014–2020) published by the Chinese government in 2014, the rate of urbanization in China is set to reach 60 per cent by 2020, up from 53.7 per cent in 2013. Large-scale modern inter-regional transport facilities such as high-speed railway (HSR) have paved the way for greater integration of the national market and forged regional economic agglomeration centred on the emergence of megacity clusters.

The development of HSR is perhaps one of the most significant technological advances for China in socio-economic terms. HSR will help to achieve more balanced regional development between the eastern, central and western regions, and it thereby could fundamentally reshape the economic geography of China in the future. The Chinese central government has promised to pour more investment into construction of HSR and other important inter-regional transportation projects to improve connectivity of the underdeveloped central and western regions with the developed eastern region in the coming decade, including the ongoing construction of the Lanzhou–Xinjiang, Chengdu–Chongqing and Yunnan–Guangxi rail lines.

The rapid expansion of HSR nationally will help the underdeveloped central and western regions to achieve more economic spillover effects from the prosperous coastal eastern region and will facilitate the communication of people, technology and information, and thus integrate the fragmented regional markets and boost development of China's under-developed cities. According to Zheng and Kahn's empirical analysis,[1] HSR has enhanced spatial economic agglomeration and improved market access in China.

China has become a major global player. Taking into account the significance of the Chinese economy to the world, its regional development and internal dynamics will have both domestic and international implications. China's regional dynamics could provide the foundation for greater domestic economic growth and a more sustainable growth model in the future. The chapters outline the importance of internal dynamics and regional diversity to China's long-term sustainable economic development.

Previous scholarly research has very much focused on regional development disparities in China and the various internal and external factors contributing to regional development (for example, Dennis Wei's book *Regional Development in China: State, Globalisation, and Inequality*[2] and Hong Yu's *Regional Economic Development and Inequality in China: The Case of Guangdong*). Meanwhile, important issues arising from such as industrial upgrading, inter-regional industrial transfer, and urbanization in different localities in China, linkages in China's regional dynamics, and potential for transformation of China's development model to one of sustainable economic growth have rarely been examined in detail. Taking this into account, it is timely to examine these urgent issues. To date, few works have considered the significance of the state's regional policies and internal dynamics to sustainable economic development in China, industrial upgrading and inter-regional industrial transfer. Neither have the impacts of problems deriving from the state's regional development policies come under scrutiny, such as the emergence of ghost cities and the land-centred urbanization.

The Chinese government has come to acknowledge the serious problems created by its ill-designed regional policies on urbanization. Xu Shaoshi, the Director of the National Development and Reform Commission of China, gave a report to the Executive Committee of the National People's Congress, China's parliament, in June 2013 in which it was admitted that over 200 million migrant workers and their families have so far failed to integrate into the cities, or to enjoy the same level of social welfare benefits as the urban population, in terms of employment, education, health care, housing and pensions, whilst at the same time the state has invested in many wasteful and redundant infrastructure projects.[3] This being the case, China needs to move away from land-centred and new city construction-driven urbanization and to focus instead on high-quality, people-centred urbanization to equalize access to public services between urban and rural populations, including social welfare and security provision, and income growth among the rural population.

China is a vast and fast developing country, with huge regional diversity; hence it is impossible to deal with all dimensions of regional development or to discuss all the associated problems and challenges. Bearing this in mind, this book, *Chinese Regions in Change: Industrial Upgrading and Regional Development Strategies*, strives to address all the major issues concerning China's regional development and government's regional policies. The chapters of the proposed book are structured to reflect the diversity, disparity and internal dynamics in the development of China's regions.

Previous scholarly studies have covered in depth the concept of the "developmental state" in relation to East Asian economic development. Robert Wade's 1990 book,[4] for example, provides detailed case study analysis on the role played by the state in supporting industrial development and economic growth in Taiwan and Japan. In addition, a World Bank study (1993)[5] has discussed the various factors contributing to the economic miracle of East Asia, with particular reference to the role of the government. However, previous research has rarely applied the concept of developmental state to examine the role of state strategies in development of regions or sub-regions in China. The active role played by local governments and provision of preferential policies by the state have contributed to the rapid industrial and economic growth enjoyed by the eastern region. In the case of Guangdong, Fan's study (1995) describes how foreign trade and financial policies offered by the Chinese central government in the post-1978 era benefited economic development in the region.[6] Yu's book (2011), meanwhile, has illustrated how state-initiated preferential treatments in various forms, such as taxation reduction, land use rights and foreign trade, have favoured the Pearl River Delta at the expense of inland northern and eastern regions within Guangdong.[7]

Based on intensive secondary and primary field research, the different chapters present an overall picture of diversified regional development in China, from industrial upgrading in the eastern region to inter-regional industrial transfer in the central and western regions. Focused critical analysis is provided on the subject of China's internal dynamics and regional economic development, including the supra-regional (Beijing–Tianjin–Hebei in Chapter 5, Central and Western China in Chapters 6 and 7), regional (Guangdong in Chapter 2 and Hainan in Chapter 6), as well as the sub-regional (Guangzhou–Foshan megacity in Chapter 3, Nansha District in Chapter 4 and Chengdu in Chapter 8), and the book assesses development initiatives implemented by local and sub-regional governments.

The examination of the internal dynamics of China and problems associated with regional policy implementations is based on case study, field interview data analysis and review of state-initiated policy measures. Different regions in China have attempted to achieve fast economic growth and move up the industrial value chain through industrial restructuring and upgrading, inter-regional industrial transfer, urbanization or seeking central government's endorsement of new regional policies. The book also examines the difference and similarities among local government policies to boost regional industrial and economic growth and assesses their implications and effectiveness. In addition, the major challenges facing China's regions in their pursuit of sustainable development are addressed, including inter-regional industrial competition, slow progress of industrial upgrading and difficulty in transferring industries among regions, emergence of ghost cities, and soaring local government debt.

Guangdong has been in the vanguard of the economic reforms and opening up that have occurred in China since 1978. Industrial production in Guangdong expanded rapidly, which in turn led to rapid growth in the economy. Chapter 2 examines this process of fast industrialization, and how Guangdong has since developed to become an industrial powerhouse for the world. It also discusses the internal and external pressures Guangdong has been under in recent years to increase its industrial competitiveness and undertake industrial upgrading. Industrial upgrading has been the focal point of the government's regional economic policies since the early 2000s. However, problematic industrial policies have thwarted the government's aspirations for industrial upgrading rather than speeding up the process, as examined in this chapter. In addition, Guangdong's aspirations to move up the value chain have met with various obstacles and challenges. Guangdong's industrial development is still mainly driven by low-end and low value-added manufacturing industry, and the status quo of Guangdong as the world's low-end assembly and processing base remains unchanged.

Guangdong is an important economic powerhouse of China and a highly developed and prosperous region. Chapter 3 discusses how the Guangdong government is seeking to speed up the urbanization process via the formation of megacities or city clusters, as in the case of the plan for Guangzhou–Foshan megacity. The inspiration for this megacity derives from the existence of close historical relations and cultural links between the two cities of Guangzhou and Foshan. Furthermore, industrial complementarity within Guangzhou–Foshan area provided a foundation for development of an integrated regional market. Moves to integrate Guangzhou and Foshan have already been initiated, in particular integration of the two cities' transportation systems. Such integration is likely to benefit the residents by bringing down living costs and will also boost inter-city business and leisure interchange. However, administrative and bureaucratic barriers will need to be broken down if this megacity is to achieve full integration.

Chapter 4 offers a detailed analysis of Guangzhou Nansha New District, another rising star of Guangdong. The Chinese central government has given Nansha the opportunity of economic rejuvenation and playing a lead role in the economic transformation of the Pearl River Delta (PRD) region. In September 2012, the Chinese central government mapped out a plan for a new national development area, featuring a new blueprint for Nansha. The economic performance of Nansha makes it a fast growing area in the PRD region. Nansha is targeted to achieve breakthroughs in key reform areas, including administration, economic and social management, involving implementation of a wide range of pilot programmes. However, the current institutional framework and administration structure reflect that the Nansha government lacks the authority to exercise real autonomy over local development, implement reform initiatives or achieve reform breakthroughs.

Chapter 5 examines another area driving the development of Eastern China, the Beijing–Tianjin–Hebei economic region (Jing-Jin-Ji). This region has tremendous political advantages with which no other region in China can compete. Its comparative political advantage derives from Beijing being the national capital and political centre of China. Close proximity to central government has hence facilitated communications for the local governments within this region in gaining support from ministries.

The Jing-Jin-Ji region has benefited from strong Chinese government support and experienced rapid economic growth over the last decade, driven by domestic investment and consumption. The rapid development of Tianjin Binhai New Area, with high-tech industry taking the lead, has boosted economic growth in the Jing-Jin-Ji region despite the global economic crisis of 2008. The economic influence of this region is expected to increase in the next decade as it has abundant human resources and well-developed infrastructure. Nevertheless, water shortage could threaten the sustainability of the region's socio-economic development.

Moreover, lack of industrial cooperation within the region has resulted in duplicated developments and cut-throat competition.

The Chinese central government has identified tourism as an important means of stimulating domestic consumption and transforming China's economic development pattern from investment and export driven to consumption led. According to the government's new plan released in 2009, development of Hainan as an International Tourism Destination has been upgraded to a national strategy. By critically discussing the Western theories on the policy-making process, Chapter 6 intends to adopt the case study of Hainan to specifically analyze its state-initiated plan for regional tourism development.

Hainan is the only province in China to clearly be identified by the government for the development of its tourism into a mainstay industry. It is intended to become a test zone for China's tourism reform and innovation and take a lead in development of tourism and associated industries. The government believes that the tourism sector is a key means of boosting regional economic development and reducing regional disparities between Hainan and the prosperous eastern provinces. Nevertheless, Hainan still faces serious obstacles to its goal of becoming a top Asia Pacific holiday destination. A lack of skilled personnel, backward transport network and poor service standards in tourism and hospitality are persistent and pressing issues.

The development of China's central regions is essential to the nation's achievement of balanced regional development. In Chapter 7, regional focus and discussion shifted to the central region. Although central China has achieved a reasonable rate of growth, it lags far behind the prosperous eastern region in terms of development, and its share of the nation's GDP is gradually dwindling. This chapter examines the Chinese central government's rejuvenation plan for the central region announced in September 2009, and it evaluates the economic competitiveness of the central region. The author suggests that state-backed efforts to reduce economic gaps have been hindered by unfavourable geography, the weak foundations of the central region's economy, and self-reinforcing industrial agglomeration in the eastern region.

Chapter 8 offers a critical discussion on the state-initiated "Great Western Development" (GWD) strategy and assesses its effectiveness. Since the late 1990s, Chinese leaders have been increasingly concerned with the huge gap between the wealthy eastern and poor western regions and the deteriorating developmental trend. In response, in 1999, Beijing adopted the GWD strategy, which is the state's key initiative in tackling the issue of China's widening regional disparity. The main policies of the GWD strategy include providing preferential treatments and facilitating huge fiscal transfers to western China. The government has also invested heavily in western transportation improvement. Compared to the pre-2000 period, the GWD strategy has slightly reversed the declining development trend in the western region vis-à-vis the eastern and central regions of China. However, Beijing's efforts since 1999 to achieve more balanced regional development have yet to bear much fruit, as by 2012, the western region still accounted for less than 20 per cent of China's GDP. Beijing has yet to find an effective solution to the issue of regional inequality.

Nevertheless, in the western region, a few cities have emerged as economic centres to boost development in the region. For example, as discussed in Chapter 9, Chengdu, the provincial capital of Sichuan, has become a rising economic star and one of the world's fastest-growing cities in recent years. Chengdu's strategic geographical location offers excellent links with other regions of China. In achieving its remarkable economic growth Chengdu has been one of the main beneficiaries of the state-driven western development initiative launched in 1999. Attracted by its strategic location and preferential state policies, multinational corporations have shown growing interest in pursuing business opportunities in Chengdu.

The inland western region has opened its doors to the world, and its local governments are keen to access the international market and attract foreign investment by participating in the economic globalization process. Chapter 10 examines the development potential of Beibu Gulf Economic Zone (BGEZ), Guangxi. The BGEZ is one of the most prosperous areas in Guangxi. The China–Malaysia Qinzhou Industrial Park, located in this zone, is a case in point. It was officially established in September 2012 and is the only government-to-government project located in western China. Guangxi is perceived as the gateway for China–ASEAN (Association of Southeast Asian Nations) cooperation as it is the only province in China with both land and sea access to ASEAN countries and the only western province with a sea gateway. The Guangxi government is very active in initiating proposals to promote bilateral cooperation between China and ASEAN member states; it is hence eager to take on the "Maritime Silk Road of the 21st Century" initiative announced by the Chinese central government in 2013. The Guangxi government is striving to make Guangxi a key part of this initiative and thereby to create new dynamics within the Beibu Gulf Zone that will boost economic development.

The Chinese government seeks to forge a local complementary network of regional industrial production for more balanced regional industrial development. Chapter 11 examines inter-regional industrial transfer (IRIT) in China, which is one of the most significant stimuli of industrial and economic growth in the central and western regions, and discusses its effectiveness and problems. The development experience of China's coastal region demonstrates that vibrant and prosperous manufacturing industries are the foundation for broad-based economic development. The IRIT is thus crucial to enhancing the industrial and economic competitiveness of China's inland regions. Labor-intensive industries in coastal China have been shifting to the country's interior since the early 2000s, and several national-level inter-regional industrial transfer zones have been successively established in the central and western regions. Statistics show that that the pace of IRIT to central China is faster than such transfer to western China. However, the remote and mountainous geography, self-reinforced agglomeration effect of the eastern region, underdeveloped educational system and international competition are hindrances to the success of IRIT.

Chapter 12 examines the issue of ghost cities. Some Chinese cities are now notoriously known as ghost cities because of their impressive but empty skyscrapers, luxury apartments, magnificent squares and wide roads. These ghost cities are a result of excessive housing and infrastructure construction and speculation on property demand. As shown in this chapter, these ghost cities are by-products of the Great Leap style of urbanization in China. To the local governments, urbanization means more big investment in large-scale development projects and building of new cities. The emergence of ghost cities is a consequence of China's land-centred urbanization which has outpaced the urbanization of people.

Land-cantered urbanization is rooted in local GDP-ism, which in turn results in aggressive developmentalism and excessive investment on the part of China's local governments. Under the state's urbanization push, local authorities have rushed to build new cities and towns, literally creating an inter-regional competition for city building. As a result of the local governments' heavy investment in public transport, real estate and new city/town building, local government debt has risen sharply since 2008. This rush to invest is explained by the fact that under fiscal law of 1994, local governments are not allowed to directly borrow money from banks or to issue bonds. Many local governments therefore circumvent this restriction by setting up local government-run financing vehicles (LGFVs) to fund local infrastructure projects.

A National Audit Office (NAO) report, published in December 2013,[8] provided a rare glimpse of the real size of local government liability. The NAO conducted a full audit of a total of 427 provincial, municipal and county-level governments within 31 provinces, covering 62,215 government departments and affiliated organizations, and 7,170 LGFVs. This local government debt includes direct and indirect liabilities, and guaranteed debt. Local government debt in China amounted to 17.9 trillion yuan in June 2013, of which nearly 60 per cent (9.8 trillion yuan) was generated by government investment in housing and transport facilities. Individually, two provincial governments, 99 city governments and 195 county governments have ratios of outstanding debt to individual annual fiscal revenue of above 100 per cent. These figures imply that nearly 70 per cent of local governments audited do not have the capacity to pay off their debt, which is an ominous sign for China. To compound this situation, more than 61 per cent of local government debt was due to be paid by 2015.

Notes

1 Zheng, Siqi, and Kahn, Matthew E. (2013). "China's bullet trains facilitate market integration and mitigate the cost of megacity growth", *PNAS Early Edition*, published online 18 March 2013, pp. 1–6.
2 Wei, Yehua Dennis. (2000). *Regional Development in China: State, Globalization, and Inequality*, London: Routledge.
3 Xu Shaoshi. (2013). "The Report of the State Council Regarding the Work of Urbanization to the Executive Committee of the National People's Congress", http://www.npc. gov.cn/npc/zxbg/czhjsgzqk/2013-06/27/content_1798667.htm (accessed 27 August 2014)
4 Wade, Robert. (1990). *Governing the Market: Economic Theory and the Role of Government in East Asian Industrialization*, Princeton: Princeton University Press.
5 World Bank. (1993). *The East Asian Miracle: Economic Growth and Public Policy*, Oxford: Oxford University Press.

6 Fan, Cindy C. (1995). "Of belts and ladders: state policy and uneven regional development in post-Mao China", *Annals of the Association of American Geographers*, 85:3, pp. 421–429.
7 Yu Hong. (2011). *Economic Development and Inequality in China: The case of Guangdong*, London and New York: Routledge.
8 National Audit Office of China, "*Quanguo zhengfuxing zhaiwu shenji jieguo*" (Audit Figures on National and Local Government Debt), 30 December 2013, Beijing, pp. 1–13.

2 Industrial upgrading in Guangdong

Introduction

Guangdong province has played an important role in China's economic reforms and opening up since 1978. It was the first province to implement reform policies that transform China's centrally planned economy to a market economy. The province has benefited from China's economic opening up and the relocation of labour-intensive and export-oriented industrial production from Asia's industrialised economies to Guangdong. Industrial production in Guangdong has expanded rapidly, which in turn led to rapid growth in the economy. The coastal Pearl River Delta (PRD) region, which refers to the province's nine major cities along the Pearl River, namely Guangzhou, Shenzhen, Zhuhai, Foshan, Jiangmen, Dongguan, Zhongshan, Huizhou and Zhaoqing, has attained exemplary rapid growth. In addition to the abundant supply of cheap labour and its geographic proximity to the neighbouring economies of East and Southeast Asia, the region has also benefited from a well-developed infrastructure. These advantages, combined with favourable government policies, provided strong incentives for foreign investors to set up production facilities in the region, during the early stages of China's economic reform. Fast industrialisation followed, and Guangdong has since developed to become the industrial powerhouse for the nation.

Nevertheless, Guangdong understands that competitive advantages based on cheap labour and land do not guarantee long-term growth for the future, because these industries will be eventually transferred to the western and inland regions of China with more abundant labour supply and lower wages and land costs. Guangdong is not only facing various internal pressures such as dramatic rise in labour and production costs and Chinese currency appreciation, but it is also under external pressures to increase its competitiveness and improve industrial performance in face of the shrinking demand in the Western markets for its manufactured goods caused by the 2008 global economic crisis.

However, many obstacles and difficulties have hindered Guangdong's aspirations to move up the value chain and achieve industrial upgrading from labour-intensive and low-end activities to that of skill intensive, high technology and high value-added. In this respect, Guangdong is at a crossroads. Its success in industrial upgrading will decide the destiny of this southern province.

A summary of literature review on industrial upgrading and Guangdong's experience

Productivity growth forms the basis for sustainable economic development. Industrial upgrading and technological improvement of existing manufacturing activities are vital ingredients to achieving productivity growth. Gereffi[1] defines industrial upgrading as "a process of improving the ability of a firm or an economy to move to more profitable and/or technologically sophisticated capital and skill-intensive economic niches". Humphrey and Schmitz's study[2] describes the three different phases of upgrading which industrial firms have to undertake – process upgrading (highly efficient transformation of input and output); product upgrading (adoption of more sophisticated forms of production); and functional upgrading (acquiring new functions in the production chain).

An economy must constantly pursue technological innovation and move up the value chain by producing value-added and high-technology products. The economic success of a region depends on its capacity to strengthen comparative advantage and compete in newly emerging industries. For a region or nation, competitive advantage based merely on cheap land and labour costs, or abundant natural resources, is closely associated with low-end and low value-added industrial activities and is deemed to be unsustainable in the long term. When labour and other production costs increase in a region, the labour-intensive and low-end manufacturing firms located in this region are compelled to relocate to other regions with lower wages and more abundant supply of cheap labour. Lall's research[3] categorises export-oriented products by technology activity. Based on Lall's study, resource-based products are classified as simple and labour-intensive production, low-technology products generally involve stable and well-diffused technologies, while many other products compete on price with little differentiation. Medium-technology products involve both skill and scale-intensive technologies in intermediate products and capital goods. On the other hand, high-technology products incorporate advanced technologies with emphasis on product design and are characterised by high level of research and development (R&D) investment.

Ozawa[4] outlines the theory on industrial upgrading and growth clustering in the East Asian context. He theorises that the evolutionary process of regional industrial upgrading will occur in five successive stages, from labour-driven, scale-driven, assembly-driven, R&D-driven to information technology-driven (IT) industrial development. Ozawa stresses that industrial upgrading process will continue until the top rung of the development ladder is reached. He further emphasises that the industrial catch-up process for developing regions is more than simply borrowing advanced knowledge and technologies from the developed regions; in fact, developing nations need to concentrate their efforts on driving indigenous innovation and supporting home-grown companies to generate original knowledge.

Developing regions cannot solely rely on transferred technologies from foreign direct investment (FDI) and overseas companies to boost industrial upgrading efforts. To maintain their technological supremacy, foreign companies are not willing to set up major research centres or conduct advanced R&D activities in emerging countries. Lall points out that to make efficient use of the imported technology, it is imperative for the host countries to create new knowledge and skills to master the technology's tacit elements. In addition, to facilitate foreign companies' transfer of technologies and more advanced equipment and functions, developing countries must be equipped with a strong educational and training base to develop the capabilities of local suppliers as well as technological skills to provide advanced services. Lall stresses that an FDI-dependent strategy cannot be substituted for domestic capability building. Dunning[5] argues that the actual contribution of inward FDI to industrial upgrading of host countries largely depends on government policies and various characteristics of the host nations. Often, inward FDI can be damaging to indigenous capability upgrading by limiting local industrial production to low value-added activities and inevitably driving large imports of high-end and value-added intermediate components.

In response to the rapid globalization and changing global distribution of consumption and production, Yeung, Henderson and others, in a series of research papers, proposed a new theoretical framework called global production network (GPN) for the analysis of regional development and industrial upgrading. According to Henderson et al.,[6] the framework of GPNs consists of three key elements, namely value (comprising the creation, enhancement and capture of value), power (corporate, collective and institutional) and embeddedness (territorial and network). Citing the case of East Asian economies, Yeung's research[7] argues that regional development is closely associated with the GPNs through the dynamic processes of strategic coupling between local actors (e.g. local firms and institutions) and leading transnational corporations (TNCs). Drawing upon the GPN perspective in manufacturing context, TNCs outsource their low-end and low value-added manufacturing activities to other independent manufacturers located in the low-cost regions to reduce cost and achieve product flexibility, while retaining control of high value-added activities.

Coe et al.,[8] however, argue that regional development is driven by the processes of value creation, enhancement and capture through the strategic coupling of GPNs. As the strategic coupling process is contingent and variable, it should not be assumed that the region will automatically benefit from the process. In the context of intensive global competition, the study outlines the interactive and complementary coupling effects between local factors and the strategic needs of lead TNCs (e.g. the agglomeration of upstream and downstream industries on the supply side, preferential tax treatments and abundant supply of skilled labour) within the global production networks in stimulating regional economic growth.

Yeung points out that whether a region can successfully achieve regional development and industrial upgrading depends on its capability to be articulated into the GPNs. In global production networks, theoretically, a region can break out from the "locked-in" development trajectory to pursue industrial upgrading and economic restructuring in times of an external economic crisis and when the region's local assets are complementary to the strategic needs of TNCs embedded within the GPNs. What GPN framework has failed to explain adequately is the evolution process of GPNs and the type of structural preconditions that will help form and shape such networks. In this respect, Henderson *et al.* also point out that "what cannot be shown, of course, is the evolution of the GPN over time (path dependency) and structural preconditions shaping it (such as different national capitalisms or national modes of regulation)".[9]

However, the GPN theoretical framework demonstrates that the government plays an important role in creating local environment and regional assets that align with the strategic needs of leading transnational corporations, and this encourages regional development whereby regions actively participate in the value-added production networks of TNCs and pursue industrial upgrading and economic development. The government also plays an important role in achieving industrial upgrading. The implementation of state industrial policy will thus create new competitive advantage, thereby nurturing and supporting emerging industries with high value-added technologies as well as achieving sustainable economic development. This is corroborated in Ozawa's study, which highlights the significance of industrial policy in achieving industrial upgrading and knowledge-driven economic growth in Japan. Michael Porter[10] also discusses the role of government in industrial upgrading and economic restructuring. According to Porter's study, the government should create an environment that is conducive for firms to introduce new technology and production methods, and to strengthen competitive advantage as entrants of newly emerging industries of higher productivity. Nevertheless, Porter argues that government alone cannot successfully create competitive and efficient industries as the onus is ultimately on the firms to put in efforts to innovate. Governments may play a crucial role, albeit an indirect one. Government policy should therefore focus on encouraging firms to pursue improved productivity and technological enhancement, and not become too directly involved in industrial upgrading per se.

The state should also encourage companies to play a prominent role in factor creation. However, in areas where individual firms are unable to invest or fail to obtain results, such as state-sponsored R&D programmes, education and infrastructure provision, the state should be called upon to play a key role to support industrial upgrading through investment and active involvement in the said areas.[11] In pursuit of technological advancement and increased productivity, it is crucial that firms have a large ready pool of skilled labour and human resources at their disposal. Therefore, achieving high industrial productivity or increase competitive advantage is impossible if there is no improvement in people's skills and general education. Porter argues that the government should work closely with the industrial sectors and research organisations to set up proper skills training centres. Companies should also invest in in-house training to continually upgrade and improve skills of their own labour force. In addition, due to technological spillovers and externalities generated from R&D, the government's industrial policy should pay more attention to R&D activities.

There are many previous studies done on Guangdong's economic development. The research conducted by Vogel[12] and Sung *et al.*[13] offers detailed discussion on the leading economic position of Guangdong in China. Cheng's research[14] highlights that Guangdong has become a testing ground for state development initiatives and measures over the past three decades after Beijing granted Guang-dong permission to implement preferential policies. Yu's research[15] provides a comprehensive analysis on Guangdong's economic development and the widen-ing disparity during the reform period. Many previous studies[16] have focused on discussion of Guangdong's economic success and the so-called Guangdong devel-opment model, which is based on preferential state policies, inflow of FDI and trade. There are, however, few studies that investigate the link between regional industrial upgrading in China and the various above-mentioned theories.

Guangdong is the core of China's economic and industrial prowess. Industries have played a crucial role in local economic development of Guangdong over the past three decades. From the long-term industrial restructuring and upgrading perspective, Guangdong's reliance on low-skill and low value-added manufac-turing industries to maintain its export competitiveness should be viewed as a transitory and temporary, rather than permanent approach. Guangdong, with its successful industrial take-off over the past three decades, needs to prove that it is still dynamic and resilient and that it still has the capability to adapt to changes. In view of its remarkable industrial development and economic take-off, Guangdong province was chosen as a case study for this chapter. This chapter analyses Guang-dong's prospects, current progress and challenges in industrial upgrading, and the problems caused by government initiatives, and at the same time, examines the theoretical explanations offered by various literature.

Industrial take-off in Guangdong

Guangdong, one of China's most developed industrial centres and a manufac-turing base of worldwide importance, has achieved economic take-off and rapid growth over the past three decades. The per capita gross domestic product (GDP) of Guangdong had increased from 370 yuan in 1978 to 54,095 yuan in 2012, reg-istering an average growth of 15.8 per cent during the period. The total regional GDP of Guangdong reached 5,706.8 billion yuan in 2012 from 18.6 billion yuan in 1978. The average economic growth rate was 18.3 per cent for the period between 1978 and 2012.[17] Guangdong is the core of China's economic and indus-trial prowess; it is not only one of the most prosperous and economically power-ful regions in China, but also a leader in terms of economic openness. In 2010, Guangdong accounted for 13.3 per cent and 11.4 per cent of national value-added industrial output and GDP, respectively; it also contributed more than 21 per cent of FDI inflow to China and more than a quarter of the total exports from and total imports to China.

Significantly, the export-oriented manufacturing industries have played a cru-cial role in the economic success of Guangdong since 1978. Guangdong's dramatic economic take-off is driven by rapid industrialisation, thereby causing a boom in the manufacturing industries which in turn contribute to Guangdong's economic wealth. Guangdong's value-added industrial output increased to 2,581.0 billion yuan in 2012 from 7.6 billion yuan in 1978. Value-added industries accounted for 45.2 per cent of provincial GDP of Guangdong in 2012, up from 36.0 per cent in 1980 (Figure 2.1).

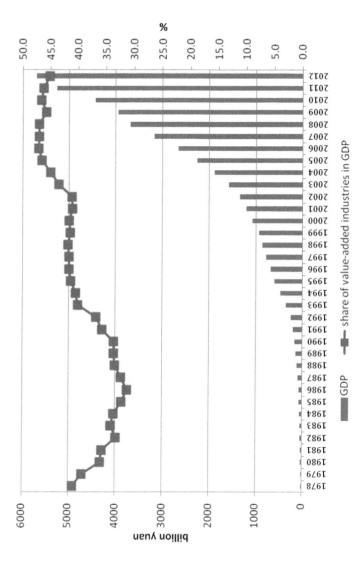

Figure 2.1 GDP and the contribution of value-added industries in Guangdong, 1978–2012

Note: Data are based on current rate.

Source: Guangdong Provincial Bureau of Statistics, *Guangdong Statistical Yearbook*, various years.

Since 1978, the huge inflow of FDI has been crucial in propelling the rapid industrialisation of Guangdong and aggressive development of export-driven manufacturing industries, particularly in several parts of the eastern coastal PRD. The inflow of FDI to Guangdong rose by more than 110 times to USD24.1 billion in 2012 from merely USD0.21 billion in 1980. This is essential in fuelling the province's industrialisation and its rapid growth. Guangdong's industries are sustained by the strong presence of foreign firms. Within the region's largest industry – the manufacturing of communication equipment, computers and other electronic equipment – foreign firms accounted for more than half of all firms, producing nearly three-quarters of the industry's total output and close to three-fifths of its value added in 2009. This industry is also highly export oriented, shipping more than three-quarters of the products to markets outside mainland China.

Foreign-invested enterprises (FIEs) also play important roles in other pillar industries in Guangdong. FIEs' contribution to total output in transport equipment manufacturing, raw materials and chemical products manufacturing, and textiles and clothing industries were 82 per cent, 62 per cent and 50 per cent, respectively.[18] Hong Kong, in particular, has played an important role in the rapid industrialisation of Guangdong over the past three decades, providing the much-needed advanced technology, capital and knowledge for Guangdong's economic modernisation. In order to reduce labour and land costs, the majority of Hong Kong-owned, labour-intensive manufacturing industries have moved to Guangdong since the early 1980s.[19]

Guangdong's industrial development at a crossroads

The industrial development in Guangdong has faced both internal and external challenges over the recent years, ranging from rising labour and production costs to weak global demand. In this increasingly hostile environment, low-end and labour-intensive manufacturing firms located in Guangdong run into difficulties, whereas local companies that have achieved consistent technological improvement and successfully move up the value chain by entering the technology-intensive and value-added industry will survive and thrive. Against this backdrop, both the central and local governments have attempted to cope with these challenges, and speed up economic restructuring and industrial upgrading by implementing various policy measures since the 2000s.

Solving the industrial development puzzle and government initiatives

Since the first half of 2010, several high-profile labour strikes over pay and conditions have occurred in foreign-owned manufacturing firms in the PRD region, forcing some to halt production or offer pay increases.[20] Guangdong further increased the minimum wage for workers from 1 May 2013 onwards (Table 2.1). These incidents reflect the rising labour power in China. As migrant workers possess greater freedom in job-seeking and choosing work location, their negotiation

Table 2.1 Regional monthly minimum wages in Guangdong, 2013 (yuan)

City Level	Monthly Minimum Wage	Affected City
1st Tier	1,600	Shenzhen
	1,550	Guangzhou
2nd Tier	1,310	Zhuhai, Foshan, Dongguan, Zhongshan
3rd Tier	1,130	Shantou, Huizhou, Jiangmen, Zhaoqing
4th Tier	1,010	Shaoguan, Heyuan, Meizhou, Shanwei, Yangjiang, Zhanjiang, Maoming, Qingyuan, Chaozhou, Jieyang, Yunfu

Source: Human Resources and Social Security Bureau of Guangzhou Archive, <http://www.hrssgz. gov.cn/tzgg/ldjy/ldgz/201302/t20130225_198292.htm> [8 February 2014]

power in wages is bolstered too. Job opportunities abound in China's inland and western regions, which enjoy impressive economic growth. The migrant workers are therefore demanding higher wages in Guangdong; otherwise, they will not hesitate to move to other regions.

The PRD economy has reached a point where achieving growth becomes difficult without increasing workers' wages. As rural-urban migration continues in China at increased pace, there is no serious shortage of migrant workers in Guangdong. As the household registration system is still in place, Wu et al.[21] argue, through empirical model analysis, that the existing pool of agricultural surplus labour in China is still significantly large. Many migrant workers are still flocking to Guangdong to seek work opportunities and a better life. One of the main issues facing migrant workers in Guangdong is the generally low average wage.

Faced with the appreciation of the Chinese yuan and the rapidly increasing labour wages and other production costs, the heavy dependence on export-oriented industries, and labour-intensive and low-technology manufacturing has left Guangdong vulnerable to both external and internal shocks. Worse still, other emerging countries with lower labour costs, such as Bangladesh, Vietnam and Cambodia, are competing with Guangdong to produce labour-intensive manufactured goods for the global market.

In addition, industrial growth had shown signs of slowing down since the 2008 global economic downturn, which also impeded the development of local manufacturing industries. Many manufacturing factories located in the PRD region have been forced to reduce production output and even shut down operations completely, mainly due to the shrinking demand from the Western markets. Most of the firms that remained have struggled to survive since then. A case in point is Houjie township, one of the main manufacturing bases in Dongguan city, where more than 300 low-end and low value-added manufacturers closed down, and consequently about 0.2 million workers lost their jobs in 2008/2009. The 2008 global economic crisis had therefore exposed the weaknesses of Guangdong's export-oriented industries, which have indeed reached a crossroads in their development.

Over the years, the PRD region has established itself as a global manufacturing base for low value-added, labour-intensive products, drawing its competitiveness from an abundant supply of cheap labour, land and resources, as well as a relatively lax environmental regulatory system.[22] This model is not sustainable as the standards of living rise and labour wages increase in the PRD region. Guangdong is facing soaring production costs with respect to land, electricity and other resources. As shown in Table 2.2, there are significant variations across regions in the minimum wage, which is considerably higher in the eastern regions than in inland regions. Shanghai has been recording the highest national minimum wage, at 1,620 yuan per month, since May 2013. The differential cost has incentivised many industries, especially those labour-intensive and low-technology manufacturing plants, to move their production facilities westward. For sustainable development in the long run, the region badly needs to reorientate its industrial and economic structure. This has sounded a warning for Guangdong to speed up industrial upgrading and restructure its economy.

In contrast to the past, the recent wage increases pose difficulties to many Guangdong-based manufacturing firms in hiring unskilled and semi-skilled workers at low pay rates, and there is also greater competition to attract migrant workers. However, wage increase is a natural development phenomenon for a region.

Table 2.2 Minimum monthly wages of workers in various regions in China (yuan) (from May 2013)

Region	Province	Minimum Monthly Wage
Eastern region	Guangdong	1,010–1,600
	Shanghai	1,620
	Jiangsu	1,320
	Zhejiang	1,470
	Beijing	1,400
	Tianjin	1,500
	Liaoning	1,100
	Fujian	1,200
	Shandong	1,380
	Hebei	1,320
Central region	Shanxi	1,290
	Henan	1,240
	Anhui	1,010
	Hubei	1,100
	Hunan	1,160
	Jiangxi	1,230
Western region	Shaanxi	1,150
	Chongqing	1,050
	Sichuan	1,050
	Ningxia	1,300
	Guizhou	1,030

Source: WageIndicator Foundation, University of Amsterdam Archive, <http://www.wage indicator.cn/main/salary/minimumwagesinchina> [8 February 2014]

Once the competitive advantage of low wages and production costs has been fully exploited, it is essential for companies to move into high technology and high value-added industrial activities. Wage increase could be viewed to bring positive outcomes as this creates pressures for industrial firms to speed up upgrading and improve productivity, which are considered greater strategic competitive advantages. Wage increase will also drive consumption demand for advanced and high value-added industrial goods produced in Guangdong. Based on Porter's "diamond" model,[23] demand conditions will influence investment priorities of an industrial sector.

In coping with the various external and internal challenges facing Guangdong's industrial development, the provincial government has launched its industrial upgrading and economic restructuring since the early 2000s to achieve sustainable economic development. Such efforts are vital to sustaining local industrial growth and strengthening competitiveness. The Guangdong government has thus introduced various preferential policies over the past years to promote local industrial upgrading and economic restructuring, from low value-added to high-end and high value-added.

Guangdong's policymaking and implementation process for industrial upgrading and restructuring has adopted a "top-down" approach that takes into the consideration of various government departments (Table 2.3). Under the supervision of the National Development and Reform Commission (NDRC) of the State Council of China, various statutory bodies and departments of the Guangdong government – the Development and Reform Commission of

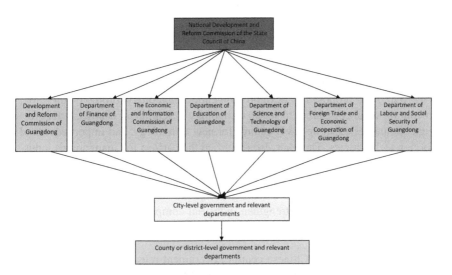

Table 2.3 An overview of policymaking and implementation structure for industrial upgrading in Guangdong

Source: Compiled by the author.

Guangdong province, the Economic and Information Commission, Department of Education, Department of Science and Technology, Department of Finance, Department of Labour and Social Security, and Department of Foreign Trade and Economic Cooperation – jointly formulated policies for Guangdong's industrial upgrading.

Various provincial government departments have participated and taken on different responsibilities in formulating state policies and initiatives. For example, the Development and Reform Commission of Guangdong province is responsible for overall policy design and approval; the Department of Finance takes charge of overall budget allocation, such as funds for technology innovation and R&D activities; and the Department of Education and Department of Labour and Social Security collaborate in providing vocational training and education development. The implementation and execution of policies will ultimately involve the different levels of Guangdong's local government.

The "top-down" approach to industrial upgrading in Guangdong resonates with the top-down administrative hierarchy in contemporary China. The Guangdong provincial government and its relevant departments under the direct administration design and formulate all the policy initiatives, and determine development strategies and goals. The responsibility for local implementation and monitoring of industrial upgrading polices, on the other hand, falls on the shoulders of different local governmental departments at various levels, from city level to district or county level. The local governments of Guangdong have introduced various specific preferential measures to encourage both domestic and foreign investors to engage in high-end and high value-added investment initiatives over the past few years. For example, Guangzhou provides tax incentives for firms to locate their operations in its economic development zone.[24]

One of the first documents that outlined government plans to restructure economic development and achieve industrial upgrading in Guangdong was *Guangdong's 11th Five-year Plan for Social and Economic Development (2006–2010)*, which was issued by Guangdong provincial government in early 2006. The *11th Five-year Plan* proposed to develop indigenous technology, promote education, encourage local companies to set up technology development centres, attract foreign companies to set up R&D centres for new technology, and import advanced foreign technologies. The plan also identified the barriers to Guangdong's industrial development, including rising labour and production costs, lack of research and indigenous innovation capacity, and overdependence on low value-added goods production (see Table 2.4 for government documents). The Guangdong government also aimed to strengthen industrial competitiveness by focusing on the development of electronic information, electric appliances and petroleum and chemical industries.

In January 2009, the Chinese central government released the *Outline of the Plan for the Reform and Development of the PRD Region 2008–2020*[25] (Box 1), which acts as the guiding state document to industrial upgrading, and maps out comprehensive development schemes for industrial restructuring and technology

Table 2.4 List of main government documents that guide industrial upgrading in Guangdong

Number	Government Documents	Issued Date
1	Guangdong's 10th Five-year Plan for Social and Economic Development (2001–2005)	February 2001
2	Decision to Jointly Promote Industrial Transfer by the Pearl River Delta Region and the Other Regions of Guangdong	March 2005
3	Guangdong's 11th Five-year Plan for Social and Economic Development (2006–2010)	March 2006
4	Guangdong's 10th Five-year Development Plan for High and New-tech Industry	June 2006
5	Plan to Speed up Industrial Development and Key Projects Construction for the Eastern Region	April 2007
6	Outline of the Development Strategy on Intellectual Property Right	December 2007
7	Outline of the Plan for the Reform and Development of the PRD Region 2008–2020	January 2009
8	Comprehensive Strategic Plan for Cooperation between Guangdong Government and China Academy of Science (2009–2015)	May 2009
9	Guangdong 12th National Economic and Social Development Five-year Plan (2011–2015)	January 2011

Source: The Guangdong Government Archive, <http://www.gd.gov.cn/govpub/jhgh/zdzx/> [20 April 2012].

upgrading within the PRD region. The plan highlighted the long-term industrial development policies and development priorities and established targets for some industries. Guangdong aims to upgrade its economy towards the capital- and technology-intensive industries, including high-end equipment manufacturing, automobile, steel, petrochemical, and shipbuilding industries. With regard to industrial upgrading, the region aims to become a centre of advanced manufacturing and modern service industries, as well as a centre for international shipping, logistics, trade, conferences and exhibitions and tourism.

Industrial upgrading is the focal point of the plan initiated in 2008 by the then Guangdong Party Secretary Wang Yang. The policy of "double transformation of industries and labour forces", as stipulated in the plan, essentially centres on industrial upgrading and aims to strengthen the long-term competitiveness of the region. The low-end manufacturing industries were expected to be relocated to the relatively underdeveloped periphery, while the PRD region was to concentrate on developing high-end manufacturing and modern service industries.[26] Guangdong hopes to undergo steady transformation into an advanced manufacturing base. The new industrial policy direction will enable Guangdong to move up the production value chain and ride on the wave of China's next phase of economic development. The local authority was expected to raise the access thresholds (e.g.

entry barrier) to traditional industrial sectors, and thereby to gradually eliminate these backward industries.

As outlined in *Guangdong's 12th Five-year Plan for National Economic and Social Development (2011–2015)*, the government intends to develop institutional system to support industrial innovation and upgrade technological innovation capability of enterprises, set up investment funds for start-up innovative firms, and establish key national-level laboratories and engineering centres to support industrial development, for example, national engineering centres on environmental production and energy conservation, biochemistry and medical equipment manufacturing. The government aims to help industries overcome barriers to obtain advanced core technology in key industrial fields, including electronic information, biomedicine, new energy vehicles and new material and energy. According to *Guangdong's 12th Five-year Plan*, the share of advanced manufacturing in Guangdong's total value-added industrial output will reach up to 50 per cent; and high-tech industrial manufacturing will account for 26 per cent of Guangdong's total value-added industrial output by 2015. For strategic emerging industrial sectors, namely, the advanced electronic information technology, new-energy vehicles, energy conservation and environmental protection, solar power, nuclear power equipment, wind power, biomedicine, new materials, aviation and aerospace, and marine, the total industrial output should reach 2 trillion yuan, and the value-added output of strategic emerging industries will account for 10 per cent of provincial GDP of Guangdong.

The Guangdong government has made attempts to attract FDI from major global multinationals. Priority has been given to investment in areas such as information and communication technologies (ICTs), biotechnology, new materials, recycling, new energy and marine industry. At the same time, the PRD region prohibits foreign investment in activities at the lower end of the production chain that cause pollution and have high-energy consumption. The plan has specified certain measures to achieve the region's structural transformation. To achieve rapid economic growth and sustainable industrial development, Guangdong's industries should seek to transform their growth model from one that relied on extensive expansion to one that focuses on intensive growth, with emphasis on both quantitative and qualitative improvement.

The Plan identified many development targets for the region over the next decade, including those for the industries. By 2020, high-tech manufacturing industries are expected to generate at least 30 per cent of total industrial output and 28 per cent of the region's GDP. The PRD region has identified the advanced technology and clean energy sectors, including high-speed rail, wind and nuclear power industries, to be given priority for industrial development. In addition to high-tech industries, the PRD region also focuses on the development of capital- and technology-intensive advanced manufacturing industries which, in broadly defined categories, include modern equipment manufacturing, automobiles, steel, petrochemicals and shipbuilding. The provincial government expects these industries to contribute over half of the PRD's overall industrial growth.

**BOX 1 The key objectives in *Pearl River Delta's (PRD)
New Development Plan***

- Industrial upgrading: (i) To encourage qualified domestic companies to be listed on stock exchanges and (ii) mergers and acquisitions (M&As) between state-owned enterprises and private companies, especially in the automobile industry.
- Industrial clustering: To develop industrial parks and clusters by improving the investment environment, attracting talents and reducing tax burdens. The government will establish special development zones, such as the Shenzhen Science Park, Guangzhou Bio-Island and the Dongguan Songshan Lake Industrial Park, to spearhead the development of various advanced industries.
- Technological capacity enhancement: (i) To encourage collaboration between industries and research institutions (and universities) in various joint technological initiatives and (ii) provide preferential policies such as tax concessions for R&D activities; the region's technological and innovative capacity will be enhanced with government's increased investments in R&D activities. The aim is to raise the rate of R&D expenditure to Guangdong's GDP to 2.8 per cent by 2020, from the current low level of under 1.7 per cent.
- The government will also adopt favourable policies, such as pre-tax deduction of R&D expenses and expanding government procurement on products with indigenous technology, to assist the development of high-tech industries.
- Attracting talent: To provide competitive salary and benefits, including housing benefits.
- Attracting high-quality FDI: To encourage FDI in key industries.
- The provincial government targets to establish up to 50 nationally renowned and 10 world-class innovative enterprises in the PRD region.

Source: National Development and Reform Commission (NDRC) of the State Council of China, *The Outline of the Plan for the Reform and Development of the PRD Region 2008–2020*, December 2008.

The Guangdong government has launched a number of policy initiatives to cope with the challenges facing local industrial development. Nevertheless, the government policies on industrial upgrading have not been effective, as evaluated by performance indicators that measure the effectiveness of policies on industrial upgrading. Guangdong's industrial upgrading and economic restructuring remain sluggish. Self-reinforcing agglomeration, a lack of government spending on R&D activities, and fierce intercity competition for industrial growth attributed to government policies have impeded Guangdong's aspirations to achieve industrial upgrading.

**An assessment of effectiveness of state policies
and problems posed by government policies**

As little is known of the channels through which government policies were implemented and the influence they exert, it is difficult to directly measure the effectiveness of government policies and initiatives on local industrial upgrading in Guangdong introduced since the early 2000s. This chapter proposes to evaluate policy effectiveness of industrial upgrading by measuring the progress of industrial upgrading as represented by three indicators: Guangdong's share in China's total value of exports of high-tech products; the percentage of value-added output of high-tech manufacturing in Guangdong's total value-added industrial output; and the total value of Guangdong's trade by product type. The chapter also assesses the availability of skilled labour in Guangdong and the effectiveness of government policies in helping enterprises to upgrade workers' skills, and therefore, the number of graduates from vocational secondary schools and technical schools – the two main types of institutions involved in skills training in Guangdong – provide a good measurement of skill upgrading.

High-quality human resources constitute an essential factor for the success of economic restructuring, which in turn depends on government-led investment in R&D and skills upgrading. For regions that lack high-tech industries and skilled labour, it is therefore imperative that the government provide vocational training to workforce to upgrade their skills. To speed up industrial upgrading and technological development process, and assist companies in expanding their skilled labour force, the Guangdong government has set up more technical schools and increased student recruitment over the past decade to provide vocational training and skills upgrading. It is one of the key strategies identified by the provincial government. According to official statistics, the number of technical schools in Guangdong increased from 171 in 1995 to 243 in 2012. The total number of graduates from vocational secondary schools increased to 0.42 million in 2012 from 0.18 million in 1995; and the total number of graduates from technical schools jumped from 0.03 million in 1995 to 0.14 million in 2012.[27] In addition, Guangdong's share in total national scientific and technology (S&T) personnel increased from 11.1 per cent in 2000 to 32.2 per cent in 2008.[28] These figures show that the government policies and measures in promoting vocational training and providing sufficient skilled labour for industrial enterprises are quite impressive.

Despite the implementation of the state-initiated plan, the progress of industrial upgrading in Guangdong has not been encouraging over the past 10 years. First, in terms of the share of Guangdong in China's total exports of high-tech products, the growth of high value-added industrial products has been slow in recent years. Although Guangdong's exports of high-tech products increased to USD221.3 billion in 2012 from USD17 billion in 2000, Guangdong's share in China's total exports of high-tech products showed a downward trend during the same period, with a dip to 36.8 per cent in 2012 from 48.0 per cent in 2001, and only rebounded since 2011 (Figure 2.2). The decline reflects Guangdong's weakening high-tech manufacturing capacity and industrial competitiveness over the past decade in comparison to the national level as well as its eroding competitive edge.

Second, as shown in Figure 2.3, Guangdong's value-added output in high-tech manufacturing industry as a proportion to its total value-added industry increased from 18.7 per cent in 2000 to 27.3 per cent in 2003, but there was a downward

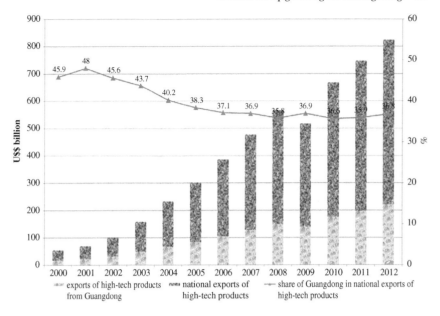

Figure 2.2 Guangdong's exports of high-tech products

Note: The *Catalog for High-technology Industrial Statistics Classification*, introduced by the National Bureau of Statistics in July 2002, categorises the following as China's high-technology industries: aircraft and spacecraft, electronic and telecommunication equipment, computer and office equipment, pharmaceuticals, medical equipment and devices manufacturing.

Sources: Data compiled by the author from:
1. Ministry of Science and Technology of the PRC, *China Science and Technology Statistics Data Book 2011*, <http://www.most.gov.cn/eng/statistics/2006/index.htm> [20 July 2011];
2. Guangdong Provincial Bureau of Statistics, *Guangdong Statistical Yearbook*, various years;
3. National Bureau of Statistics of China, *The 2012 Statistics Public Report for the National Economic and Social Development of China*.

trajectory since 2003 from 27.3 per cent in 2003 to 21.2 per cent in 2012, and only rebounded in recent years.

Third, in terms of total value of trade by product type, Guangdong recorded trade deficits in the high value-added and technology sectors in 2011 – USD62.7 billion in the electronic technology sector, USD9.8 billion in instruments and devices sector, USD3.4 billion in aerospace technology sector, and USD4.4 billion in computer-integrated manufacturing sector.[29] In fact, compared to 2005, Guangdong's trade deficits in 2010 in the electronic technology sector, instruments and devices sector, and computer-integrated manufacturing sector increased by USD28 billion, USD4.4 billion and USD1.38 billion, respectively. These data illustrate that Guangdong's firms have to import large quantities of high-tech and high value-added components for final production assembly of goods, and in fact, their contribution to the final industrial output constitutes merely the input of cheap labour. A large proportion of industrial products made in Guangdong, such as clothing, toys and shoes, involve low-skilled and labour-intensive production

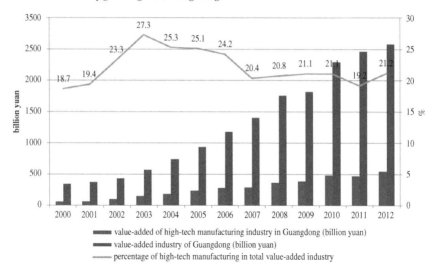

Figure 2.3 Value-added output of high-tech manufacturing industry in Guangdong

Sources: Data compiled by the author from:
1. Guangdong Provincial Bureau of Statistics, *Guangdong gongye tongji nianjian* (*Guangdong Statistical Yearbook of Industry*), various years from 2001–2010 (Beijing: China Statistics Press);
2. *Guangdong Statistical Yearbook*, 2012 and 2013.

processes. Even among China's other exports involving medium- to high-level technology, manufacturers in Guangdong have largely contributed to the low value-added segment of the overall production process, such as processing and assembly of imported parts and components. The high value-added aspects of production, such as product design, manufacturing of key components, and R&D are often carried out elsewhere. Guangdong is primarily a low-end assembly and processing base.

These performance indicators attested to Guangdong's slow progress in industrial upgrading. Obviously, government policies introduced to promote local industrial upgrading and economic restructuring since the mid-2000s have not been very effective. The main goals set by the Guangdong government regarding industrial restructuring are indeed ambitious. The main objectives are to transform "Made in Guangdong" products to "Invented in Guangdong" products by 2020, labour-intensive, low value-added local industries to high value-added, technology-based manufacturing, as well as to strengthen industrial competitiveness. However, data have demonstrated that Guangdong's industrial development is still mainly driven by low value-added manufacturing industry, and the status quo remains that Guangdong is the world's low-end and labour-intensive manufacturing factory.

The implementation of the state plan remains challenging as promoting new technology and industrial restructuring to enterprises in Guangdong is not easy. First, to ensure social stability, Guangdong has to create many jobs for the large number of rural migrant workers from both the poor regions of Guangdong and other regions in China. In this context, the local governments have to help keep a sizeable number of low value-added and labour-intensive enterprises survive.

Second, the existing industrial structure and particularly enterprises that have benefited from industrial agglomeration in the region tend to resist changes. Such resistance endangers the region's competitive edge over other regions in China. Industrial agglomeration exhibits strong self-reinforcing features and has led to the dominance of low-end industries in Guangdong. The traditional industrial structure, which may impede the realisation of goals set by the government, is a double-edged sword. One of the government's initiatives is to create a new industrial cluster of high-tech and technology-driven companies surrounding the PRD region by relocating low-end and labour-intensive industries to other regions. However, this policy would probably fail as the emergence of industrial clusters not only requires the presence of industrial production firms, but also consumers, suppliers, and other related upstream and downstream industries. Moreover, the current government policies work more effectively in reinforcing existing clusters rather than creating new clusters. Although the export-oriented and low-end manufacturing industries have contributed to Guangdong's rapid economic growth since 1980, this model is unsustainable due to environmental pollution and land shortage. The backward industrial structure has become a roadblock to the industrial restructuring of the PRD region. Besides, the local enterprises' resistance to industrial modernisation should not be underestimated. For enterprises in low-end industrial sectors, transformation will be a long drawn-out process as these companies built their past successes largely on the export of cheap and low-end manufacturing products. The low requirement for capital and human resource is still an attractive option since industrial upgrading is costly, and many firms in Guangdong are already facing financial difficulty in their efforts to enhance productivity.

There are two main problems that beset the government initiatives. First, the government paid scant attention to and invested too little in R&D. Government's investment in R&D activities, which will boost innovation, technological advancement and regional competitiveness, is crucial to promote industrial upgrading. During the field trips to the PRD region in 2009 and 2012, the author interviewed several local privately owned enterprises and foreign-owned companies. These companies are facing obstacles in carrying out technological upgrading and moving up the value chain. There is a lack of support for research and innovation caused by funding shortages. Many small and medium-sized manufacturing enterprises have difficulty engaging in and sustaining R&D activities, which require long-term, high-capital investment. Moreover, the economic returns of investing in R&D will only be discernible in the long run. It is therefore essential for the government to take the lead by investing in R&D.

However, since 2000, the Guangdong government has not injected adequate investment in R&D. The provincial government lacks commitment to support R&D activities and today, it still spends too little on R&D. Although there is an uptrend in R&D expenditure since 2005, the percentage of R&D outlay in regional GDP of Guangdong was still a mere 1.85 per cent in 2011. According to the figures from the Organisation for Economic Co-operation and Development (OECD), the R&D outlay as a percentage of total GDP of developed nations such as Finland, Germany, Japan, South Korea, Sweden and the United States were 3.87 per cent, 2.82 per cent, 3.26 per cent, 3.74 per cent, 3.43 per cent and 2.83 per cent, respectively, in 2010 (Table 2.5). Compared to these developed nations, Guangdong has spent far less on R&D. In addition, although there is an increase in the number of patent applications granted in Guangdong, the number of patents granted for important inventions are few and far between (Figure 2.4). The percentage of new inventions that are granted patents only accounted for about 14.4 per cent of the total patent applications granted in 2012.

To achieve sustainable economic growth and expedite industrial restructuring, Guangdong should initiate to hasten its economic restructuring by engaging in home-grown innovation and developing the potentials of local firms with strong R&D capacity. Instead of shutting down existing industries or relocating them, Guangdong should increase R&D spending and upgrade these enterprises. The approaches to keep these traditional and mature industries relevant include enhancing their productivity, improving the production process, and acquiring new technology to improve product quality. There are two key components to industrial upgrading in Guangdong: (i) to speed up the development of new industries that will increase Guangdong's industrial competitiveness in the long term; and (ii) to restructure, reorganise and upgrade existing industries.

Second, fierce intercity competition for industrial growth attributed to the government policies has posed challenges to achieving industrial upgrading. Industrial competition and duplication in cities within Guangdong due to a lack of industrial coordination between cities are serious issues that demand action from

Table 2.5 Comparison of R&D outlay as a percentage of GDP in Guangdong and the OECD countries (%)

Country	2003	2004	2005	2006	2007	2008	2009	2010	2011
Denmark	2.58	2.48	2.46	2.48	2.58	2.87	3.02	3.06	3.09
Finland	3.44	3.45	3.48	3.48	3.47	3.72	3.96	3.87	3.78
France	2.17	2.15	2.10	2.10	2.07	2.11	2.21	2.26	2.25
Germany	2.52	2.49	2.49	2.53	2.53	2.68	2.82	2.82	2.84
Sweden	3.80	3.58	3.56	3.68	3.40	3.70	3.62	3.43	3.37
Japan	3.20	3.17	3.32	3.40	3.44	3.44	3.36	3.26	n/a
South Korea	2.49	2.68	2.79	3.01	3.21	3.36	3.56	3.74	n/a
United States	2.61	2.54	2.57	2.61	2.67	2.79	2.90	2.83	2.77
OECD Total	2.21	2.18	2.21	2.24	2.28	2.34	2.40	2.38	n/a
Guangdong	1.34	1.14	1.12	1.19	1.30	1.41	1.60	1.74	1.85

Sources: Organisation for Economic Co-operation and Development (OECD), *Gross Domestic Expenditure on R&D*, Main Science and Technology Indicators, May 2013, <http://www.oecd-ilibrary.org/science-and-technology/gross-domestic-expenditure-on-r-d_2075843x-table1> [8 February 2014]; and the data on R&D Outlay as a Percentage of GDP in Guangdong were compiled by the author.

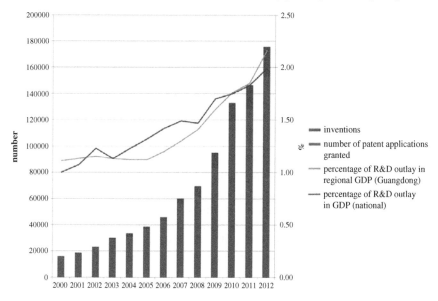

Figure 2.4 Number of patent applications granted and R&D outlay of Guangdong

Sources:
1. Guangdong Provincial Bureau of Statistics, *Guangdong Statistical Yearbook*, various years;
2. China Statistical Yearbook 2013;
3. National Bureau of Statistics of China, *The 2011 Statistics Public Report for the National Economic and Social Development of China*.

the provincial government. Furthermore, to obtain preferential treatment and pursue rapid GDP growth, local governments on the city-level often resort to playing games with the provincial and central governments to gain bargaining power in industrial development policies. Many cities have focused their efforts on developing industries such as steel, automobile and electronic information, which can boost local GDP growth and employment rate within the shortest period, and thus leading to cut-throat competition. Such unhealthy competition results in low efficiency in industrial resource distribution and allocation, diminishing economies of scale and poor financial performance for many enterprises. Consequently, industrial development priorities for most cities become quite similar. For example, in terms of advanced manufacturing industries, Guangzhou, Shenzhen and Foshan focused to develop similar industries such as electrical equipment and machinery manufacturing, and food and beverages. Further to that, Guangzhou, Foshan, Zhanjiang and Maoming openly compete in developing their steel industries; Huizhou, Zhongshan, Zhanjiang and Shantou are rivals in port-related equipment and machinery manufacturing; and Dongguan, Foshan, Zhanjiang, Yangjiang and Jieyang are competitors in the textiles and garment industry. In addition, competition is the most intense in the emerging and high-tech industries between Guangzhou and Shenzhen. Their development priorities are virtually the same. The two cities also share very similar development priorities in advanced manufacturing industry and traditional industries. Guangzhou and Shenzhen are on equal footing in economy size and share similar characteristics in economic structure. As both cities attempt to outperform each other to be the dominant player in the region, the more pertinent objective of seeking industrial and economic integration has been shelved and overlooked, leading to duplication of investment. Apart from that, Dongguan and Foshan have also been concurrently promoting industrial sectors such as electronic information, biomedicine, environmental protection, and new materials (Table 2.6).

Developing newly emerging industries requires heavy investments and support from the government, ranging from subsidies to favourable policies. This inevitably causes intense competition among regions in clamouring for resources and governmental support. Similar difficulties are also anticipated in restructuring and transforming existing industries, which involve business consolidation across administrative boundaries as well as seeking policy support from the state. A number of coastal cities, with comparable industrial structures and similar economic clout, are therefore locked in stiff competition in both new and existing industries.

Table 2.6 Competing development priorities among cities in Guangdong

City	Advanced Manufacturing Industries	High-tech and Emerging Industries
Guangzhou	Automobile, transport equipment, electrical equipment and machinery, steel, ocean-engineering equipment, food and beverages	Electronic information, biomedicine, new materials, environmental protection, new energy (wind and solar power), financial services
Shenzhen	Electrical equipment and machinery, food and beverages	Electronic information, biomedicine new materials, environmental protection, new energy (wind and solar power), financial services
Dongguan	Electrical equipment and machinery, textiles and garment	Electronic information, biomedicine, new materials, environmental protection, new energy (wind and solar power)
Foshan	Automobile, transport equipment, electrical equipment and machinery, steel, food and beverages, textiles and garment	Electronic information, biomedicine, new materials, environmental protection, new energy (wind and solar power)
Huizhou	Port-related equipment and machinery, petroleum and chemicals	Electronic information, new materials
Zhongshan	Port-related equipment and machinery, fine and precise chemistry	Biomedicine, new materials, environmental protection

(Continued)

City	Advanced Manufacturing Industries	High-tech and Emerging Industries
Zhanjiang	Port-related equipment and machinery, petroleum and chemical, steel, shipbuilding, electrical equipment and machinery, logging and paper-making, textiles and garment	X
Maoming	Petroleum and chemical, steel, Shipbuilding, electrical equipment and machinery	X
Yangjiang	Smelting and pressing of ferrous metals, food, textiles and garment, furniture-making	Electronic information, biomedicine, new materials, environmental protection
Shantou	Port-related equipment and machinery, petroleum and chemical, ocean-engineering equipment, food and beverages, textiles and garment	X
Jieyang	Food and beverages, textiles and garment, electrical equipment and machinery, transport equipment, smelting and pressing of ferrous metals	X
Chaozhou	Food, electrical equipment manufacturing, printing, pottery and china	X
Shanwei	Electrical equipment manufacturing, clothing and garment	X

Note: "X" indicates there is no plan for development.

Sources: Data compiled by the author from:
1. National Development and Reform Commission (NDRC) of the State Council of China, *Outline of the Plan for the Reform and Development of the PRD Region 2008–2020*, 2009.
2. Provincial Government of Guangdong, *The Rejuvenation Plan for the Eastern, Western and Northern Regions of Guangdong*, 2005.

Conclusion

Over the past three decades, Guangdong has developed into one of the key industrial powerhouses for China and the world. However, Guangdong's industrial strengths based on cheap land and labour costs are vulnerable to both external and internal pressures. Most of the high value-added aspects of production are carried out elsewhere. Guangdong is, primarily, a low-end assembly and processing base. The global economic downturn has exposed the weaknesses of Guangdong's industries. Wage increase is a natural development phenomenon in the case of Guangdong. Rising labour and production costs have sounded a warning that Guangdong's industries have reached a critical turning point. Guangdong is at a crossroads – it faces challenges in industrial upgrading and economic transformation as well as maintaining fast industrial growth. Its success in industrial upgrading will be pivotal to the future and wealth of this southern province.

To cope with the challenges facing Guangdong's industrial development, the provincial government has implemented a number of policies and initiatives with industrial upgrading at the core. However, the government policies are not discernibly effective and local industrial upgrading remains challenging and slow. Although the State's new initiatives are in place, the process of industrial upgrading and development of high technology and value-added industries in Guangdong have been slow over the past decade. Guangdong's manufacturing capacity and industrial competitiveness in comparison to the national level has weakened over the past decade. Guangdong's competitive edge in comparison to other Chinese regions is also gradually eroding.

Self-reinforcing agglomeration, a lack of government spending on R&D activities, and fierce intercity competition for industrial growth attributed to government policies have impeded Guangdong's aspirations to achieve industrial upgrading. Due to various inherent problems and the fact that industrial restructuring, it is highly unlikely that Guangdong achieves and completes its industrial upgrading in the near future.

Notes

1 Gereffi, Gary. (1990). "International Trade and Industrial Upgrading in the Apparel Commodity Chain", *Journal of International Economics*, 48:1, pp. 37–70; see pp. 51–52.
2 Humphrey, John and Schmitz, Hubert. (2000). "Governance and Upgrading: Linking Industrial Cluster and Global Value Chain Research", *Working Paper 120*, Institute of Development Studies, pp. 1–37.
3 Lall, Sanjaya. (2000). "The Technological Structure and Performance of Developing Country Manufactured Exports, 1985–1998", *Working Paper 44*, Queen Elizabeth House, University of Oxford, pp. 1–39.
4 Ozawa, Terutomo. (2005). *Institutions, Industrial Upgrading, and Economic Performance in Japan*, Cheltenham and Northampton, MA: Edward Elgar.
5 Dunning, John H. (1994) "Re-evaluating the Benefits of Foreign Direct Investment", *Transnational Corporations*, 3, pp. 23–51.
6 Henderson, Jeffrey, *et al.* (2002). "Global Production Networks and the Analysis of Economic Development", *Review of International Political Economy*, 9:3, pp. 436–464.
7 Wai-Chung Yeung, Henry. (2009). "Regional Development and the Competitive Dynamics of Global Production Networks: An East Asian Perspective", *Regional Studies* 43:3, pp. 325–351.
8 Coe, Neil M., *et al.* (2004). " 'Globalizing' Regional Development: A Global Production Networks Perspective", *Transactions of the Institute of British Geographers*, 29, pp. 468–484.
9 Henderson *et al.*, 2002, p. 457.
10 Porter, Michael E. (1990). *The Competitive Advantage of Nations*, New York and London: The Free Press.
11 Porter, *The Competitive Advantage of Nations*; and Ozawa, Terutomo. (1992). "Foreign Direct Investment and Economic Development", *Transnational Corporations* I, 1, pp. 27–54. World Bank. (1991). *World Development Report*, Washington, DC: World Bank Publications. Rodrik, Dani. (2004). "Industrial Policy for the Twenty-First Century", prepared for United Nations Industrial Development Organization (UNIDO), Harvard University, pp. 1–41.
12 Vogel, Ezra F. (1989). *One Step Ahead in China: Guangdong Under Reform*, Cambridge and London: Harvard University Press.

13 Yun-Wing, Sung, *et al.* (1995). *The Fifth Dragon: The Emergence of the Pearl River Delta*, Singapore: Addison-Wesley Publishing Company.

14 Cheng, Joseph Y. S. (1998). *The Guangdong Development Model and Its Challenges*, Hong Kong: The City University of Hong Kong Press.

15 Hong, Yu. (2011). *Economic Development and Inequality in China: The Case of Guangdong*, London and New York: Routledge.

16 Cheng, *The Guangdong Development Model and Its Challenges*; and Fulong, Wu. (1999). "Intrametropolitan FDI Firm Location in Guangzhou, China: A Poisson and Negative Binomial Analysis", *The Annals of Regional Science*, 33, pp. 535–555. Bui Tung X., *et al.*, eds. (2003). *China's Economic Powerhouse: Reform in Guangdong Province*, London: Palgrave Macmillan.

17 Guangdong Provincial Bureau of Statistics, ed. (2013). *Guangdong tongji nianjian 2013 (Guangdong Statistical Yearbook 2013)*, Beijing: China Statistics Press.

18 East Asian Institute, "China's National and Regional Industrial Development", an internal research report to Singapore's Ministry of Trade and Industry for reference, submitted in 2012.

19 Fung, Victor. (2002). "Hong Kong's Economic Integration with the Pearl River Delta", *EAI Background Brief no. 129*, East Asian Institute, National University of Singapore. Wong, John, and Sarah Chan, "CEPA to Deepen Hong Kong's Economic Dependence on China", *EAI Background Brief no. 175*, 2003, East Asian Institute, National University of Singapore.

20 "China: Foxconn Wage Increases Highlight Rising Pay Levels", *The Financial Times*, 8 June 2010. "Workers in China Accept Deal, Honda Says", *The New York Times*, 4 June 2010.

21 Yanrui, Wu, Kwan, Fung and Shuaihe, Zhuo, "Re-examination of Surplus Agricultural Labour in China", paper presented at the China's Growth and the World Economy international conference, Association for Chinese Economic Studies Australia (ACESA) and UWA Business School, 7–8 July 2011.

22 Junkuo, Zhang and Yongzhi, Hou. (2008). *Xietiao quyu fazhan (Coordinating Regional Development)*, Beijing: China Development Publisher.

23 Porter, *The Competitive Advantage of Nations*.

24 Guangzhou Economic and Technological Development Zone, ed. (2010, July). *Guangzhou jingji jishu kaifaqu youhui zhengce (Preferential Policies for Investment in Guangzhou Economic and Technological Development Zone)*, Guangzhou.

25 "Zhujiang sanjiaozhou diqu gaige he fazhan guihua gangyao" *(Outline of the Plan for the Reform and Development of the PRD Region 2008–2020)*, The National Development and Reform Commission, People's Republic of China, 2009, pp. 1–57, http:// www.gdep.gov.cn/hbgh/ghjh/ghjh/201008/P020100804604719020540.pdf (accessed 18 July 2011]).

26 Yu Hong and Zhang Yang, "New Initiatives for Industrial Upgrading in the Pearl River Delta", *EAI Background Brief no. 464*, 2009, East Asian Institute, National University of Singapore.

27 Guangdong Provincial Bureau of Statistics, *Guangdong Statistical Yearbook 1996*; and Guangdong Provincial Bureau of Statistics, *Guangdong Statistical Yearbook 2013*.

28 Ministry of Science and Technology. (2009). *China Statistics Yearbook on High Technology Industry 2009*, Beijing: China Statistics Press.

29 Guangdong Provincial Bureau of Statistics. (2011). *Guangdong tongji nianjian 2011 (Guangdong Statistical Yearbook 2011)*, Beijing: China Statistics Press.

3 China embarks on ambitious megacity plans in Guangdong

Are cities in China not big enough?

Wang Yang, party secretary of Guangdong, has big ideas for furthering provincial development. The creation of Guangzhou–Foshan megacity is one of the key agendas of the Guangdong government in its pursuit of sustainable and coordinated regional development within Guangdong, particularly in the Pearl River Delta (PRD) region.

As the Chinese government's priority is on rural-urban integration, Guangdong has to build on its own strengths if it were to achieve this goal. Wang Yang has been working on integrating cities within the province for the past few years, with Guangzhou and Foshan as the key elements. He believes that the integration of Guangzhou and Foshan is the answer to achieving closer socio-economic cooperation within the PRD region in the future.

The Guangzhou–Foshan metropolis, a combination of two prefectural-level cities of Guangzhou and Foshan within Guangdong Province, had a combined land area of 11.13 thousand square km and a total population of 19.9 million in 2010, accounting for 6.2 per cent and 19.0 per cent respectively of provincial totals. Both Guangzhou and Foshan are located at the centre of the prosperous PRD region and the provincial transportation networks of railway, highway and waterway.

Given favourable geographic locations and state policy treatment, Guangzhou and Foshan have achieved rapid industrialization and economic development in the past three decades. Guangzhou–Foshan has now become one of the most prosperous regions in China. Its per capita gross regional product (GRP) was 83,886 yuan in 2010, which was almost twice as high as the provincial average.

Guangzhou and Foshan have developed strong manufacturing industries, such as the manufacture of food, raw chemical materials and chemical products, smelting and pressing of nonferrous metals, and the manufacture of transport equipment, over the years. The value-added industrial output of these two cities had increased to 798.8 billion yuan in 2010 from merely 111.0 billion yuan in 2000. Guangzhou–Foshan accounted for nearly 35 per cent of total value-added industrial output of Guangdong in 2010[1] and played a crucial role in Guangdong's export-oriented manufacturing. Its industrial output ranges from the highly productive manufacture of transport equipment to the relatively low share of papermaking and paper products.

The two cities are also leading industrial players in Guangdong. In 2010, the Guangzhou–Foshan megacity accounted for a respective 74.9 per cent and 46.6 per cent of value-added industrial output of transport equipment and general-purpose equipment manufactured in Guangdong; this area accounted for 49.2 per cent and 45.1 per cent of Guangdong's value-added output of beverages and food produced. It also accounted for up to 57.1 per cent of value-added industrial output of raw chemical materials and chemical products manufactured in Guangdong (Figure 3.1).

The municipal governments of Guangzhou and Foshan signed the Cooperation Framework Agreement on the Guangzhou–Foshan Integration in March 2009. In December 2009, the Chinese central government approved the *Development Outline for Guangzhou–Foshan Integration (2009–2020)* (referred to hereafter as the Outline) to guide overall socio-economic integration between the two cities. Many initiatives to promote inter-city integration have been implemented since then. In the face of an uncertain global economic outlook and fragile global economic recovery, there is evidence of a strong willingness on both sides to forge closer mutual collaboration.

The Chinese government has ambitious state plans and policy initiatives for the Guangzhou–Foshan megacity project. The Chinese government seeks to transform Guangzhou–Foshan into a major global metropolis and an international base for modern service and advanced manufacturing industries.

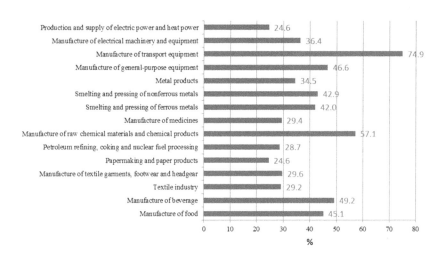

Figure 3.1 Share of value-added output for the selected industries by the Guagzhou–Foshan megacity in Guangdong, 2010

Source: *2011 Guangdong Statistical Yearbook*

Through such integration, Guangzhou–Foshan has the potential of becoming one of the most influential metropolises in China. The economic power of Guangzhou–Foshan megacity in terms of GRP (1,640.0 billion yuan) far exceeds that of Beijing (1,411.4 billion yuan), Tianjin (922.4 billion yuan) and Chongqing (792.6 billion yuan), and it is almost on par with Shanghai (1,716.6 billion yuan), China's key economic centre. The Guangzhou–Foshan megacity maintains strong manufacturing capacity. Its value-added of manufacturing output was 706.4 billion yuan in 2010, which was much higher than that achieved by other major megacities in China (Table 3.1).[2]

In spite of the promulgation of a state outline to merge the two cities and the existence of a well-developed inter-city infrastructure framework, maximizing the full economic potential of Guangzhou–Foshan remains a challenging task. For a fully integrated megacity to be successful, Guangzhou and Foshan have to not only develop a coordinated and complementary industrial structure, but also unify their pricing policies on the provision of public goods and services and distribute them more equally.

To reap the full benefits of a major megacity, Guangzhou and Foshan will need to cooperate closely to cross administrative and bureaucratic barriers. The

Table 3.1 Comparison of development indicators among China's major metropolises, 2010

Indicator	The Guangzhou–Foshan Megacity	Beijing	Shanghai	Tianjin	Chongqing
Total Population (year-end) (million persons)	19.9	19.6	23.0	13.0	28.9
GRP (billion yuan)	1,640.0	1,411.4	1,716.6	922.4	792.6
Share of GRP in national GDP (%)	4.1	3.5	4.3	2.3	2.0
Total value-added of manufacturing output (billion yuan)	706.4	276.4	653.6	441.1	369.8
Share of manufacturing industry in GRP (%)	43.1	19.6	38.1	47.8	46.7
Total value-added of tertiary output (billion yuan)	856.1	1,060.1	983.4	423.9	288.1
Share of tertiary industry in GRP (%)	52.2	75.1	57.3	46.0	36.4
Total value of foreign trade (US$ billion)	155.4	301.7	369.0	82.1	12.4
Share of foreign trade in nation (%)	5.2	10.1	12.4	2.8	0.4
Inward FDI (US$ billion)	5.9	6.4	11.1	10.8	6.3
Share of foreign direct investment in total FDI inflow to China (%)	5.6	6.1	10.5	10.2	6.0

Source: Compiled by the author based on the *China Statistical Yearbook 2011*.

authorities will also need to devote greater efforts in facilitating free inter-city movement of human talent, capital and information. The support of the local community and acceptance at the grass-roots level are crucial to ensuring the sustainability of this megacity in the long term. In spite of the official enthusiasm over the megacity project, responses from the public have been mixed.

Although the Guangzhou–Foshan megacity is likely to benefit local residents economically, concerns over its potential consequences have been raised by various interest groups. Local residents are not likely to support the creation of this megacity unless 'bread and butter' issues, such as unification of provision of public goods and services, have been resolved.

The role of the state in inter-city integration

The Chinese government had set accelerating the socio-economic integration of Guangzhou and Foshan as a major task in the *Outline for the Reform and Development of the Pearl River Delta (2008–2020)* in 2008. In December 2009, the Chinese government approved the *Development Outline for Guangzhou–Foshan Integration (2009–2020)*, a key state plan that sets the guiding principles to pushing forward the development of Guangzhou–Foshan megacity (see chronology of events in Appendix 3.1).

Since 2008, Wang Yang, party secretary of Guangdong, and Zhu Xiaodan, the then party secretary of Guangzhou, have actively promoted an ambitious plan to merge the two municipal-level cities of Guangzhou and Foshan. With the recent promotion of Zhu Xiaodan to governor of Guangdong, it is widely expected that the Guangdong government will endorse the development plan of a Guangzhou–Foshan megacity and intensify its support in the coming years.

Many initiatives to promote inter-city integration have been implemented since then. The government also anticipates forging a new growth pole through the development of Guangzhou–Foshan megacity based on industrial agglomeration and socio-economic integration. In so doing, it is also seeks to speed up the urbanization process of the sub-urban and rural areas of Foshan and Guangzhou.

Officials making the announcement of the Outline also detailed measures for translating the Outline into reality. A formal Inter-city Coordination Committee led by the mayors of Guangzhou and Foshan has been set up to coordinate the integration process of both cities. In this committee, four separate working groups were set up to look after the specific issues of integrated urban planning, inter-city infrastructure connectivity, industrial planning and allocation, and regional environmental protection.[3] Officials from the two cities have met regularly to lay out the detailed annual working plan and discuss the ongoing major inter-city development projects. The governments of both cities will also harmonize local policies and establish a proper and effective institutional framework of governance for the megacity.[4]

The intra-city transportation network between Guangzhou and Foshan has gradually taken shape over the past few years. The first inter-city metro line in

China, the 32-km-long Guzhou–Foshan Inter-city Metro Line has been in operation since November 2010. According to the Outline, the municipal governments of Guangzhou and Foshan will invest heavily in transportation construction projects to further improve the intra-city transport network and reduce transport costs for businesses. Major infrastructure projects include Guangzhou–Sanshui Expressway, the metro line connecting Foshan West Station and Guangzhou South Rail Station, Guangzhou–Zhaoqing Expressway, Pingnan Expressway and West Circle Expressway. These transportation projects will facilitate free and efficient intra-city movement of human talent, capital and information.

The two governments also seek to provide a more efficient public bus service to passengers by unifying the different bus pass cards (*yangchengtong* and *guangfotong*) which can be used and topped up in both cities. More cross-border buses and 45 more routes by 2012 are in the pipeline. These measures will help cut down inter-city transport costs and make cross-city communications more efficient and convenient. At the same time, the travel time by bus between the downtown areas of Foshan and Guangzhou will be cut to within half an hour, and between other parts of both cities to within an hour.

According to the Outline, the priority will be to develop advanced service industries, including finance, conferencing, logistics, cultural and creative industries. In particular, Guangzhou and Foshan will build on each other's strengths and develop an integrated financial sector. The central and provincial governments will support Guangzhou's ambition to become a regional financial centre that will provide frontline financial services, with Foshan providing backup financial service for Guangzhou. The Chinese central government will also boost the development of a logistics industry cluster in the Guangzhou–Foshan megacity, particularly in Guangzhou Nansha Bonded Zone, Guangzhou Bonded Logistic Park, Guangzhou Baiyun Airport Bonded Zone, Foshan Sanshan International Logistics Park and Foshan Jiujiang Logistics Park.

The municipal governments of Guangzhou and Foshan are seeking to promote the development of service industry to reduce their economic dependence on the manufacturing sector. The local authorities anticipate that the service industry can play a more important role in promoting local GDP and in gradually transforming the Guangzhou–Foshan megacity from a polluting and manufacturing-led economy to an environment friendly centre driven by the high value-added service industry. The government efforts have started to bear fruit in some areas. The service-dominated tertiary industry has become an important engine of local economic growth in Guangzhou and Foshan. The share of this megacity in total value-added tertiary output of Guangdong increased to 41.3 per cent in 2010 or 856.1 billion yuan from 38.1 per cent in 2000, and came down to 36.7per cent and 37 per cent in 2011 and 2012 individually (Figure 3.2). Specifically, this region accounted for 49.5 per cent, 38.6 per cent and 32.3 per cent of value-added output of transport and storage and post, wholesale and retail trades, and finance sectors respectively in Guangzhou in 2010.

Guangzhou and Foshan have become strong manufacturing bases in China over the years. As released in the Outline, the government has identified four

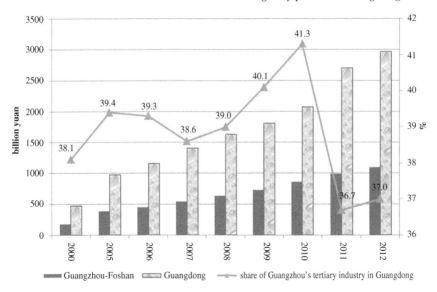

Figure 3.2 Value-added of Guangzhou–Foshan's Tertiary Industry
Source: 2011 Guangdong Statistical Yearbook

key industries – automobile, advanced equipment manufacturing, shipbuilding and petrochemicals – for further expansion. Moreover, the Guangzhou–Foshan megacity will promote the development of high-tech industries, with focus on electronic information, biomedicine, new materials, environmental protection and new energy. In addition, traditional industrial sectors such as home appliances, food, textiles and clothing will be reformed and upgraded to improve on product quality and strengthen overall competitiveness (see Table 3.2 for details).

Moreover, according to the Outline, the local governments of Guangzhou and Foshan will have to work together to standardize the provision of public goods in the fields of health care, education, electricity and labour skills training, and distribute them more equally. For example, the authorities in Guangzhou will share their vocational school resources and provide pre-job training for Foshan residents. The governments also strive to lower inter-city phone bills by unifying regional calling codes and make efforts to protect the environment and build a "regional eco-corridor alongside Guangzhou and Foshan". Guangzhou and Foshan residents will also be able to share their public amenities, parks and other leisure spaces, and will have access to the same premium public services and public goods by 2020.

However, even though these detailed measures are in place and a preliminary inter-city infrastructure framework has been developed, the state Outline will need time to deliver significant results. As a first step, the authorities are stepping up efforts to forge sub-regional integration between Fangcun District of Guangzhou and Guicheng, Nanhai. A fully integrated megacity to be successful, both

Table 3.2 Industrial development priorities for the Guangzhou–Foshan megacity

Automobile	The focus would be on the manufacturing of automobile and auto parts with indigenous core technology. The government will promote the formation of several super-sized automobile makers with industrial output value above 100 billion yuan. The government encourages the forging of large industrial giants through mergers and acquisitions. The Guangzhou–Foshan megacity is expected to become a national exporting base for automobiles and auto parts.
Shipbuilding	The government aims to strengthen competitiveness by going through an industrial restructuring and boosting the manufacturing of luxury yachts offshore oil drills and other high-end and high value-added products.
Modern equipment manufacturing	The focus would be on digital-control equipment and related systems, mechanical engineering, nuclear power equipment and wind power equipment.
Petrochemical	The government will give priority to high value-added chemical products and electronic chemical products by developing the industrial clusters in the Guangzhou Eastern Petrochemical Base, the Precise Chemical Production Base of Guangzhou Development Zone and Shunde Paint Base.
High-tech industries	The development priorities would be on electronic information, biomedicine, new materials, environmental protection and new energy. The state encourages the forging of four large industrial clusters with industrial output capacity of 100 billion yuan each.
Modern service industry	The focus would be on finance, conference, logistics, service outsourcing, and tourism, cultural and creative sectors.

Source: The Chinese central government, *Development Outline for Guangzhou–Foshan Integration (2009–2020)*

cities have to standardize the pricing of public goods and distribute services such as education, medical care, transportation and energy supply more equally. These weighty tasks will involve much bargaining, argument and conflict. Both munici-palities face serious challenges in pursuing coordinated regional development and achieving integration.

Motivation for the megacity development initiative

One of the main motivations behind the forging of this megacity is the existence of close historical relations and cultural links. Guangzhou and Foshan have a long history of close socio-economic relations and mutual interaction and exchange, and the two cities were under the same administration during the Qin Dynasty (lasting between 221 and 207 BC). Guangzhou and Foshan inherited the *Lingnan* culture; their people share the same customs, cultural activities, dialect and other traditions. Therefore, the potential for integration of these two municipalities is far stronger than in any other regions in China.

The Guangdong government believes that the development of Guangzhou–Foshan megacity will serve as a breakthrough for achieving closer socio-economic cooperation within the PRD region in the future.[5] The megacity is also expected to improve the quality of urban planning within the Guangzhou–Foshan area and achieve coordinated development of local physical and social infrastructure. The Guangdong government hopes that this megacity could generate spillovers to surrounding areas and thus speed up the overall integration of the PRD. The significance of the Guangzhou–Foshan megacity in Guangdong's economy has increased over the last decade. This megacity's GRP rose to 2,016.4 billion yuan in 2012 from 354 billion yuan in 2000; its share in Guangdong's total GRP increased from 33.0 per cent in 2000 to 35.3 per cent in 2012 (Figure 3.3). It has now become one of the richest regions in the nation. Per capita GRP of the Guangzhou–Foshan megacity was up to 98,584 yuan in 2012 from 22,929 yuan in 2000, which was almost two times higher than the provincial average (Figure 3.4).

As two of the most open economies in Guangdong, Guangzhou and Foshan have benefited tremendously from foreign investment and trade since the reform and opening up in 1978. In 2010, actual foreign direct investment (FDI) inflow to Guangzhou–Foshan was US$5.9 billion, accounting for nearly 30 per cent of total FDI inflow to Guangdong. Moreover, the value of foreign trade conducted by the Guangzhou–Foshan megacity rose from merely US$33.7 billion in 2000 to US$155.4 billion in 2010; it alone accounted for nearly 20 per cent of the total value of foreign trade from Guangdong.[6]

Another major motivation behind the Guangzhou–Foshan megacity is the two cities' industrial complementariness. The industrial complementariness of Guangzhou and Foshan thus provides the foundations for closer industrial cooperation and developing an integrated regional market. The two cities have low involvement in primary industry in terms of GRP. Nevertheless, although a certain level

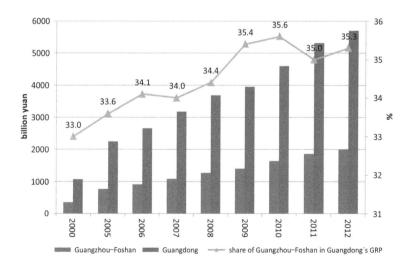

Figure 3.3 Share of Guangzhou–Foshan's GRP in Guangdong

Note: The figures are based on the current price.

Source: 2011 Guangdong Statistical Yearbook

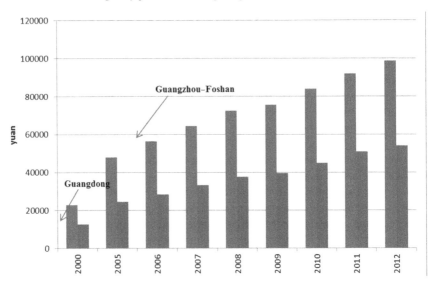

Figure 3.4 Average per capita GRP of Guangzhou–Foshan

Note: The figures are based on the current price.

Source: *2011 Guangdong Statistical Yearbook*

Table 3.3 Indicators of economic development of Guangzhou and Foshan, 2010

Indicator	Guangzhou	Foshan
GRP (billion yuan)	1,074.8	565.2
Share of primary industry in GRP (%)	1.8	1.9
Share of secondary industry in GRP (%)	37.2	62.7
Share of tertiary industry in GRP (%)	61.0	35.4
Freight throughput of ports (billion tons)	0.43	0.05
Share of total freight throughput of ports in Guangdong (%)	34.8	4.4
Possession of private vehicles (million)	1.26	0.79
Share of total possession of private vehicles by Guangdong (%)	20.1	12.6

Source: Compiled by the author base on various information sources.

of industrial competition exists, independent industrial structure and the duplication of development are not serious issues for Guangzhou and Foshan. The two cities have developed quite complementary industrial structures, with Guangzhou being dominant in service-led tertiary industry (61 per cent of GRP) and Foshan having a clear advantage in manufacturing-driven secondary industry (62.7 per cent of GRP) (Table 3.3).

Guangdong and Foshan differ considerably in their manufacturing activities. Guangzhou's manufacturing is well developed in the sectors of food, beverages, raw chemical materials and chemical products, medicines and transport equipment, which accounted respectively for 35.7 per cent, 36.6 per cent, 47.3 per cent, 23.7 per cent and 68.4 per cent of the provincial totals for 2010. Foshan tends to be much weaker in these sectors but has enjoyed relative superiority in the textile industry, and plastic products, nonmetal mineral products, smelting and pressing of nonferrous metals and manufacture of electrical machinery and equipment sectors, which accounted respectively for 18.8 per cent, 20.2 per cent, 29.3 per cent, 34.7 per cent and 30.0 per cent of the provincial totals in 2010 (Table 3.4).

Table 3.4 Value-added of selected manufacturing industries by Guangzhou and Foshan, 2010 (billion yuan)

Sector	Guangzhou		Foshan		Provincial Total
	Value-added Output	% of Provincial Total	Value-added Output	% of Provincial Total	Value-added Output
Manufacture of food	14.3	35.7	3.8	9.5	40.1
Manufacture of beverage	7.0	36.6	2.4	12.6	19.1
Textile industry	7.3	10.5	13.1	18.8	69.8
Petroleum refining, coking and nuclear fuel processing	15.2	21.7	4.9	7.0	70.0
Manufacture of raw chemical materials and chemical products	60.7	47.3	12.6	9.8	128.2
Manufacture of medicines	6.6	23.7	1.6	5.7	27.9
Plastic products	7.6	8.8	17.5	20.2	86.8
Nonmetal mineral products	4.4	5.1	25.2	29.3	86.1
Smelting and pressing of nonferrous metals	4.1	8.1	17.5	34.7	50.4
Metal products	7.7	7.3	28.5	27.1	105.3
Manufacture of special-purpose equipment	3.7	8.7	9.1	21.4	42.5
Manufacture of transport equipment	103.1	68.4	9.9	6.6	150.8
Manufacture of electrical machinery and equipment	15.3	6.4	71.5	30.0	238.6
Manufacture of communication equipment, computers and other electronic equipment	40.2	9.3	15.0	3.5	430.6
Production and supply of gas	8.4	51.2	0.6	3.7	16.4

Source: Compiled by the author.

A case in point is in the cooperation of developing the automobile industry. The two cities have formed a relatively complementary automobile production network with upstream and downstream industrial enterprises. Guangzhou has developed automobile production lines with strong capacity, while Foshan focuses on developing manufacturing capacity for auto parts, as is reflected by the presence of up to 300 auto parts makers in Nanhai, Shunde and Sanshui within Foshan. For example, FAW-Volkswagen, one of the leading automobile enterprises in China, invested up to US$2 billion and set up a manufacturing plant in Foshan in mid-2010.[7] By tapping on each other's advantages, the Guangzhou–Foshan megacity can potentially forge an automobile cluster with strong capacity in manufacturing and product design.

The complementary industrial linkages therefore provide a solid foundation to forging closer industrial cooperation and developing an integrated regional market thus effectively reducing duplication of industrial developments and avoiding excessive competition. The central government is expected to formulate additional favourable policy measures to boost the overall economic growth of this megacity.

On the part of the Guangdong government, it hopes that the creation of Guangzhou–Foshan megacity will help local industrial enterprises pursue technological upgrading and strengthen product competitiveness, and encourage mergers and acquisitions of enterprises across the two cities. To help local industrial upgrading and provide research funding for the small and medium-sized enterprises, the government is expected to increase spending on research and development (R&D) activities (the share of R&D in total GRP is expected to reach above 2.7 per cent by 2012) and developing key technologies. The Guangdong government intends to turn the Guangzhou–Foshan area into an important global base for advanced manufacturing industries through fostering research, innovation and indigenous core technology.

Forging a fully integrated megacity: issues and challenges

The merger of Guangzhou and Foshan is an initiative of the Guangdong government. The role of the state in this project is essential, particularly in the construction of inter-city transportation network and other infrastructure; however, it cannot replace the role of the private sector. Without the support of the local community and wide acceptance at the grass-roots, the megacity project would hardly be sustainable from the long-term perspective. Despite official enthusiasm over the megacity project, responses from residents tend to be quite mixed.

Financially, the Guangzhou–Foshan megacity is likely to benefit local residents. First, inter-city living costs in transportation, health care and education, for instance, are expected to decrease. It will help boost inter-city business and leisure interchange. Second, Guangzhou and Foshan can capitalize on each other's strengths. The large consumer market in Guangzhou will provide more business opportunities for Foshan's manufacturing-enterprises, while Guangzhou's service enterprises will find more room to develop in Foshan. It will help both cities' industrial enterprises to weather the negative impacts deriving from global economic uncertainties, thus reducing their dependence on foreign markets and achieving long-term development.

Nevertheless, residents will not support this megacity project unless inter-city phone and medical services and education, issues which directly affect their daily lives have been properly addressed. Some local people have expressed strong concerns and oppose the development of such a megacity.

To ensure the success of the megacity, Guangzhou and Foshan will need to cooperate to eliminate administrative barriers, which hinder the integration process. The authorities have to make more effort to facilitate free inter-city movement of human talent, capital and information, and to unify the provision of public goods across the two cities. Bureaucratic resistance of local officials would also need to be addressed. The creation of Guangzhou–Foshan megacity will lead to the mergers of related government organizations and departments in both cities. Certain workers will be axed with this downsizing. More government efforts are needed in the redeployment of workers affected.

The redistribution of local public finance and government revenue between Guangzhou and Foshan would also need to be amiably settled. Guangzhou, the capital city of Guangdong and one of the richest cities in China, has to be prepared to share its local financial and other resources with the relatively poor Foshan. In 2010, Guangzhou's contribution to the government's general budgetary revenue was at 87.3 billion yuan, more than twice that of Foshan's 30.6 billion yuan. In terms of per capita government budgetary revenue in 2010, the relative figures for Guangzhou and Foshan were 7,101 yuan and 4,349 yuan respectively (Table 3.5).

Some local officials and residents in Guangzhou have already voiced their concerns and anger on this issue. Wang Yang has called on Guangzhou officials to have the spirit of a 'big brother' and be magnanimous in sharing public goods resources with

Table 3.5 Government general budgetary revenue in Guangzhou and Foshan

City	Indicator	2000	2004	2006	2008	2010
Guangzhou	Government budgetary revenue (billion yuan)	20.1	30.3	42.7	62.2	87.3
	Percentage of total provincial government budgetary revenue (%)	22.1	21.4	19.6	18.8	19.3
	Per capita government budgetary revenue (yuan)	2062	3124	4389	5736	7101
Foshan	Government budgetary revenue (billion yuan)	6.0	9.5	15.7	22.8	30.6
	Percentage of total provincial government budgetary revenue (%)	6.6	6.7	7.2	6.9	6.8
	Per capita government budgetary revenue (yuan)	1147	1673	2653	3543	4349

Source: 2011 *Guangdong Statistical Yearbook*

the 'little brother', Foshan, if the city is to become the core area of the PRD region.[8] Key issues such as education, medical care, and pensions and society security will test the willingness and determination of both cities to pursue regional integration. Response from Foshanese citizens has not been encouraging either. Given the strong economic power of Guangzhou and its privileged status as provincial capital, Foshanese citizen fear that Foshan will be gradually marginalized, and its ancient cultural, art and social traditions will eventually be lost. Foshan is the birthplace of the *Lingnan* culture and over its long history, it has developed many unique and distinguished Cantonese cultural traditions and products. It is renowned, for instance, for Huang Feihong martial arts, Cantonese opera, dragon boat racing, cuisine, poetry and china. Many of these traditions are treasured by not only the local people but also people from other areas such as the PRD, Hong Kong, Macau and Southeast Asian countries.

In addition, due to their rapid urbanization and industrialization, Guangzhou and Foshan are suffering from serious environmental pollution. The devastating environmental report published by Greenpeace in 2010, an independent and non-profit organization, demonstrated serious water pollution in Guangzhou and other cities within the PRD caused by wastewater discharge from local industrial factories. The wastewater containing hazardous materials and toxic metals has heavily polluted the Pearl River and other surrounding rivers and is a threat to the environment and human health.[9]

The local environment in Guangzhou and Foshan has deteriorated significantly with the sprouting of numerous export-oriented manufacturing factories in recent years. Massive industrial and economic development has come at an unacceptable environmental cost. The creation of Guangzhou–Foshan megacity will further boost industrial growth and attract more enterprises. In terms of environmental protection and human health, it is questionable if it is wise or affordable for Guangzhou and Foshan to forge a megacity.

In terms of car ownership, Guangzhou and Foshan are currently two of the most crowded cities in Guangdong and in China with deteriorating problems of traffic congestion. As shown in Table 3.3, the combined ownership of private vehicles in these two cities exceeded two million, representing 32.7 per cent of total ownership of private vehicles in Guangdong. Given the serious traffic congestion and over-crowded conditions, it is debatable if Guangzhou–Foshan can cope with the projected increase in population and traffic. This would only add extra pressure to the social burdens of public goods provision, a situation which Guangzhou–Foshan may not have the capacity to handle.

Despite the aforementioned issues of bureaucratic resistance among local officials, local pollution and traffic congestion, many features of integration are already in place in Guangzhou and Foshan. Transportation and other physical infrastructure are well coordinated, while the industrial complementariness between Guangzhou and Foshan is working well to strengthen the competitiveness of local industrial enterprises. In standardizing the provision of public goods, particularly in the areas of education and health care, the local governments are also making progress. Nevertheless, more needs to be done over a long time span before a fully integrated Guangzhou–Foshan megacity, could be operational.

Appendix 3.1 Chronology of events

2000	The Guangzhou government had devised a development strategy to provide a 'west link' in order to strengthen the economic cooperation with Foshan.
2002	The concept of "Guangzhou–Foshan Economic Circle" was proposed.
2003	The Foshan government proposed an 'east link' to strengthen economic cooperation with Guangzhou and benefit from the spillovers.
December 2005	The forum on The Regional Cooperation and Development between Guangzhou and Foshan was held to discuss the specific proposals and measures to form close inter-city cooperation.
June 2007	Construction started on the Guangzhou–Foshan Inter-city Metro Line.
December 2008	The State Council of China approved the *Outline of Reform and Development for the Pearl River Delta Region (2008–2020)*. The Chinese central government projects that the Guangzhou–Foshan integration can serve as a model to drive coordinated regional development within the PRD region.
March 2009	The municipal governments of Guangzhou and Foshan signed the Cooperation Framework Agreement on the Guangzhou–Foshan Integration.
December 2009	The Chinese government approved the Development Outline for Guangzhou–Foshan Integration (2009–2020).
November 2010	The 32-km-long Guzhou–Foshan Inter-city Metro Line came into operation; it is the first inter-city metro line in China.

Source: Compiled by the author.

Notes

1 Data source from *Guangdong Statistical Yearbook 2011*.
2 Beijing and Shanghai have maintained their superiority over the Guangzhou–Foshan megacity in terms of their appeal to foreign investors. The figures for foreign trade by Shanghai and Beijing, and FDI inflow to these two cities were higher than those for the Guangzhou–Foshan megacity.
3 "Guangfo tongcheng chengli siren lingdao xiaozu, jianli guangfo shizhang lianxi huiyi zhidu" (Leader's group and inter-city mayor coordination committee have been established to facilitate the development of Guangzhou–Foshan megacity), *Guangzhou Daily*, 19 March 2009, http://news.dayoo.com/finance/66655/66657/200903/19/66657_5506677. htm (accessed 28 January 2012)
4 "Development in China: The Pearl River Mega-city," *The Economist*, 12 February 2011, http://www.economist.com/blogs/gulliver/2011/02/development_china (accessed 29 January 2012)
5 "Wang Yang: Zhusanjiao guihua yi guangfo tongchenghua wei shifan" (Wang Yang: The Guangzhou–Foshan megacity will be the role model for the implementation of the Outline of Reform and Development for the PRD), *Xinhua*, 21 May 2011, http://news. xinhuanet.com/politics/2011-05/21/c_121442094.htm (accessed 23 January 2012)
6 *2011 Guangdong Statistical Yearbook*.
7 "Foshan attracting investors with many advantages," *China Daily*, 29 September 2011, http://www.chinadaily.com.cn/cndy/2011-09/29/content_13814032.htm (accessed 27 January 2012).
8 "*Wang Yang litui zhusanjiao yitihua*" (Wang Yang pushes forward the integration of the Pearl River Delta region), *Hong Kong Mingpao*, 4 February 2009, http://life.mingpao. com/cfm/dailynews3b.cfm?File=20090204/nalca/caa1.txt (accessed 25 January 2012).
9 "Poisoning the pearl: An investigation into industrial water pollution in the Pearl River delta" (2nd edition), *The Greenpeace*, January 2010, pp. 1–68.

4 Nansha new district in Guangdong

State initiatives and perspectives

Background to Nansha and the unveiling of the state plan

Nansha New Area is located in the southern region of Guangzhou, the capital city of Guangdong. It has a total land area of 803 square km and a population of 0.74 million.[1] In the past, little was known of this tiny fishing town. The backward transportation facilities and relative remoteness have earned for Nansha the unflattering nickname of the "Siberia of the Pearl River Delta". Nevertheless, with Beijing's blessing, Nansha has now remade itself to play a lead role in the economic transformation of the Pearl River Delta region (PRD). Its gross regional product (GRP) grew from 6.2 billion yuan in 2002 to 57.1 billion yuan in 2011 at an average annual growth rate of 28 per cent (Figure 4.1).

In September 2012, Nansha was mapped out as a new national development area and a new blueprint for Nansha New Area of Guangzhou (广州南沙新区发展规划) (referred to as the Plan) by the Chinese central government. It is the sixth new national development area, after Pudong in Shanghai, Binhai in Tianjin, Liangjiang in Chongqing, Zhoushan in Zhejiang and Lanzhou in Gansu. The development of Nansha has now been upgraded to a national strategy. The Chinese authorities are expected to provide a wide range of preferential policies to support Nansha's development and reforms, including measures on taxation, land use, finance and industrial upgrading.

After years of policy debates, the Chinese authorities have finally decided on the direction and positioning of Nansha's future development. Nansha was initially designated for heavy manufacturing industries and a national base for steel and petrochemical industries. The concern over environmental pollution had caused the Guangdong government to suspend the scheme and some huge projects for petrochemical and steel factories in Nansha funded by China's state-owned enterprises in the early 2000s.[2]

The authorities aim to have Nansha as a reform pioneer and growth engine to boost the future economic development of Guangzhou, strengthening its domestic and international competitiveness, particularly in the modern service industry. Nansha is set to become a service outsourcing base for activities such as IT outsourcing, logistics outsourcing and software business outsourcing for the PRD.

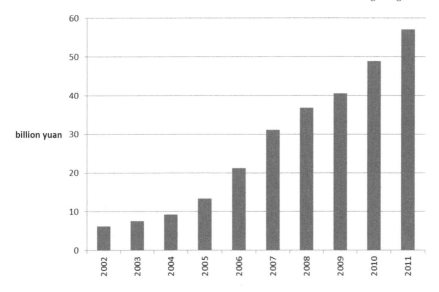

Figure 4.1 GRP of Nansha new district

Source: Nansha Statistics Bureau

The development of Nansha at the state level is to speed up the rather sluggish pace of industrial upgrading of Guangdong[3] as well as developing Guangzhou into a key national city of global significance.

Nansha enjoys various unique advantages. First, Nansha Port is Guangzhou's only gateway to the sea. It will pave the way for Guangzhou to participate in the international production chain and pursue industrial upgrading by tapping into its premium port facilities. It will facilitate foreign trade for Guangzhou as well as the entire PRD region.

Second, Nansha is strategically located in the centre of the PRD region, one of the most developed and dynamic economic regions in China. It is also only 70 km from Hong Kong and is linked to the PRD road network encompassing all 14 large cities within the PRD that connects to Hong Kong and Macao by expressway, sea or high-speed metro link. Twelve passenger ships run daily between Nansha and Hong Kong. PRD's booming manufacturing-led economy and domestic consumption is a huge hinterland and enormous development potential for Nansha, particularly for its service industry.

Third, in 1993, Nansha was designated by Beijing as a national economic and technological development zone, high-tech industrial development zone and bonded zone. Its potential is further enhanced by the implementation of the Closer Economic Partnership Arrangements (CEPA) between the Mainland, Hong Kong and Macao in 2010. By tapping into this, Nansha is a step ahead of other regions in its service sector cooperation with Hong Kong and Macao, thus speeding up the development of its service-driven economy.

Nansha: a fast developing area of Guangdong

Nansha's economy has achieved spectacular growth during the past 10 years, registering a GRP of 57.1 billion yuan in 2011 from 6.2 billion yuan in 2002, an average annual growth rate of 28 per cent. The economic performance of Nansha makes it a fast growing area in Guangzhou and the PRD as a whole; it accounted for 4.6 per cent of Guangzhou's GRP in 2011 from less than 2 per cent in 2002 (Figure 4.2). Although the figures are still relatively small, they indicate Nansha's increasing importance to Guangzhou's economy.

The industrial output value of Nansha increased to 170.3 billion yuan in 2011 from 10.8 billion yuan in 2002, an annual growth rate of 35.8 per cent (Figure 4.3). This is particularly attributable to its relatively strong manufacturing industries. The output value of the advanced manufacturing industry of Nansha was 93.7 billion yuan in 2011, dominated largely by the automobile industry at 72.6 billion yuan in 2011, a growth spearheaded by Guangzhou's Toyota automobile factory. The automobile sector accounted for more than 42 per cent of total industrial output of Nansha in 2011. Nansha is emerging as one of the three key automobile production and export bases in China. The output values of the shipbuilding and petrochemical industries were 8.7 billion yuan and 23.5 billion yuan in 2011, accounting for 5.1 per cent and 13.8 per cent respectively of the industrial output value of Nansha (Figure 4.4).

Nansha Longxue Island will be developed as a key national shipbuilding base and repair shipyard when the project is completed and operational. China State

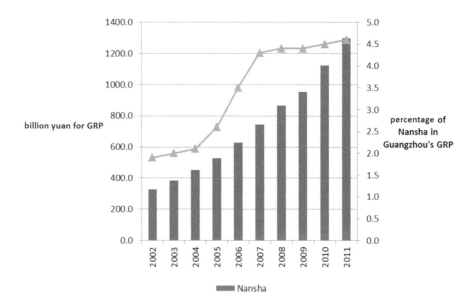

Figure 4.2 Nansha's GRP in Guangzhou

Source: Nansha Statistics Bureau, *Guangdong Statistical Yearbook*, 2009 and 2012

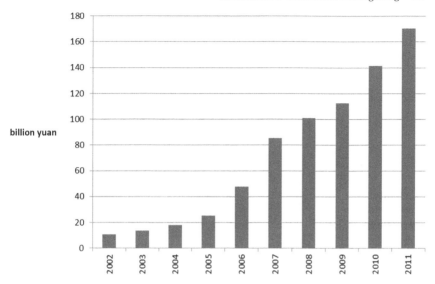

Figure 4.3 Industrial output value of Nansha

Source: Nansha Statistics Bureau

Shipbuilding Corporation has been commissioned to build 300,000-ton large ships, containers and other marine engineering projects for Guangzhou to conduct ocean resource exploration of the South China Sea.

With 48 domestic and international freight routes covering Southeast Asia, Middle East, Africa, Europe as well as the Americas, Nansha's deepwater port is taking shape; it now has 10 deep docks of 50,000–100,000 tons capacity. In 2011, Nansha port completed 147 million tons of cargo throughput and 8.92 million TEU (twenty-foot equivalent unit). Due to its premium port facilities and geographical superiority, exports from Nansha increased to US$4.02 billion in 2011 from US$0.5 billion in 2002; the total value of foreign trade from Nansha increased from only US$1.13 billion in 2002 to US$10.67 billion in 2011.

Most of Nansha's investment will be financed by bank loans, particularly for transportation and other infrastructure facilities. China Development Bank will loan a total of 62 billion yuan to Nansha during the 12th Five-Year Program period (2011–2015).[4]

Nansha is no stranger to Hong Kongers, who are the top foreign investors in Nansha. The economic cooperation between Hong Kong and Nansha could be traced back to the 1980s when some Hong Kong-funded foreign enterprises were already in joint venture with local partners in Nansha.[5] The inflow of utilized foreign direct investment (FDI) to Nansha had risen from US$0.65 billion in 2002 to US$672 million in 2011 (Figure 4.5).

The development of Nansha is closely associated with the late Dr Fok Ying-tung (1923–2006), a powerful tycoon in Hong Kong. Fok forged close political ties

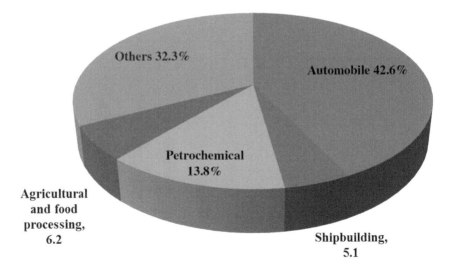

Figure 4.4 Composition of secondary industry in Nansha, 2011 (by percentage)

Source: Nansha Statistics Bureau

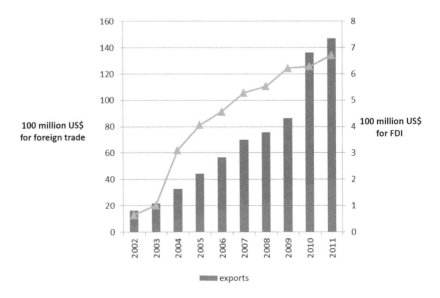

Figure 4.5 FDI and foreign trade of Nansha

Source: Nansha Statistics Bureau

with Beijing and was a politically well-connected businessperson. He was an ex-vice chairman of the National Committee of the Chinese People's Political Consultative Conference of China. Nansha was his hometown. Developing Nansha was Fok's lifelong dream. Fok had lobbied Beijing for special treatment and state initiatives for years. Fok and his family have spent billions of dollars on infrastructure construction, recreational facilities, real estate and other business activities in Nansha since the early 1990s.[6]

New state blueprint for Nansha

The central government's release of a number of regional development plans, along with various initiatives and preferential policies since 2008 has pressured Wang Yang and other Guangdong leaders to promote the development of Nansha to strengthen the regional competitiveness of Guangdong. From the local officials' perspective, Guangdong will lose ground and its unique position without a boost from new state initiatives. Wang Yang, the then party secretary of Guangdong, played an important role in pushing for the grand development of Nansha by lobbying for national support and endorsement.

The provincial and municipal governments submitted a draft of the development plan for Nansha. In 2012, the State Council of China approved the Nansha Development Plan. A national coordinating mechanism led by the National Reform and Development Commission (NDRC) with the participation of other relevant ministries, Hong Kong and Macao governments, Guangdong provincial and Guangzhou municipal governments was established to oversee Nansha's development, solve problems over coordination within different governments, and provide comprehensive support.

The Guangdong authorities have high hopes for Nansha to take the lead in overcoming institutional barriers and achieving breakthroughs in key reform areas, including administration, innovation, economic and social management with the implementation of a wide range of pilot programs. In administration, Nansha can lead in reforming administrative approval procedures for business registration, business operations and business supervision through promoting online review and approval systems. For instance, to prevent and counter official corruption, officials in Nansha are required to report on their personal income and property, and strictly implement an official property declaration system. The system has been expanded to include all top and middle-ranking local officials. Nansha will institutionalize this practice and allow public supervision and oversight.[7]

As outlined in the Plan, Nansha will be the first to have the autonomy to facilitate immigration checks and relax visa controls on length of residence for skilled foreigners in Nansha. The government will also facilitate cross-border passenger travel between Nansha, Hong Kong and Macao. These policies aim to facilitate human and information flow and exchange, attract more foreign investment and foreign talent to Nansha to work, establish a business presence and conduct export and import trade via the Nansha port.

The central government has approved the setting up of a national pilot zone for reforming human talent management in Nansha, along with Qianhai and Hengqin (广州南沙-深圳前海-珠海横琴粤港澳人才合作示范区). The local government is expected to introduce various measures including tax concession on personal income, flexible visa controls across Hong Kong and Macao, education, health care and housing allowance to attract creative and high-skilled talent. Nansha aims to attract up to 5,000 creative and high-skilled talents or 15 per cent of total high-skilled talent working in Nansha by 2015.[8]

To build a truly international port, Nansha is expected to intensify its custom clearance reforms, improve the inspection and service system of bonded logistics, and increase overall port efficiency for foreign trade. In order to forge close cooperation with Hong Kong, the state plans to introduce Hong Kong practices of advanced economic and social management, urban planning and public service provision as well as its administrative governance and institutional framework to Nansha.[9]

As outlined in the Plan, Nansha is designated as a key comprehensive cooperation platform for forging closer ties between mainland China, Hong Kong and Macao in service outsourcing, innovation and education. The local government goes even further and plans to create a "mini-Hong Kong" in Nansha.

According to the Plan, Nansha will focus on promoting shipping logistics, high-tech innovation, tourism, automobile and shipbuilding (ship manufacturing, overhaul and repairs) as advanced manufacturing and service industries. The government will encourage the development of new generation electronic information products and services (e.g. integrated circuits, flat panel displays and electronic appliances) and marine engineering industries (e.g. manufacturing of marine engineering equipment, and oil and gas exploration equipment). The development of high value-added shipping-related services, including shipping finance, insurance, settlement, brokerage and ship trading, will also receive state priority.

The government will issue a variety of preferential policies, such as industry investment funds and land use preference, to promote the growth of these five strategic industries. The authorities will lower investment thresholds and ease investment qualifications to pave the way for the private sector. The government will open the market wide for qualified medical service providers and personnel to do business in Nansha and provide a level playing field for both state-owned and private investors.

According to the Plan, the government will initiate measures to build an environmentally friendly and energy-saving society in Nansha. By tapping on this opportunity, the local government will boost the development of the service industry. A case in point is the development of the cruise and boating industries. Efforts will be made to speed up the construction of an international cruise wharf and homeport to develop Nansha into a high-end tourist attraction for businesspersons and leisure seekers.

The government has targeted the value-added output of the tertiary industry to account for more than 65 per cent of GRP in Nansha by 2025. Nansha has to reduce the volume of energy consumption per unit of GRP by 20 per cent and the land utilization size per unit of GRP by 30 per cent in comparison to the 2010 figures, as well as reduce the volume of water usage per unit of value-added industrial output.

The Plan emphasizes the need to improve people's well-being and give them a greater share in economic growth. The government has plans to have Nansha take the lead in developing an inclusive economic growth model to ensure more equitable sharing of benefits of economic growth by all people, thereby increasing social harmony.

The Plan encourages the local Nansha government to implement new initiatives to become an innovation and reform zone for social management and public services (社会管理服务创新试验区). The local government needs to work out new measures to transform a stability and maintenance-driven social management system to a people-first system. The government aims to implement a street and household-based rural-urban integrated social management framework.

The government will forge cooperation with Hong Kong and Macao on social management and import social organizations from Hong Kong to Nansha and transfer certain social management responsibilities to them. The government will bid for and buy social services from these social organizations and enhance their self-development capability. It seeks to improve the public service system and build efficient and modern public services in Nansha.

On health care, the Plan has designated Nansha as the pioneer in establishing a premium health care system covering both urban and rural residents. The government will encourage non-governmental and private organizations to invest in the health care sector and provide high-end medical services to residents.

Challenges and perspectives for Nansha

Several new regional development plans for Guangdong have been approved by the Chinese central government, including those for Hengqin in Zhuhai (珠海横琴), Qianhai in Shenzhen (深圳前海) and Nansha in Guangzhou (广州南沙). According to their individual state plans, the areas will be developed into three key platforms to stimulate the economic restructuring and industrial upgrading of Guangdong, and forge close cooperation with Hong Kong and Macao. The Guangdong government believes that these regions can take the lead in creating a new type of provincial development. Though Qianhai and Hengqin have been designated as platforms for cooperation with Hong Kong and Macao respectively, Nansha has a bigger role to play being the platform for forging cooperation with both Hong Kong and Macao.

The local government's expectations of Nansha are high. Local officials of Guangzhou have labelled Nansha as the best area for Guangzhou's future development.[10] The authorities would want Nansha to lead in the implementation of various reform initiatives, from economic openness to social and administrative management. Besides its new state initiatives for Nansha, the Guangdong government has already announced that all special policies offered to Qianhai and Hengqin will be granted to Nansha as well.[11]

Nansha will also be granted various new autonomous powers via the provincial government of Guangdong, as announced by Zhu Xiaodan, governor of Guangdong province. Compared to the other two new regions, Nansha enjoys more state preferential treatments. The development of Nansha will be coordinated by a NDRC-led national mechanism, unlike the other regional development plans for Qianhai and Hengqin.

Although top Guangdong officials promised that the local authority in Nansha would be granted more freedom and authority to implement new reform initiatives and development proposals, the real extent of the autonomy remains unknown. As Nansha is under the jurisdiction and administration of the municipal government of Guangzhou, local public finance and taxation collection are supervised by the Guangzhou municipal government.

Local official personnel change and cadre management affairs are approved by the municipal government. Nansha officials have to seek the approval of the municipal government for any big local development projects. The Nansha government thus lacks the authority to exercise real autonomy over local development, implement reform initiatives or achieve reform breakthroughs.

During a press conference organized by the State Council Information Office in 2012, Guangzhou Mayor Chen Jianhua clearly stated that the Guangzhou municipal government, rather than the local government of Nansha, would be the dominant player in the development of Nansha.[12] Unless the Nansha government is allowed to execute municipal-level administrative power over local affairs, its ability to play a lead role in initiating and implementing reforms will be limited.

The structure of the Nansha government administration is also far too cumbersome. There are up to 23 government departments, each with different responsibilities (Table 4.1). To further complicate the situation, the Chinese authority has even set up separate but similar administrative units in the Nansha Economic and Technological Development Zone, a part of Nansha. A "super-ministry" style of institutional restructuring and reform, similar to that implemented in several areas of Guangdong (e.g. Shenzhen and Shunde), is badly needed in Nansha to reduce red tape and the burden of bureaucracy.

The Nansha government has yet to meet the increasing challenge posed by its rural and urban populations to provide equal and standard basic public services and good social management. The Nansha government would have to streamline its departments through adjustments, mergers and dissolution if it is to become more service oriented, while ensuring economic regulation and market supervision. The kind of new pilot schemes and reform measures the Nansha government will introduce, and the extent to which it can implement such initiatives remain to be seen. The problems of the national institutions and political system will make it difficult for the local government to implement new policy initiatives.

Another serious challenge for Nansha to forge cooperation with the two neighbouring SAR regions is the increasingly strong resistance from the local community in Hong Kong. Some Hong Kongers fear that the Plan would diminish Hong Kong's leading position in the service industry. Despite the good intentions and state-initiated efforts, the development of close regional cooperation between

Table 4.1 Administration structure of the Nansha government

The Nansha Government (广州市南沙区政府)	➢ Development and Reform Bureau (发改局) ➢ General Office (政府办公室) ➢ Bureau of Economy and Information (经信局) ➢ Bureau of Education (教育局) ➢ Bureau of Justice (司法局) ➢ Bureau of Finance (财政局) ➢ Bureau of Human Resources and Social Security (人力资源和社保局) ➢ Bureau of Environmental Protection (环保局) ➢ Bureau of Supervision (监察局) ➢ Bureau of Water Affairs (水务局) ➢ Bureau of Agriculture and Forestry (农林局) ➢ Bureau of Culture, Press, Publication, Radio and Television (文广新局) ➢ Bureau of Health (卫生局) ➢ Bureau of Audit (审计局) ➢ City Administration Bureau (城管局) ➢ Bureau of Work Safety (安监局) ➢ Bureau of Public Security (公安局) ➢ Bureau of Urban Planning (规划局) ➢ Bureau of Construction (建设局) ➢ Bureau of Industry and Commerce (工商局) ➢ Bureau of Local Taxation (地方税务局) ➢ Bureau of Quality and Technology Supervision (质量技术监督局) ➢ Bureau of Food and Drug Safety Supervision (食品药品监管局)

Source: Compiled by the author.

Hong Kong and Nansha will be a difficult and lengthy process due to their different institutional systems, governance and development.[13]

After the Plan for Nansha was unveiled, the local Hong Kong media has frequently reported on the threat of Nansha International Port to Hong Kong in terms of weakening its status as the world's leading port and international shipping centre.

Nansha will also have to map out a path to stimulate its service industry and upgrade its tertiary industry. Despite the state plan to promote the service industry, the share of tertiary industry in total GRP of Nansha sharply decreased to 16.9 per cent in 2011 from 23.1 per cent in 2002. This indicates that the service sector has grown slowly and is relatively weak. The manufacturing-led secondary industry accounted for a much larger portion of Nansha's GRP (Figure 4.6). A regional comparison based on the percentages of tertiary industry in GRP shows that the development of the service industry in other new development areas has been faster than that of Nansha (Table 4.2). Table 4.2 shows that of the six national-level new areas designated by the Chinese central government, Nansha's current position in terms of various performance indicators among regions is disappointing. Nansha's economy is relatively small, and its industrial output value, exports and

Table 4.2 Comparison of main economic indicators among China's six national-level new areas

Indicator	National New Development Area					
	Nansha	Pudong	Binhai	Liangjiang	Zhoushan	Lanzhou
Geographical location	Guangdong	Shanghai	Tianjin	Chongqing	Zhejiang	Gansu
Land size (square km)	803	1,210	2,270	1,200	1,440	8,208
Permanent residential population (million persons)	0.27	5.05	2.43	1.60	1.14	0.55
Gross regional product (billion yuan)	57.1	548.4	620.7	105.5	76.5	9.8
Secondary industry (billion yuan) (percentage of GRP)	45.9 (80.4%)	230.6 (42.0%)	343.3 (55.3%)	57.3 (54.3%)	34.5 (45.1%)	5.0 (51.0%)
Tertiary industry (billion yuan) (percentage of GRP)	9.6 (16.8%)	314.3 (57.3%)	158.9 (25.6%)	46.4 (43.9%)	34.4 (44.9%)	3.6 (36.7%)
Industrial output value (billion yuan)	169.1	925.3	1065.3	198.5	111.5	3.9
Total value of foreign trade (US$ billion)	10.6	226.0	58.6	4.1	13.2	n.a.
Exports value (US$ billion)	4.0	88.9	n.a.	2.0	7.4	n.a.
FDI (US$ billion)	0.7	5.3	8.5	1.6	0.1	n.a.
Local government budget revenue (billion yuan)	3.1	42.5	62.3	24.5	12.7	0.2

Source: Compiled by the author based on various information.

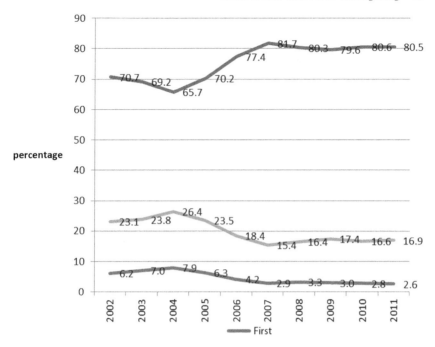

Figure 4.6 Composition of GRP in Nansha

Source: Nansha Statistics Bureau

inflow of FDI are much lower than those of Pudong in Shanghai and Binhai in Tianjin. This means that there is a lot more for Nansha to work on.

Notes

1 Nansha New District covers 10 township-level administrative units, including Nansha, Zhujiang, Longxue, Huangge, Hengli, Wanqingsha, Dongchong, Lanhe and Dagang.
2 "Nansha to drive Guangzhou development", *South China Morning Post*, 9 March 2011, http://www.scmp.com/article/740306/nansha-drive-guangzhou-development (accessed 22 February 2013)
3 Yu Hong and Zhang Yang. (2009, 17 July). "New initiatives for industrial upgrading in the Pearl River Delta", *EAI Background Brief No. 464*, National University of Singapore.
4 "Guangzhou plans $28b investment to develop Nansha", *South China Morning Post*, 30 October 2002, http://www.scmp.com/article/395911/guangzhou-plans-28b-invest ment-develop-nansha (accessed 22 February 2013)
5 "*Guowuyuan pifu nansha chengwei guojiaji xinqu dazao jingdeqi jianyan de weida zuopin*" (State Council approved Nansha as a new national development area), *Southern Daily*, 18 October 2012, http://news.southcn.com/g/2012-10/18/content_56400964. htm (accessed 20 February 2013)
6 "A bigger picture for Guangzhou's Nansha", *China Daily*, 9 May 2012, http://www. chinadaily.com.cn/china/2012-05/09/content_15242058.htm (accessed 19 February 2013)
7 "*Nansha chuji ganbu jiang naru caichan shenbao fanwei*" (The top and middle-ranking local officials working in Nansha will have to report personal property and be included

in the official property declaration system), *Southern Daily*, 21 November 2012, http://news.southcn.com/g/2012-11/21/content_58565320.htm (accessed 21 November 2012)
8 *"Nansha qianhai hengqin jian rencaitequ huo zhongyang pizhun"* (The Chinese central government has approved the building of a pilot zone of human talent in Nansha, Qianhai and Hengqin), *Southern Daily*, 19 December 2012, http://news.southcn.com/g/2012-12/19/content_60434463.htm (accessed 1 February 2013)
9 *"Guangzhou nansha ni dazao xiaoxianggang litui yuegang yitihua"* (Nansha aims to build mini-Hong Kong and promote the integration of Guangdong and Hong Kong), *Lianhe Zaobao*, 11 October 2012, http://www.zaobao.com.sg/wencui/2012/10/hongkong121011d.shtml (accessed 11 January 2013)
10 "Guangzhou plans $28b investment to develop Nansha", *South China Morning Post*, 30 October 2002, http://www.scmp.com/article/395911/guangzhou-plans-28b-investment-develop-nansha (accessed 22 February 2013)
11 *"Wangyang qinzi duzhan: Guangzhou nansha xinqu guihua fangan gongbu"* (The role of Wang Yang and the publication of the development plan of Nansha new area), *21st Century Business Herald*, 13 October 2011.
12 *"Guoxinban jiu guangzhou nanshaxinqu fazhan guihua juxing fabuhui"* (State Council Information Office holds press conference to outline the development plan for Guangzhou Nansha), STCN, http://finance.ifeng.com/stock/zqyw/20121010/7126988.shtml (accessed 11 January 2013)
13 Yu Hong. "Hong Kong broadening its economic linkages with Guangdong", *EAI Background Brief* No. 645, East Asian Institute, National University of Singapore, 28 July 2011.

5 Development of the Beijing–Tianjin–Hebei economic zone

A rising economic zone

Backed by strong state support, the Beijing–Tianjin–Hebei Economic Circle (Jing-Jin-Ji) (北京–天津–河北经济圈或京津冀经济圈)[1] has experienced fast economic growth over the last decade. The contribution made by Jing-Jin-Ji region to China's total gross domestic product (GDP) was around 11 per cent in 2008 from 10 per cent in 2000. In 2008, its contribution to China's GDP exceeded that of the Pearl River Delta (PRD) for the first time.

The Jing-Jin-Ji region enjoys a comparative political advantage because Beijing is the national capital and political centre of China. Close proximity to the central government has allowed the local governments within this region to make use of communications to gain support from ministries. The other economic regions do not have the benefit of such accessibility.

Public infrastructure investment has been an important driving factor for the development of the Jing-Jin-Ji region. Investment has stimulated its industrial growth, particularly in the steel and automobile sectors. Total infrastructure investment in this region rose to around 680.2 billion yuan in 2012 from merely 61.1 billion yuan in 2003. The ratio of infrastructure investment to total regional GDP were up to 12.5 per cent in 2009 from 4.2 per cent in 2003, and then slightly decreased to 11.9 per cent (Figure 5.1).

Particularly, the public investment for the Beijing Olympic Games has updated and improved the entire system of local infrastructure. With new job creation and the long-term boost for service industries, consumption demand and overall economic growth of Beijing have been stimulated. By investing billions of dollars in Beijing, the central government did not only hope for the success of the Olympic Games and the projection of a modern image of China, but also intended to bolster the overall development of the Jing-Jin-Ji region. It is expected that this region will continue to enjoy the spillover effects of the Beijing Olympic legacy in the years to come.

The Jing-Jin-Ji region has spent more on research and development (R&D) than the other regions. In 2008, total government expenditure on R&D in this region was 86.4 billion yuan and amounted to 2.6 per cent of its GDP, considerably higher than the corresponding figures for the PRD (1.4 per cent) and Yangtze River Delta (YRD) (2.0 per cent) (see Table 5.2).

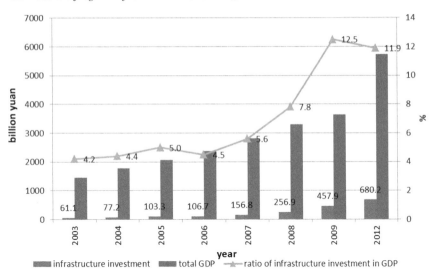

Figure 5.1 Growth of infrastructure investment in the Jing-Jin-Ji region

Source: The author compiled this figure using annual statistical yearbooks and public reports of national economic and social development statistics for the relevant regions.

The PRD and YRD regions' economic recovery has heavily relied on foreign trade and investment. In contrast, Jing-Jin-Ji region's economic growth is mainly fuelled by domestic investment and consumption (see the detailed discussion in the following section). The economic development of this region has not been badly affected by the global crisis. The quarterly rate of GDP growth in this region dropped only slightly in the third quarter of 2008 to 10.8 per cent from 12.9 per cent in the first quarter of that year.

The fact that a relatively high proportion of its exports are high technology products has also helped to mitigate the effects of global economic slowdown in the Jing-Jin-Ji region (see Table 5.1). The development of high-tech industries has been impressive in this region over the last few years. Its output value of high and new technological industry was 727.7 billion yuan in 2008, and this sector accounted for 30.6 per cent of total industrial output of the Jing-Jin-Ji region in 2008.

One of the main centres of development for high-tech industries is the Tianjin Binhai New Area (TBNA) (天津滨海新区). A high and new tech industry-led economy has gradually emerged in this region, with development of aviation at the core. Tianjin aims to become the major aviation centre of China.

The rapid development of TBNA has fuelled the economic growth of the Jing-Jin-Ji region despite the global economic crisis of 2008. Plan for development of this region as a key growth engine of China has been gradually taking shape since the TBNA became part of national strategy, as highlighted in the 11th Five-year Development Plan (十一五发展规划) adopted in 2006.

The Overall Plan for the Comprehensive Supporting Reform Pilot in Tianjin Binhai New Area (天津滨海新区综合配套改革试验总体方案) was finally

Table 5.1 Indicators of economic openness in the Jing-Jin-Ji region

Indicator	GDP (billion yuan)	Exports (US$ billion)	Ratio of Exports to GDP (%)	Exports of High-Tech Industrial Products (US$ billion)	Ratio of High-Tech Products in Total Exports (%)
2007	2,789	104	29	33	31
2008	3,303	124	26	38	31
2009	3,639	94	18	34	37
2012	5,735	137	15	38	28

Source: The annual statistical yearbooks and public reports of national economic and social development statistics for the relevant regions within the Jing-Jin-Ji (the ratio figures are the author's calculations).

Table 5.2 R&D expenditure in selected regions (billion yuan)

Year	Jing-Jin-Ji		PRD		YRD	
	R&D Expenditure	Ratio of R&D Expenditure to GDP (%)	R&D Expenditure	Ratio of R&D Expenditure to GDP (%)	R&D Expenditure	Ratio of R&D Expenditure to GDP (%)
2007	70.8	2.54	40.5	1.30	102.6	1.90
2008	86.4	2.61	49.0	1.37	123.3	1.98
2012	160.9	3.12	120.2	2.11	306.5	2.97

Source: The author compiled this figure using the statistical yearbooks for the relevant regions.

approved by the State Council in April 2008.[2] The TBNA is expected to exert economic leverage similar to that of Shenzhen Special Economic Zone in the PRD and Shanghai Pudong New Area in the YRD. The TBNA will become the driving force for the economic growth of the Jing-Jin-Ji region.

Huge challenges still remain for the Jing-Jin-Ji region in the coming years. Particularly, the economic cooperation and integration of Beijing, Tianjin and Hebei is weaker than that of the cities within the YRD and PRD regions. Independent industrial structures, weak industrial linkages and duplication of economic competition are the pressing problems. They also limit the development of an integrated domestic market.

Impacts of the global economic crisis

The GDP per capita in the Jing-Jin-Ji region increased to 72,411 yuan in 2012 from merely 1,109 yuan in 1980, with annual growth of 21 per cent (see Appendix 5.1). In contrast to areas relying more on exports such as the coastal PRD and

YRD regions, the economic growth of this region has not been badly affected by the global economic downturn. In 2009, the value of its exports in relation to GDP was merely 18 per cent (Table 5.1).

The quarterly rate of GDP growth in this region dropped only slightly in the third quarter of 2008 to 10.8 per cent from 12.9 per cent in the first quarter of that year. Thanks to the government stimulus package announced in November 2008, its economic growth increased to 11.8 per cent in the third quarter of 2009 from 10.2 per cent in the first quarter (Figure 5.2).

The rapid economic growth of this region has been largely driven by investment and consumption over the past 10 years. Therefore, it has helped to mitigate the potentially severe effects of global crisis in this region.

The growth of foreign trade and inflow of foreign direct investment (FDI) has also bolstered economic development of the Jing-Jin-Ji region. The total exports value had increased to US$137.5 billion in 2012 from only US$32.8 billion in 2000, with annual growth of 12.7 per cent. Value of inflow of FDI went up to US$29.0 billion in 2012 from US$6 billion in 2000 (Figure 5.3). Following the sharp decline of inflow of FDI to the PRD and YRD regions, there are clear signs that foreign capital is moving north in China toward the Jing-Jin-Ji region.

A relatively large share of the Jing-Jin-Ji region's total exports is made up of high technological products. Development in these industries has been impressive over the last few years, and this has also helped the region to withstand the global economic downturn. One of the main centres of development for high-tech industries is the TBNA. The output value of high and new technological industry in this economic zone was 1004.6 billion yuan in 2012. High and new technological sectors accounted for 25.4 per cent of its total industrial output in 2012 (Figure 5.4).

The Jing-Jin-Ji region has shown stronger capability in technological innovation than the other regions and has spent more on R&D. In 2012, total government expenditure on R&D in this region was 160.9 billion yuan and amounted to 3.12 per cent of its GDP, considerably higher than the corresponding figures for the PRD (2.11 per cent) and YRD (2.97 per cent) regions (Table 5.2).

The rapid increase in the numbers of patents granted also reflects the strong technological capacity in the Jing-Jin-Ji region. In 2012, a total of 85,829 patents were granted, which was a 8.3 fold increase from 10,328 in 2000 (Figure 5.5).

Strong research capability and an abundant supply of highly skilled workers offer the Jing-Jin-Ji region extra edge in strengthening its competitiveness. Educational advantages provide golden opportunities for scientific research, high technological innovation, and above all, the practical application of technology. With Beijing as the key educational centre, there are more than 230 universities and 700 research institutions and a cluster of scientists and researchers within this region.

Furthermore, these universities are turning out large numbers of highly qualified graduates, and the total number of students in higher education institutions increased to 2.27 million in 2012 from merely 0.45 million in 2000, with an annual growth rate of 14.4 per cent (Figure 5.6). The Jing-Jin-Ji region will likely further expand and serve as one of the key growth engine for China's economic development in the future.

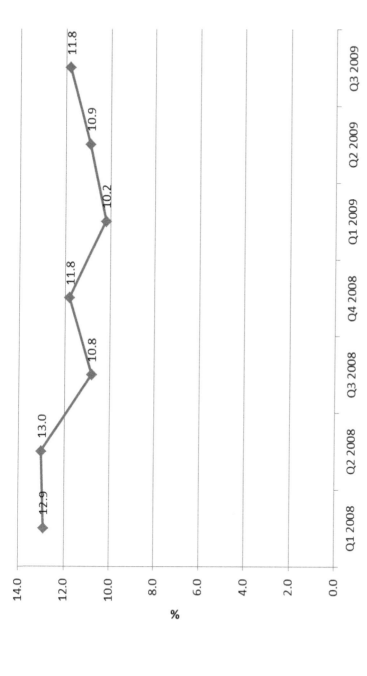

Figure 5.2 Quarterly GDP growth in the Jing-Jin-Ji region

Source: The author compiled this figure based on statistics bureau data for the relevant regions within the Jing-Jin-Ji.

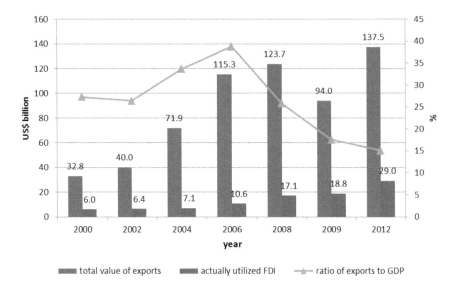

Figure 5.3 Growth of exports and inflow FDI in the Jing-Jin-Ji region

Source: The author compiled this figure using statistical yearbooks for the relevant regions.

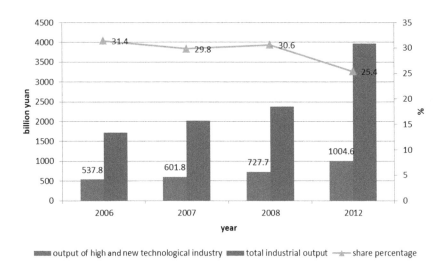

Figure 5.4 Share of high and new technological industry in industrial output in the Jing-Jin-Ji region

Source: Statistical yearbooks for the relevant regions, various years (the share percentages are the author's calculations).

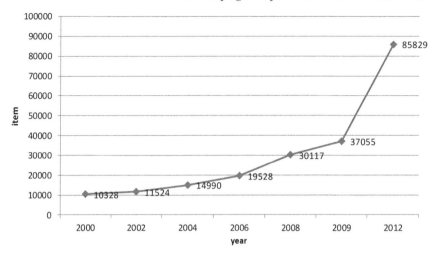

Figure 5.5 Growth of patent applications granted in the Jing-Jin-Ji region

Source: The author compiled this figure using statistical yearbooks and public reports of national economic and social development statistics for the relevant regions.

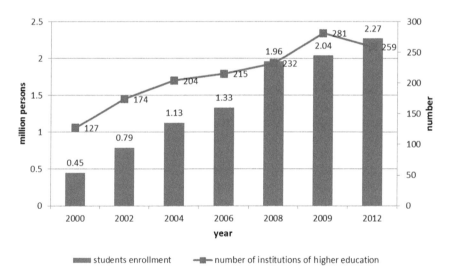

Figure 5.6 Educational development indicators in the Jing-Jin-Ji region

Source: The author compiled this figure using the statistical yearbooks and public reports of national economic and social development statistics for the relevant regions.

Beijing's Olympic legacy

During the period of preparation for the Beijing Olympic Games of 2008, both the central and municipal governments had offered huge capital investment in transportation and other infrastructure construction (Table 5.3). In total, 116 km of

Table 5.3 Total construction investment for the Beijing Olympic Games, 2008 (US$ billion)

Construction Investment	2001	2002	2003	2004	2005	2006	2007	2008	Total
Planned Non-Olympic Specific Expenditure									
Highways and railways	0.54	0.59	0.63	0.63	0.63	0.31	0.31	0	3.64
Airport	0.01	0.03	0.03	0.01	0	0	0	0	0.08
Environmental protection	1	1	1.5	1.5	1.5	1.3	0.8	0	8.6
Olympic Related Expenditure									
Sports venues	n/a	n/a	0.21	0.42	0.49	0.28	0.01	0	1.41
Olympic village	n/a	n/a	n/a	n/a	0.11	0.15	0.13	0.03	0.42
Total	**1.55**	**1.62**	**2.37**	**2.56**	**2.73**	**2.04**	**1.25**	**0.03**	**14.15**

Source: The Beijing Organizing Committee for the Games of the XXIX Olympiad (BOCOG), 2008

municipal railway and 402 km of highway have been added to the city's transport network. In many ways, Beijing has experienced a complete makeover for the Olympic Games.

Compared to the infrastructure investment for the 1992 Barcelona and 2000 Sydney Olympic Games, expenditure for the 2008 Beijing Olympic Game was more than 1.7 and 4.6 times higher, at US$14.2 billion.[3] The spectacular opening ceremony, meticulous organization, and state-of-the-art facilities led Jacques Rogge, the president of the International Olympic Committee (IOC), to praise the Beijing Games as being "truly exceptional".[4]

The government's eyes were not simply focused on the Games themselves. This public investment has updated and improved the entire system of local infrastructure including subway, highways, airport, and also the sewage system. More importantly, with new job creation and the long-term boost for tourist, cultural, and exhibition industries, consumption demand and overall economic growth of Beijing has been stimulated. Around 4.5 million foreign tourists travelled to Beijing during the summer games period, bringing in a total of US$4.8 billion.[5]

By investing billions of dollars in Beijing, the Chinese government did not only hope for the success of the Olympic Games and the projection of a modern image of China, but also intended to bolster the overall development of the Jing-Jin-Ji region. In fact, beneficial economic effects of the Beijing Games have radiated to other adjacent regions over the past few years.

In terms of the Chinese economy as a whole, the proportion of it tied to the Games is too small to generate significant influence on national economic development. Nevertheless, the Olympic economy is likely to have a large spillover effect on the economic growth of Beijing and the whole Jing-Jin-Ji region and to create a legacy which will guarantee sustainable growth of this region for years to come.[6]

However, hosting the Olympic Games was not a cost-free meal for China. The modes of living for many local residents in Beijing have been affected by the Games. According to the estimation made by the Centre on Housing Rights and Evictions, a Geneva-based non-governmental organization (NGO), around 1.5 million residents were displaced for urban re-development between 2000 and

2008 (see Appendix 5.2). Some of them were even forcibly evicted by the authorities and their houses demolished.[7] Such practices were often accompanied by brutality and bloodshed and reflect a lack of transparency and justice in China.

Binhai new area: a new growth pole

Before 1978, economic growth of Tianjin was slow due to a lack of state preferential policies. It could not keep pace with national economic development. Nevertheless, Tianjin was to benefit substantially from the development of the TBNA in terms of its political and economic status in China.[8]

The rapid economic growth of the Binhai New Area has been impressive since its establishment in 2002. The GDP was up to 720.5 billion yuan in 2012 from 132.3 billion yuan in 2004, with annual growth of 23.6 per cent (Figure 5.7). One in four of the global 500 enterprises had invested and set up factories in the TBNA region by 2009.[9] China and Singapore's new joint development project of Tianjin Eco-city is also located in this region. The rapid development of TBNA fuelled economic growth of this region in 2008 in spite of the global economic crisis.

Development of the Jing-Jin-Ji region as a key growth engine of China has been gradually taking shape since the TBNA was integrated into the national strategy, as highlighted in the 11th Five-year Development Plan of 2006. The State Council of China gave the green light for the TBNA to develop into a "national experimental zone for comprehensive reforms" (国家综合配套改革试验区) in 2006.

The Overall Plan for the Comprehensive Supporting Reform Pilot in Tianjin Binhai New Area was finally approved by the State Council in April 2008.[10] The

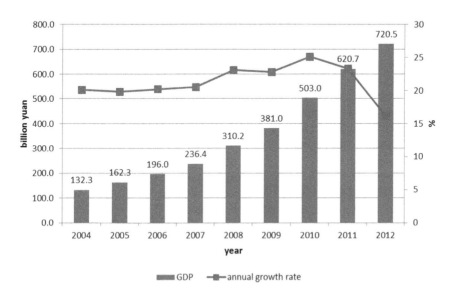

Figure 5.7 GDP growth in Binhai New District 2004–2012

Source: Public Reports of Economic and Social Development Statistics for Tianjin, various years

TBNA is expected to exert economic leverage similar to that of Shenzhen Special Economic Zone in the PRD and Shanghai Pudong New Area in the YRD.

The Chinese government has offered preferential policies (e.g. finance) to the TBNA region.[11] Wen Jiabao, premier of China, was born in Tianjin and spent his youth there. During his speech at the 2008 Summer Davos held in Tianjin, Wen confirmed that the government would make efforts to promote the development of the TBNA.[12]

However, an uncoordinated and complicated administrative system has hampered the development of the TBNA. The Binhai New Area has not functioned as an integrated region since its establishment in 2002. It consists of Tanggu (塘沽), Hangu (汉沽) and Dagang (大港) administrative districts, parts of Jinnan (津南) and Dongli (东丽) districts and the functional zones of Tianjin Port, Tianjin Economic and Technological Development Area, and Tianjin Port Free Trade Zone. It is hard to see how the TBNA region can amount to anything without a unified administrative institution.

It was difficult for local governments to cooperate and communicate with each other due to their remote location and separate administrative boundaries. It was also impossible for the municipal government to implement the unified policies across the whole TBNA region. Nevertheless, the administrative boundary readjustments for the TBNA announced by the Tianjin government in November 2009 are expected to provide a breakthrough on this pressing issue.

As defined by the new readjustment plan, Tanggu, Hangu and Dagang districts would be merged to form the new Binhai New Area District. The TBNA government would be granted more authority over reform and development. The important development projects in this area are expected to be under direct supervision of the central government.[13] This marks the new state effort to establish a coordinated, high effective and unified administrative and management system in the TBNA.

A high and new-tech industry-led economy has gradually emerged in this region, with development of aviation and other relevant industries, such as aircraft maintenance, logistics, and commercial services at the core. The high-profile manufacturing factory for Airbus A320 airplane located in the TBNA is the only European Airbus assembly line outside Europe.[14] The first A320 jetliner was assembled by Airbus's Tianjin factory and delivered to Sichuan Airlines in June 2009. Backed by the central government, Tianjin is expected to become the major aviation centre of China.

The three giants of China's aeronautical industry: the Aviation Industry Corporation of China (AICC), China Aerospace Science and Technology Corporation (CASTC), and China Aerospace Science & Industry Corporation (CASIC), have all been constructing their own development projects in the TBNA, with a total investment of 22.9 billion yuan.[15]

Challenges

The Jing-Jin-Ji region faces three main challenges. First, the economic integration of Beijing, Tianjin and Hebei is weaker than that of the cities within the YRD and

PRD regions and this lack of cooperation represents a serious challenge to the Jing-Jin-Ji region. Although this has been an issue since the early 1990s, concrete progress has not yet become apparent. Independent industrial structures and duplication of economic competition are the pressing problems. Beijing, Tianjin and Hebei each seek to thrive as an independent economy and implement different development strategies. Unlike the cities within the PRD and YRD regions, both Beijing and Tianjin are centrally administrated municipalities, which is likely to make it more difficult for the Jing-Jin-Ji region to forge close socio-economic ties.

Maintaining coordination of the economic growth of the two core cities of Beijing and Tianjin would be an important task for the local governments. Although Beijing is the political and educational centre of the Jing-Jin-Ji region, Tianjin and Hebei do not regard themselves as subordinate players. There are currently no formal regional administrative mechanisms or regular government meetings to coordinate the development of this region and there appears to be a lack of willingness on the part of the local governments to forge closer collaboration between the different cities.

Regional cooperation requires a leading core place and other supplementary peripheral regions. Nevertheless, it is hard to single out a core or dominant region. Neither Beijing nor Tianjin is powerful enough to lead the whole Jing-Jin-Ji region. Even Hebei, with its strong industrial base, is unlikely to assume leading status.

Due to administrative boundaries and underdevelopment of their inter-regional transport network, Beijing and Tianjin were unable in the past to radiate large-scale agglomeration effects to the neighbouring areas. The free movement of human talent, capital and information between cities has been hampered. For example, Beijing has so far offered only weak economic trickle-down effects to Hebei.[16]

However, the operation of the Beijing–Tianjin high-speed railway is expected to change this scenario. It could greatly increase integration and commercial interaction between these two large municipalities. A Beijing–Tianjin high-speed-railway–centred express network is expected to substantially improve overall inter-city transport within the Jing-Jin-Ji region, and contribute to closer regional cooperation. This 120-km-long high-speed rail running at a speed approaching 350 km per hour has cut travel time between the two cities to 30 minutes from 90 minutes. During the first month of operation, from August 2008, the passenger traffic recorded for this train was 18.3 million, which represented growth of 128.4 per cent compared to the corresponding figure in the previous year.[17]

Second, duplication of industrial structure is another unresolved problem. All regions have developed similar traditional industries: for example, steel, petrochemical, electronic information, and automobile manufacturing sectors. They are also competing in the new industries such as finance, biotechnology, medicine, and aerospace industries.[18] The industrial linkages within the Jing-Jin-Ji region are loose and weak.

This lack of industrial cooperation may result in duplicated development and cut-throat competition. It also limits the development of an integrated domestic market, which is badly needed in the aftermath of a sharp fall in external demands caused by the global economic crisis.[19]

Policy regarding the construction of ports also reflects the absence of coordination. Both Tianjin and Hebei have viewed the building of ports as a crucial means of strengthening competitiveness and development of trade. Tianjin Port (天津港), with 142 berths and 309.4 million tons of handled freight, is the largest sea port in the Jing-Jin-Ji region. However, along the merely 640-km-long coastline of this region, Tianjin Port has been facing fierce competition from the emerging Qinghuangdao (秦皇岛港), Tangshan (唐山港), Huanghua (黄骅港) and Caofeidian (曹妃甸港) ports.

Third, the population and the industrial growth of this region are affected by a water shortage.[20] For example, the annual local water output is below 300 m per capita in Beijing, which is significantly less than the international definition of a dangerously low level of water supply as 1,000 m per capita per year.

Almost all surface water sources have either dried out or become polluted in the Jing-Jin-Ji region.[21] Fast industrial growth requires plentiful supplies of water: particularly in the steel and automobile sectors. Although this region has abundant human resources and developed its infrastructure, water shortage could become a fatal constraint to its sustainable development.

Nevertheless, the Jing-Jin-Ji economy remains robust in fundamentals and enjoys the strong central support. Therefore, this "Third Growth Engine" is expected to become a more influential force for national economic development. It could become the most promising region in China for the next decade. Particularly, the economic growth of Tianjin could serve as a new development model for China.[22]

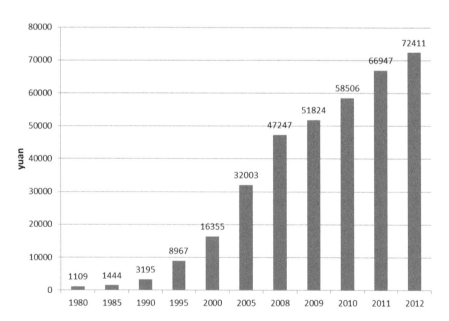

Appendix 5.1 GDP per capita in Jing-Jin-Ji Region, 1980–2012

Source: The author compiled this figure using the statistical yearbooks for the relevant regions.

Appendix 5.2 Households and persons affected by demolitions in Beijing 2000–2008

Year	Households Affected by Demolitions	Persons per Household	Persons Affected by Demolitions
2000	58,550	3	175,650
2001	58,550	3	175,650
2002	69,000	3	262,200
2003	50,000	2.9	145,000
2004	24,000	2.9	69,600
2005	72,000	2.6	187,200
2006	60,000	2.6	156,000
2007	60,000	2.6	156,000
2008	60,000	2.6	156,000
Total	512,100	n/a	1,483,300

Source: Centre on Housing Rights and Evictions, 2009

Notes

1 The Jing-Jin-Ji region is dually centred on the two centrally administrated municipalities of Beijing and Tianjin, surrounded by the other cities within Hebei province, and has a total land area of around 216,000 square km and 96.9 million in population. Geographically, this region, with its vast hinterland, is located in the core area of the Circum–Bohai Bay Region.
2 "State Council's Approval on the Overall Plan for the Comprehensive Supporting Reform Pilot in Tianjin Binhai New Area," *People's Daily*, http://www.022net.com/2008/4-1/492048112518172.html (accessed 11 January 2009)
3 Brunet, Ferran, and Zuo, Xinwen. (2008). *"The Economy of the Beijing Olympic Games: An Analysis of First Impacts and Prospects"*, Barcelona: Centre d'Estudis Olímpics UAB, http://olympicstudies.uab.es/pdf/wp116_eng.pdf (accessed 11 January 2009)
4 "Beijing Olympics – China's come-of-age show," *Xinhua*, http://www.chinadaily.com.cn/sports/2008-12/24/content_7336619.htm (accessed 4 April 2009)
5 "Will China's economy perform at the Games?" *BBC News*, http:news.bbc.co.uk/2/hi/7445980.stm (accessed 4 January 2009)
6 There are potential problems of post-Olympic economic slowdown in the Jing-Jin-Ji region arising from the burden of high maintenance and operational costs for the sports venues, the underutilization of games-related infrastructure facilities, and worsening local environmental situation.
7 "Fact Sheet – Forced evictions and displacements in future Olympic cities," *Centre on Housing Rights and Evictions*, http://www.cohre.org/mega-events-report (accessed 4 January 2009)
8 Zhu Xufeng and Sun Bing. (2008). "Tianjin Binhai New Area: Process, Problems, and Prospects," *EAI Working Paper No. 141*, East Asian Institute, National University of Singapore.
9 "China has taken 60 years to forge three economic growth engines, namely the YRD, PRD and Jing-Jin-Ji regions," *Xinhua*, http://www.gov.cn/jrzg/2009-09/13/content_1416563,htm (accessed 11 November 2009)
10 "State Council's Approval on the Overall Plan for Support of the Comprehensive Reform Pilot in Tianjin Binhai New Area," *People's Daily*, http://www.022net.com/2008/4-1/492048112518172.html (accessed 1 November 2009)

11 "Binhai: Taiwan's new investment focus," *China Daily*, http://tianjin.chinadaily.com. cn/m/tianjin/e/2009-08/03/content_8511242.htm (accessed 11 November 2009)
12 "Full text of Chinese Premier Wen Jiabao's speech at 2008 Summer Davos in Tianjin," *Xinhua News*, http://news.xinhuanet.com/english/2008-09/27/content_10122832.htm (accessed 1 January 2010)
13 "Tianjin to establish new Binhai district," *China Daily*, http://tianjin.chinadaily.com. cn/m/tianjin/e/2009-11/10/content_8948675.htm (accessed 1 January 2010)
14 "Airbus delivers first A319 assembled in China," *China Daily*, http://tianjin.chinadaily. com.cn/m/tianjin/e/2009-07/24/content_8475570.htm (accessed 1 January 2010)
15 "Airport industrial park becoming important base of aeronautical and astronautical industry in Tianjin," *China Daily*, http://tianjin.chinadaily.com.cn/m/tianjin/e/2009-05/ 18/content_8087148.htm (accessed 11 November 2009)
16 Yu, Danlin, and Wei, Yehua Dennis. (2008). "Spatial-data Analysis of Regional Development in Greater Beijing, China, in a GIS Environment", *Papers in Regional Science*, 87:1, pp. 97–117.
17 "The speed of Beijing – Shanghai's high-speed railway could reach 380 km per hour," *BBC News*, http://news.bbc.co.uk/chinese/simp/hi/newsid_7590000/newsid_ 7592600/7592676.stm (accessed 5 April 2009)
18 Deng, Lishu. (2007). "Strategic Analysis on Industrial Coordinative Development in the Jing-Jin-Ji Economic Zone", Beijing Academy of Social Science, *Productivity Research* (In Chinese), 3, pp. 117–120.
19 An encouraging sign for regional industrial cooperation would be the relocation of Beijing-based Shaogang Group, one of the biggest steel makers in China. Shaogang Group is constructing a new steel-making base in Hebei.
20 Dong, Jiang *et al.* (2008). "Integrated Evaluation of Urban Development Suitability Based on Remote Sensing and GIS Techniques – A Case Study in Jingjinji Area, China", *Sensors*, 8, pp. 5975–5986.
21 Zhai, Baohui, Jia, Yuliang and Xu, Qingyun. (2004). "*A Long Way to Go: the Coordinative Development in the Capital Region of China*"? 40th ISoCaRP Congress, pp. 1–11.
22 Bo, Zhiyue. (2009). "Tianjin City: Leadership Reshuffle and Economic Development", *EAI Background Brief No. 470*, East Asian Institute, National University of Singapore.

6 Developing China's Hainan into an international tourism destination

Introduction

According to the Chinese central government's new plan released in 2009, Hainan was identified as the key area for promotion of tourism in China. Development of Hainan as an international tourism destination (*hainan guoji lüyoudao*) has been upgraded to a national strategy. Hainan is the only province in China to clearly be identified for development of its tourism into a mainstay industry by the central government. Hu Jintao, president of China, remarked in April 2008 that it was the intention for tourism to become a pillar industry for Hainan.[1] Hainan aims to become a test zone for China's tourism reform and innovation and take a lead in development of tourism and associated industries. The government also believes that the tourism sector is a key means of boosting regional economic development and reducing regional equalities between Hainan and the prosperous eastern provinces.

Theoretical framework

In the context of an administrative and political hierarchy, the *top-down* policy decision-making process refers to key policies and strategies made and introduced by the policymakers in the top-level central government, while the bottom-level governments have the duty and responsibility to implement and enforce these policies. The policy decision-making process of this approach is characterized by heavy intervention of the top policymakers and other powerful external factors, and in contrast, by under-representation of local community and governments. The policy decisions, formulation and implementation are separated from each other. The top-down approach stresses that the top governmental officials are the key to achieving objectives of policy formulation and implementation, while the various bottom-level officials and private participants are largely unimportant or even impediments to policy decisions. This approach is widely perceived as a form of policy implementation which neglects proper consideration of all parties' interests and representation of interests and views from the local community. In other words, the voice of the local community in policy-making is largely marginalized and their participation in policy-making is virtually non-existent. In contrast, the *bottom-up* decision-making process indicates that the top-level policymakers must consult and work closely with the bottom-level officials in making and introducing policies and strategies; its emphasis lies in policy implementation at the bottom level.[2] The bottom-up policy-making process focuses on the policy implementation interaction between various actors at the bottom level and their strategies to achieve policy objectives.[3] The intensive communication and interaction between the top policymakers, local government, private investors and local community are the key strengths of this approach.

Some scholars argue that, in the face of diverse interests and increasingly influential interest groups, the top-down style decision-making process enables the central government to effectively impose state development plans by wielding its considerable resources and power. Krutwaysho and Bramwell[4] point out that the diverse views and interests among stakeholders (government agencies, society and individuals) form impediments to policy formulation and implementation. However, many scholars[5] have criticized the weakness of top-down decision-making by arguing that the central government lacks up-to-date local knowledge of development conditions; the top policymakers rarely engage in proper negotiation and communication with the local community on social, economic and cultural issues. The top-down policy-decision approach neglects the issues of communication and cooperation between various actors in policy implementation, diverse values and interests among different participants, which would affect their motivation for policy implementation, and also limits on the control of policy interpretation and implementation by the top officials over the bottom bureaucrats[6]. They believe that the top-down style decision-making process make it difficult for the central government officials to properly evaluate the effectiveness of state policy, and can easily lead to the failure or unsustainability of regional development planning.

The top-down style policy-making process, lacking proper coordination and collaboration among all parties fails to take into account the local community's interests and needs, and limits local participation. Both from the process (democratic and good governance by the state of society) and technical (the inputs from the bottom-level participants in designing and exercising policy) perspectives, Brinkerhoff[7] points out that participation is crucial to policy implementation. Due to the top decision-makers' lack of awareness of local conditions, they often fail to develop a successful and best-fit tourism development plan. Studies such as that of Byrd[8] on Akamas, Cyprus, have demonstrated that, in tourist regions, policy formulation via the top-down approach is much less effective and productive than formulation on a bottom-up and collaborative basis.

The top-down planning approach is adversely affected by a lack of local knowledge on the part of the main policymakers and lack of participation by the local community; and these two issues tend to reduce the chances of success for state plans. On the other hand, the complicated and multi-level communication and bargaining involved in the bottom-up planning approach tends to make state policy implementation a time-consuming business, and the policy produced tends to be weak and ineffective, mainly due to the lack of resources and power within the bottom community. Both of the approaches seem to be inadequate to provide a good framework and model for state policy planning and strategy-making process.

As tourism plays an important role in many regions' development, state-initiated tourism plans will affect local people's lives, either positively or negatively. Local people's voices cannot be ignored or rejected in the policy-making process. It is natural for different groups to have different views and priority agendas on development issues. Therefore, it is essential to have proper debate and discussion on state-initiated policy in order to achieve a generally acceptable conclusion, with consensus among the majority of people, and consequently, a sound, effective and sustainable state development plan.

The stakeholder theory, originally developed in 1984 by Freeman,[9] combined the intrinsic value of both top-down and bottom-up approaches and was also characterized by strong community participation. It was developed in the western world to assess the effectiveness and sustainability of national tourism plans and their impact on local communities.[10] The stakeholder theory indicates that it is crucial to incorporate all stakeholders (government, private investor, local citizen, employee, and customer) into the policy-making process. This collaborative decision-making, incorporating the wisdom of all participants has the potential to offer effective policy enforcement and implementation. Freeman[11] gives the definition of stakeholders as "any group or individual who can affect or is affected by the achievement of the firm's objectives".

According to the stakeholder theory, all parties affecting or affected by the policy-making should decide and implement policies in a collective manner. Any affected actor could damage or even break the sustainability of policy planning. The entire decision-making process should be based on the maximum benefits for all affected stakeholders without showing preference for any particular policy or giving priority to any individual group. Sautter and Leisen[12] point out that

> Often, planners underestimate the complexity of this step and default to a cursory report of only the most obvious stakeholders, chiefly tourists, business owners and government officials. Today, however, organizations and/or planning bodies must be more careful to take a hard look at the various types of persons/groups which affect or are affected by the tourism services.

They further argue, "With this in mind, it is important to reiterate the basic premise that all stakeholders' interests have intrinsic value".[13] The involvement of various stakeholders with diverse values, opinions and interests would make the policy decision-making process complicated and time-consuming. However, the stakeholder decision-making approach is essential to produce useful results. Without a collaborative decision-making process, the formulation of a community-oriented tourism plan can never be achieved.[14] Dwyer, Forsyth, and Spurr state that

> Cross-sectoral collaboration for destination planning among key stakeholders should help to reduce turbulence in the domain and increase the likelihood of sustainable tourism development.[15]

In order to gain maximum returns from the tourism industry for regional economic development, it is necessary for the top policy planners to communicate with all affected groups and consider their diverse interests before forming a tourism development plan. Gunn[16] argues thus:

> Expansion of tourism depends greatly upon the local attitude toward expansion. If the local electorate and leadership fully understand the implications of tourism and favor its development, further expansion has support. However, if attitudes and cultural norms are antagonistic or hostile, it will be difficult to develop tourism.

How well can the western policy-making theories fit into an explanation of the emergence of developing regions? There are, in particular, very few studies on linkage of regional tourism plans in China with planning formulation theories. This chapter attempts to address the capacity of popular policy-making theories to explain China's tourism planning by critically assessing Hainan's economic development and the plan newly released by the Chinese central government for tourism in this region. Hainan province was chosen as a case study for this chapter because of its long history of tourism and the problems it has experienced with development policies and economic and tourism strategies. However, there is so far little English-language documentation available on the socio-economic development of Hainan. The limited amount of knowledge of this island is mainly focused on its tropical fruits, rubber production or notorious housing speculation.

A case study of Hainan fits well in testing the western theories of the tourism policy planning process. Tourism has played an increasingly important role in the economic development of Hainan over the past two decades. The tourism-dominated tertiary sector accounted for 45.1 per cent of regional GDP of Hainan in 2009. The percentage of people employed in Hainan's tertiary sector increased to 35.6 per cent in 2009 from 20.6 per cent in 1990. Significantly, the majority of this employment is directly associated with tourism.

Background to Hainan

Hainan is located in southern China, and it is China's sole tropical island province, with a land area of 35,354 square km and 8.45 million in population. It is close to Vietnam, the Philippines, Malaysia and other Southeast Asian countries. It is one of the easiest and nearest entry-points in China to Southeast Asia. Historically, Hainan has been firmly under Chinese rule since as far back as the end of the Song Dynasty.[17] Hainan is the only Special Economic Zone (SEZ) approved by the State Council of China in 1988; it covers the whole province and is the largest SEZ in China.

Around two million Hainan-origin Chinese are living abroad, mainly in Southeast Asia countries like Vietnam, Malaysia and Singapore. The majority of the local population is Han Chinese, and it also has officially recognized ethnic minorities mainly from Li and Miao. The Li are the largest minority group on this island. The minority people mainly inhabit the central and southwest regions of Hainan. Thanks to their poor living environment featuring mountainous and inland geography, the local minority people tend seldom to be involved in the formal industrial, commerce and tourism sectors, and their living standard is relatively very low compared to that of the Han Hainanese.[18] The majority of minority people are engaged in the agricultural and farming sector. They are largely marginalized and still very poor, being largely excluded from the benefits of local economic development. The economic and tourism development story of Hainan has now been questioned and criticized with little involvement by the local minority community and their little gains from local tourism boom.

The Hainan authority has adopted a pro-tertiary industry strategy to accelerate local economic growth over the past three decades, with particularly emphasis on tourism. The share of tertiary industry in gross domestic product (GDP) increased to 46.9 per cent in 2012 from 26.2 per cent in 1982. In contrast, the ratio of primary industry to GDP was down to 24.9 per cent in 2012 from nearly 60 per cent in 1982 (Table 6.1).

Hainan's tourism sector has developed rapidly over the past 12 years. Domestic tourism receipts rose to 35.7 billion yuan in 2012 from 6.9 billion yuan in 2000, with annual growth of around 14.7 per cent. An increasing number of foreign visitors have come to Hainan for oriental-style sightseeing. International tourism receipts on this island had increased to US$0.35 billion in 2012 from US$0.1 billion in 2000 (Figure 6.1).

Table 6.1 Composition of gross domestic product of Hainan

Year	GDP (billion yuan)	Share of Primary Industry (%)	Share of Secondary Industry (%)	Share of Tertiary Industry (%)	Per Capita GDP (yuan)
1982	2.8	59.7	14.0	26.2	510
1985	4.3	50.3	21.5	28.1	729
1990	10.2	44.6	19.7	35.6	1,562
1995	36.3	35.4	21.6	42.9	5,063
2000	52.6	36.4	19.7	43.8	6,798
2005	90.5	32.9	26.1	40.9	10,998
2008	145.9	29.9	29.7	40.2	15,981
2009	164.6	28.0	26.9	45.1	19,166
2010	205.2	26.3	27.6	46.1	23,644
2011	252.3	26.1	28.3	45.6	28,898
2012	285.6	24.9	28.2	46.9	32,377

Sources:
1. Hainan Statistical Bureau. *Hainan tongji nianjian (Hainan Statistical Yearbook)*, (2008, 2009, 2013). Beijing: China Statistics Press.
2. Hainan Statistical Bureau. *Hainan guomin jingji he shehui fazhan tongji gongbao (Public Record of Economic and Social Development Statistics of Hainan)*, (2008, 2009, 2010).

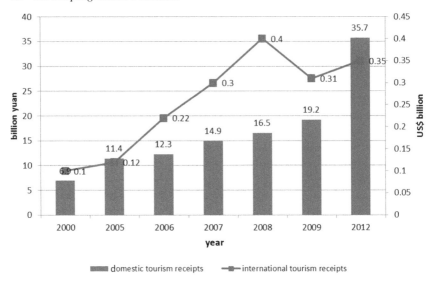

Figure 6.1 Domestic and international tourism receipts by Hainan

Sources:
1. Hainan Statistical Bureau. *Hainan tongji nianjian 2008 (Hainan Statistical Yearbook)*, (2008, 2013). Beijing: China Statistics Press; Hainan Statistical Bureau.
2. Hainan Statistical Bureau. *"Hainan guomin jingji he shehui fazhan tongji gongbao"* (Public record of economic and social development statistics of Hainan), (2008, 2009, 2010).

Nevertheless, due to the global financial crisis and widespread H1NI pandemic, 2009 was a difficult and challenging year for international tourism. After experiencing a robust growth of international tourist arrivals from 534 million persons in 1995 to 920 million persons in 2008, the number of international tourist arrivals decreased to 880 million persons in 2009, a drop of 4.4 per cent compared to 2008. However, in 2010, it was recorded a strong recovery, the number of international tourist arrivals rose to 935 million persons, an increase of 6.2 per cent compared to 2009 (Figure 6.2). The total numbers of inbound visitors and international tourism receipts for China were also down to 130 million person-times and US$40.8 billion respectively in 2008, a drop of 1.4 per cent and 2.6 per cent compared to the previous year.

Hainan's tourism industry was unable to escape from the global economic slowdown and fall in the demand for tourism. Nevertheless, domestic tourism, to some extent, weathered the storm which has affected international inbound tourism to Hainan and, overall, figures for tourism growth were acceptable in 2009. However, as the global economic recovery in major western nations is still sluggish and fragile, domestic tourism is likely to remain a major source of tourism in Hainan for years to come.

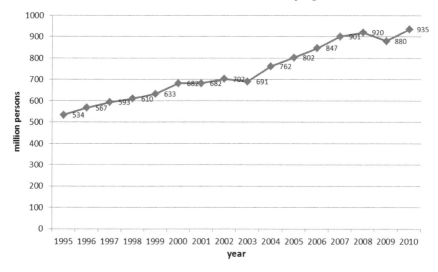

Figure 6.2 International tourist arrivals, 1995–2010

Sources:
1. The United Nations World Tourism Organization. (2009). *2009 International tourism results and prospects for 2010*, 18 January 2010, Spain, pp. 1–12.
2. The United Nations World Tourism Organization. (2011). International tourism 2010: multi-speed recovery. http://www.eturbonews.com/20600/international-tourism-2010-multi-speed-recovery (accessed 7 March 2011)

A new state development blueprint for Hainan

The boom in the Chinese economy and fast industrialization have greatly increased the wealth and prosperity of Chinese people, and triggered population mobility over the past two decades. This has contributed to the rapid development of the tourism industry in China. Between 1994 and 2012, tourism expenditure had increased from 102.3 billion yuan to 2270.6 billion yuan, with annual growth of 18.8 per cent. Per capita tourism expenditure had increased to 767.9 yuan in 2012 from 195.3 yuan in 1994 (Figure 6.3). Recreation and holidays are becoming a priority for China's growing middle and wealthy classes.

Demand for high-quality tourist destinations from the increasing number of rich Chinese people has been enhanced by their experiences of visiting international tourism destinations. Due to its inherent advantages and potential, Hainan was chosen by the Chinese central government for development into a high quality and lucrative tourism destination which would satisfy this growing domestic demand. The central government has identified tourism as a key means of stimulating domestic consumption and transforming China's economic development pattern from investment and export-driven to consumption-led. Tourism could also make an important contribution to transforming China into a low-carbon

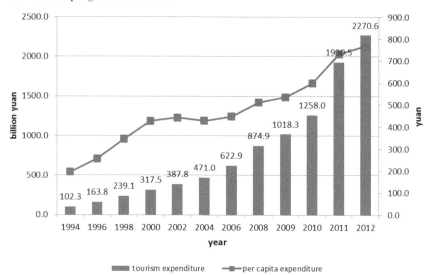

Figure 6.3 China's domestic tourism development indicators

Sources:
1. National Statistical Bureau of China. *Zhongguo tongji nianjian (China Statistical Yearbook)*, (2009, 2010, 2013). Beijing: China Statistics Press.
2. Hainan Statistical Bureau. (25 January, 2010). *"2009 nian Hainan guomin jingji he shehui fazhan tongji gongbao"* (Public record of economic and social development statistics of Hainan 2009). http://www.tjcn.org/tjgb/201001/3620.html (accessed 8 March 2011)

economy. According to the figure given by China Tourism Academy,[19] energy consumption per unit value-added in the tourism sector is merely 0.202: 11 times lower than the corresponding figures for other industrial sectors.

The policy-making process for the new tourism development plan in Hainan has followed a typical top-down style through the directives from various central ministries (Table 6.2). Under the supervision and authority of the Chinese central government, the National Development and Reform Commission (NDRC), Ministry of Finance (MOF), National Tourism Administration (NTA), Ministry of Land Resources (MLR), Ministry of Environmental Protection (MEP) have jointly worked on and decided the regional development plan for Hainan, with limited consultation with the provincial government in Hainan. Different central government ministries have taken on different jobs and responsibilities in formulating this plan. For example, the NDRC is responsible for overall plan design, development review and physical plan approval; the MOF is responsible for working out overall budgets for transportation and other infrastructure development; the NTA is required to coordinate tourism development issues in Hainan and market local tourism internationally, and the MEP deals with local environmental protection and resource preservation, whilst involvement of different levels of Hainan government is required for the full implementation of this plan.

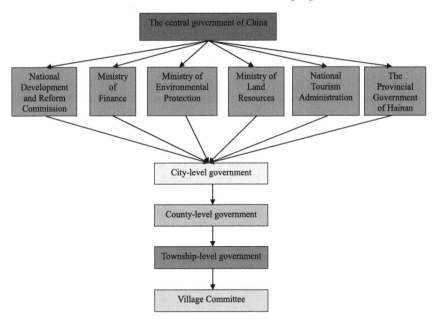

Table 6.2 An overview of decision-making structure for Hainan's tourism development plan

Source: Compiled by the author.

Not surprisingly, the top-down style of tourism development plan in Hainan reflects the long-standing top-down administrative hierarchy and highly central-ized political system in contemporary China. The ruling Chinese Communist Party (CCP) leadership in Beijing makes all important policy decisions and sets up policies and strategies. Tourism plans and policies are not immune, and are largely influenced by the CCP and reflect its will. However, policy responsibil-ity for implementation falls on the shoulders of different levels of local govern-ment: from provincial, city, country, township to village level. Historically, the central government has often played a supervisory role in directing the activities conducted by the local governments in China. The local governments, let alone the local community, have very little say on policy decisions and formulation. Although the bargaining power of the local state has gradually strengthened over the past 10 years due to limited decentralization and the beginnings of devolution of authority from the central state to local administrative bodies, the top central government is still powerful and maintains the highest authority in China.

The central government is developing Hainan as an international tourism des-tination in the belief that the tourism sector is a key means of increasing local employment, boosting regional economic development and reducing regional disparities between Hainan and the prosperous eastern provinces. Since 1988, the local governments in Hainan have failed to impose a clear and successful development strategy to stimulate local tourism growth. Therefore, in seeking to boost local economic growth and creating more jobs in the tourism-linked service sector, including food, accommodation, transport, souvenir products, entertainment activities and travel agencies, the Chinese central government has largely by-passed the Hainan government and taken the initiative to formulate a new 'tourism-first' regional development plan for Hainan. Nevertheless, historically, the development of Hainan has proved problematic, and the island still faces serious obstacles to its goal of becoming a top holiday destination in Asia Pacific. In the past, the government frequently changed the direction of development policies, from industry and agriculture towards tourism. Misguided government policies have led to the boom-to-bust housing bubble and lack of socio-economic development in Hainan over the past two decades.

Under this top-down tourism planning, a triangular axis of the central government, various ministries and powerful external force such as property developers has overwhelmingly dominated regional tourism development in Hainan and enjoyed the majority of economic benefits contributed by tourism growth. The local community in Hainan has been denied the opportunity to participate in the decision-making process or to voice their interests and demands, and this is particularly the case with minority groups. It is not my intention to argue that the local people have not been involved in tourism planning at all. What I suggest is that local community participation has been weak and seriously inadequate, while property developers and other external private entrepreneurs have exerted far too

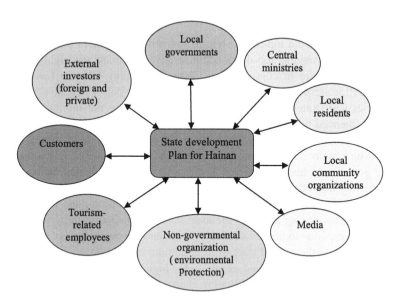

Table 6.3 An overview of potential stakeholders affected by the state tourism development plan for Hainan

Source: Compiled by the author.

much influence over Hainan's development. Due to poor education and short-age of knowledge, the local community and minority groups are disadvantaged and lack adequate information about the regional tourism development plan. In order to get involved in the policy-making process and achieve a collaborative policy-making process among all stakeholders, local citizens need to be properly educated with regard to tourism development.[20]

Achieving a sustainable tourism industry in Hainan is quite a complicated undertaking, and one that needs to accommodate all the various parties with relevant stakes and interests (Table 6.3). Normally, these parties have dramatically different views on the direction and goals of regional tourism development. Any process of formulation that is dominated by the powerful central ministries, local governments and property developers is bound to result in a tourism plan which is unsustainable and doomed to failure. In seeking to achieve maximum socio-economic benefits and improvement of welfare for the disadvantaged local residents and minimize the negative impacts they incur from, there is a need for a sound tourism development plan based on the interests of the local community rather than those of the government and property developers. Unfortunately, with this current new tourism plan for Hainan this seems not to be the case.

An overview of Hainan's development: an 'up and down' style

The economic development history of Hainan has shown a typical "up and down' style during the reform period (Table 6.4). The Chinese central government gave approval for Hainan to become a province and establish a Special Economic Zone (SEZ) in 1988. At that time, Yangpu region was key to the development of Hainan. The newly formed provincial government anticipated that Yangpu would accelerate its export-oriented industrial development via inward foreign direct investment.

From 1988 onwards, besides all the state-owned special policies shared by the other SEZs, the Chinese central government provided numerous unique preferential policies for this island, from tax reduction and exemption of low income taxes, duty-free privileges of input imports for industrial production and bank loans to foreign exchange retention and generous land-use rights. Particularly, the foreign investors were allowed to enjoy up to 70 years of land-use rights based on leasehold. These packages of preferential policies have created favourable investment environment in Hainan for foreign investors. Meanwhile, despite its relatively impressive economic growth since 1988 in contrast to that of the pre-reform period, in general, Hainan remains largely undeveloped.

The share of tertiary industry in GDP increased to 46.1 per cent in 2010 from 26.2 per cent in 1982. In contrast, even though the ratio of primary industry to GDP decreased substantially from 1982 to 2010, primary industry still accounted for around 26 per cent of regional GDP in 2010 (Table 6.1). Yeh[21] argues that a large proportion of local people still make a living through farming and other agriculture-related economic activities.

Table 6.4 Summary of key development events in Hainan

Year	Event
1983	The Chinese central government decided to open up Hainan to the outside world, as outlined by the "No. 11 Central Document".
January 1984–March 1985	Hainan spent US$1 billion in national foreign currency to import 79,000 tax-free foreign vehicles and then resold them to other provinces; this led to the so-called Vehicle Importation Incident and shocked the central government in Beijing. Lei Yu, the provincial leader of Hainan was sacked by the central government.
April 1988	Hainan was separated from Guangdong and became an independent province and China's largest special economic zone.
June 1988	Due to a lack of development capital, the newly formed provincial government of Hainan signed a cooperation agreement with a Hong Kong-based subsidiary of a Japanese company, and proposed to lend land of 30 square km within Yangpu to this company, and entrust its land development rights to it for a period of 70 years. This so-called Yangpu Model gave rise to strong criticisms from Chinese scholars and members of national parliament, who called it a national humiliation and a loss of national sovereignty. The proposed deal was finally scrapped.
1992	The central government approved the establishment of Hainan Yangpu Economic Development Zone.
1993	The central government suddenly tightened its monetary policy and forced the commercial banks to reduce lending to the real estate sector. The housing bubble in Hainan finally went bust.
1996	The provincial government of Hainan planned to develop Hainan into a newly industrial province, and tropical agricultural base. Significantly, for the first time, the local government wanted to develop tourism in Hainan, and transform it into a premium island resort.
2001	The Boao Forum for Asia was established in Hainan.
2003	Hainan hosted the annual Miss World pageant.
2007	The State Council of China approved the establishment of Hainan Yangpu Bonded Area.
2009	According to the Chinese central government's new development plan "Several Opinions on Development of Hainan as an International Tourism Destination", Hainan was identified as the key area for promotion of tourism in China.

Source: The author's summary, based on various information.

Due to a lack of development capital, the provincial government signed a cooperation agreement with a Hong Kong-based subsidiary of a Japanese company, and proposed to lend land of 30 square km within Yangpu to this company, and entrust this place's land development rights to it for a period of 70 years. However, this so-called Yangpu Model has given rise to strong criticism from certain Chinese scholars and members of the national parliament, who called it a national humiliation and a loss of national sovereignty. The proposed deal was finally scrapped. As a result, the economic development of Hainan was stagnant until 1992 when the Hainan Yangpu Economic Development Zone (HYEDZ)[22] approved by the State Council of China, was established. Despite various state-initiated preferential policies granted since then, the economic growth of HYEDZ has still not been promising. Economically, it has never really taken off.

During January 1984 and March 1985, Hainan spent US$1 billion in national foreign currency to import 79,000 tax-free foreign vehicles, and then resold them to other mainland provinces for profits. This led to the so-called Vehicle Importation Incident and shocked the central government in Beijing. Lei Yu, the provincial leader of Hainan was sacked by the central government. This event also negatively affected Hainan's foreign trade and economic growth. What is worse from the historical perspective, Hainan has become a land of rampant real estate speculation. It had had a painful experience of property boom and bubble during the early 1990s.[23] When the central government suddenly tightened its monetary policies and forced commercial banks to reduce and cancel loans to the real estate sector in June 1993, this caused property developers to abandon hundreds of newly started or unfinished buildings and vacant construction sites, and eventually led to the property bubble and collapse of local housing markets. Many foreign investors also cancelled their business development projects and withdrew investment. Hainan had suffered from slow economic growth for several consecutive years after the housing bubble collapse in the 1990s (Figure 6.4). Hainan

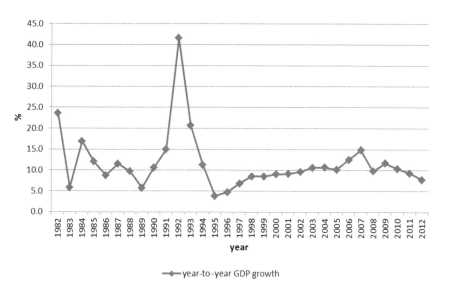

Figure 6.4 Economic growth of Hainan 1982–2012

Sources:
1. Hainan Statistical Bureau. *Hainan tongji nianjian (Hainan Statistical Yearbook)*, (2009, 2013). Beijing: China Statistics Press.
2. Hainan Statistical Bureau. (25 January, 2010). *"2009 nian Hainan guomin jingji he shehui fazhan tongji gongbao"* (Public record of economic and social development statistics of Hainan 2009). http://www.tjcn.org/tjgb/201001/3620.html (accessed 8 March 2011).

recorded the lowest economic growth among all provinces within China between 1995 and 1997.[24] Despite its SEZ status and superior coastal advantage, Hainan has remained one of the poorest provinces in China throughout the three reform decades since 1978.

Contradictions in development strategy

Hainan has been failed to find the right direction for its local economic growth and implement a clear development strategy since 1988. A few local officials and scholars have advocated that agricultural development is the key for Hainan based on local comparative climate advantages. They argue that Hainan's strengthen lies in developing tropical and subtropical agriculture by planting rubber and tropical fruits such as coconuts, sugarcane and pineapples. As a result, several agriculture-led development strategies in the form of 'tourism-directed agriculture', 'eco-agriculture' or 'high-quality tropical agriculture' were proposed. A large portion of Hainan's agriculture output has been produced by the state-owned farms rather than local peasants. As also outlined by the new development plan, the central government anticipates that Hainan will become a national base of tropical agricultural production. However, 7.5 tons of cowpeas: a typical agricultural product from Hainan, containing highly toxic pesticides, flowed into several other provinces in China in February and March 2010.[25] This new round of food safety scandals has triggered national public outrage and badly hit Hainan's agricultural sector. This case not only reflects serious problems of pesticide management regulation in Hainan, but also exposes loopholes in the entire supervision process of agricultural production and sales.

On the other hand, in rejecting the idea of agriculture as a dominant sector for Hainan, several other officials and economists have argued that industry is the crucial factor in its long-term and sustainable economic development. They insisted that Hainan could only achieve rapid economic growth and catch up with more advanced Chinese regions through fast manufacturing growth and industrialization.[26] However, no manufacturing-led industrial development strategy was designated until 1992.[27] Economically, Hainan has relied heavily on its agricultural sector since the 1980s. Industrial growth in this region has been slow due to its historically weak industrial foundations and state policy restrictions. Due to the principle of defence-oriented and nuclear war preparation designated by Mao Zedong, the then leader of China, Hainan was prohibited from developing large manufacturing industries. Identifying Hainan as strategically important for national defence, the Chinese central government was very reluctant to invest heavily in local industrial development and infrastructure during the pre-reform period. Total investment from the central government was merely 4.3 billion yuan between 1952 and 1980, which was equal to around 10 per cent of state investment into Baoshan Iron & Steel Company in Shanghai. In addition, most of the state investment was allocated to resource extraction rather than local industrial development and infrastructure construction in Hainan. Many local people believe that Hainan's resources are being exploited for the sole benefit of mainland China.[28]

The local industrial base was weak in Hainan, mainly relying on small agriculture-based and food processing industries. In fact, Hainan is rich in natural resources; many of them are rare in other regions of China, ranging from rubber, timber oil and gas to iron and copper. It is estimated that total crude oil reserves in Beibu Gulf, Yingge Sea and the southeastern basin of Hainan are as much as 91.2 billion tons. Gas deposits discovered in the Yingge area amount to around 104 billion cubic metres.[29] These natural and strategic resources lay down a solid foundation for developing heavy and manufacturing industries. However, the Chinese central government has maintained full control of the exploitation of natural resources. In the decades since 1949, instead of developing local resource-processing industries, the state-owned enterprises have mainly extracted these strategic resources from Hainan and then shipped them on to other regions of China for processing and manufacturing. For example, Hainan Island contains iron mines; ironically, it has not developed a local iron and steel industry. In other words, the central government has taken too much out and contributed too little to Hainan.

The local government in Hainan has very little say on processing or industrial development based on these resources. In addition, due to the relatively small size of its market and population, and the lack of an educated and skilled labour force, foreign companies have been relevant to putting investment and setting up manufacturing industrial plants in Hainan. As a result, in general, local industries have been limited and underdeveloped. To be fair, besides a lack of central state support and capital investment, unbalanced economic structure with over dependence on the agricultural sector has made the manufacturing-based economic takeoff difficult to achieve. This situation has been exacerbated by a serious shortage of educated and qualified skilled labour. To achieve real economic takeoff, it is crucial for Hainan to decrease the reliance of its economy on the agricultural sector and to focus rather on the industrial and tourism-based service sectors. The share percentage of the primary sector to regional GDP needs to fall; in contrast, the importance of the industrial and service sectors to the local economy should increase. Besides food processing and agriculture-based light industrial sectors such as rubber products, soft drinks and candy, resource-based heavy and manufacturing sectors could provide other important sources of local industrial growth.

Some of the top local leaders and government-affiliated scholars have for many years advocated developing tourism into a leading industrial sector in Hainan. The provincial government of Hainan has adopted a pro-tertiary industry strategy to accelerate local economic growth over the past decade, with particularly emphasis on tourism. When the new development plan for Hainan was released by the Chinese central government in 2009, Hainan was chosen as the key area for promotion of tourism in China. Development of Hainan as an International Tourism Destination has been upgraded to a national strategy. After nearly three decades of development strategy controversy and debate, it seems that the emphasis of the local government's strategies to boost economic development will be finally shifted to the tourism-based service sector. However, realistically speaking, compared to its many counterparts in mainland China, Hainan's status as a popular tourist destination for foreign tourists remains modest to date.

In sum, the development path of Hainan was not made clear. The Hainan government frequently changed the direction of development policies, from industry and agriculture towards tourism. Worse still, these failed government policies caused the boom-to-bust housing bubble and slow socio-economic development in Hainan of the past two decades. In Hainan, advertisements and marketing signs for luxury housing and apartment buildings and construction sites of high-end building are apparent everywhere. The figure in Table 6.5 shows that the investment on real estate sector in Hainan has increased substantially over the past few years.

The local government leased far too many land lots for high-end housing construction in the 1990s. Hainan took more than ten years to bottom out floor space under construction or completion. Real estate boom-to-bust has become a shameful feature of Hainan's economy. Ironically, today, the spotlight is once more focused on its soaring housing prices. After the new tourism development plan for Hainan was issued by the Chinese central government, many real estate developers from home and abroad flowed into this island in the hope of making huge profits. As a result, local property speculation re-emerged. Housing prices in Hainan have surged. Haikou and Sanya, the two major cities in Hainan, both showed an astonishing 50 per cent year-on-year increase of housing prices in February 2010: the highest growth rate in China.[30] In particular, the sale price per square meter on Fenghuang Island, a housing development project developed by a Zhejiang company, was up to 70,000 yuan (US$10,249) in January 2010. China's top property developers including Vanke and Poly have put major capital investment into Hainan, speculating on its good development potential. Chi Fulin, the Director of China Institute for Reform and Development, a local government-affiliated think tank, warned that the real estate market was overheating in Hainan.[31]

The new state plan, speculation-driven property developers and newly rich Chinese people are the major sources behind the recently rocketing growth of housing price in Hainan. With too much hot money flowing into the real estate sector, the emergence of a new housing bubble is a real concern. If this trend continues, the destiny of such a housing bubble is inevitably to bust. Hainan is likely to repeat its trajectory of real estate boom-to-bust circle of the 1990s, and the real economy

Table 6.5 Sources of investment funds in real estate development in Hainan (billion yuan)

Year	2005	2006	2007	2008	2009
Domestic loans	0.8	1.0	2.6	3.2	9.1
Foreign investment	0.1	2.2	0.1	1.5	3.0
Self-raising funds	3.4	3.5	8.4	8.4	10.8
Others	4.6	4.6	7.2	14.1	20.2
Total investment	8.9	11.3	18.3	27.2	43.1

Source: Hainan Statistical Bureau. (2010). *Hainan tongji nianjian 2010 (Hainan Statistical Yearbook 2010)*. Beijing: China Statistics Press, see p. 132.

will be badly hit. Unless this pressing real estate issue is addressed by the local government in the form of tighter regulation and supervision of land development, it could not only trigger another run of property bubble, but also, harm Hainan's economy by affecting its future development as an international tourism centre.

Hainan's development advantages and Beijing's rationale

The traditional food and cultural performances by the local ethnic minority communities in Hainan have a great appeal for both domestic and foreign visitors. In this unique island region, tourists can experience the cultural and ethnic diversity of Hainan, as well as its marvellous, unspoilt scenery. Natural geographic advantages and local tourist attractions have given Hainan a regional and international edge in tourism development. As unveiled by the new state plan, the government is keen to develop a kind of tourism agglomeration in Hainan of all associated elements, including sightseeing attractions, shopping malls, hotel accommodation and tourist resorts, catering, tourism agencies and tourism-oriented research institutions. The government is seeking to stimulate development of all tourism-related industries. Hainan would enjoy the privileges and policies listed in the "Western Development" programme. The central government is expected to designate further preferential policies and provide capital funding and subsidies. The central government would not only play a crucial role in coordinating development of tourism-related local infrastructure, but also it would attempt to construct a local tourism brand and promote Hainan as a tourist destination throughout the world.

Hainan would become the key forum and region for China's international economic cooperation and cultural exchange mainly via Boao Forum for Asia. Hainan may further develop its developed brands such as hosting this Forum and Miss World pageant to promote its tourism and international communication. Tourism product development also would be based on its island-style characteristics. Hainan is expected to concentrate on developing its unique tourist attractions (e.g. Yalong Bay, Boao), typical local products, for example, hand-made textiles and pottery. Leisure-oriented sports such as sailing and diving would be further expanded. The construction has started in Wenchang City, Hainan, of a new space centre, which is expected to mainly focus on international commercial space launches.[32] With the growing interest in space exploration, Hainan is planning to build a space-oriented theme park to boost its tourist attractions. The government also aims to expand the lottery industry in Hainan, and strict lottery regulations would be relaxed in this region, fuelling speculation that this island might be transformed into one big casino in the future. However, Wei Liucheng, the Chinese Communist Party secretary of Hainan, brushed off concerns over a possible casino in Hainan, saying that the development of the lottery business would not affect China's anti-gambling rules and laws.[33] In consideration of gambling-related corruption, crime and social instability, the central government has officially banned all gambling in China.

Development of duty-free shopping for travellers is also high on the development agenda. The tertiary sector would be given more freedom to develop duty-free shops and build large shopping malls in Hainan. The Ministry of Finance is considering giving tax refunds to foreign tourists in Hainan and possibly offering duty-free goods to all its domestic and foreign tourists in the future. It is believed that such preferential treatment of Hainan would affect Hong Kong's status as an international shopping paradise.[34] The government hopes that Hainan will become an international shopping centre by 2020. However, the value of duty-free goods in Hainan was merely US$5.3 million in 2007, compared to the corresponding figure of US$6.4 billion in Hong Kong.[35]

Apart from the specific development goals identified in Table 6.6, first, the government intends to develop Hainan's backward and inadequate transportation system by putting more capital investment into local transportation construction. Second, it will put more efforts into local eco-system protection and develop an economy characterized by environmentally friendless and energy conservation. If the ambitious state plan comes to fruition, it has the potential to shape the future economic development of Hainan.

As outlined in the new state plan, aside from the tourism sector, Hainan is also expected to accelerate its industrial development. In particular, the central government hopes that the HYEDZ can become a logistics centre for oil and gas exploration, and other resource development and services in the South China Sea, and a key storage base for national strategic and commercial oil reserves. This would stimulate Hainan's industrial growth through expansion of oil and gas exploration. To this end, in September 2007, the State Council of China gave the green light to establish a bonded area within the HYEDZ. The petroleum, gas and chemical industries in this area were the major sectors identified by the government for development. The industrial development potential of Hainan largely relies on the performance of the Yangpu economic zone. By leveraging on its advantages

Table 6.6 Highlights of the new development plan for Hainan

General Development Goal

1   Hainan is declared a test zone for national tourism reform and innovation by the central government. Hainan would take a lead in developing tourism and associated industries in China.

2   The value-added output of tourism in Hainan is expected to account for more than 8 per cent of its GDP, and the value-added output of its tertiary sector would account for more than 47 per cent of its GDP by 2015. The ratio of persons employed in tertiary industries in the total number of employed persons in Hainan is expected to reach 45 per cent by 2015.

3   The value-added output of tourism in Hainan is anticipated to reach more than 12 per cent of its GDP, and the value-added output of the tertiary sector would account for more than 60 per cent of its GDP by 2020. The ratio of persons employed in tertiary industries in the total number of employed persons in Hainan is expected to reach 60 per cent by 2020.

4   The government intends to promote the development of other tourism-related industries in Hainan, including cultural, creative, sports and conference sectors. In order to accelerate growth of this sector, Hainan's tourism market is due to open up further to private and foreign companies.

(Continued)

Table 6.6 (Continued)

Typical Local Tourist Products

5   Hainan is expected to concentrate on developing premium tourism attractions (e.g. Yalong Bay, Boao), typical local tourism products, for example, hand-made textiles and pottery. Leisure-oriented sports such as sailing and diving would be further expanded. Also, Hainan is expected to build the world's largest array of golf courses.

Infrastructure

6   The government aims to build a fast, convenient and comprehensive transportation network in Hainan. The construction of cross-Qingzhou Strait tunnel and Guangzhou–Haikou highway is expected to be accelerated. Building the Haikou–Wuzhishan–Sanya and Wanning–Danzhou–Yangpu inter-regional highways is another important task.

7   The government would further develop power stations, water irrigation, information and other infrastructure facilities.

Environmental Protection

8   Heavily polluted, high water and energy-consumption industries would not be allowed to develop in Hainan. In contrast, ocean, high-tech, software and creative industries would be encouraged to develop on this island.

9   The ratio of forest cover to total land area would account for 60 per cent by 2015. Hainan is expected to become a model of national eco-friendly construction and development in the future.

Education and Manpower Training

10   Training an abundant workforce skilled in tourism and hospitality is expected to be an important task for the government.

Duty-free Shopping

11   The tertiary sector would be given more freedom to develop duty-free and brand shops, and build large shopping malls. The Ministry of Finance is considering giving tax refunds to foreign tourists in Hainan, and potentially allowing non-Hainanese domestic tourists to benefit from duty-free shopping on this island. Duty-free goods may be offered to all domestic and foreign tourists in the future.

Lottery Business

12   The government is expected further open up the lottery industry in Hainan, and strict lottery regulations would be relaxed in this region. The central government gave the green light to Hainan to explore the lottery market, and develop pari-mutuel and instant sports lotteries on large international events.

Visa-free Policy Expansion

13   The Chinese government would broaden its current visa-free policy to Hainan from 21 to 26 nations. The newly approved nations include Finland, Denmark, Norway, Ukraine and Kazakhstan.

14   The tour group requirement from South Korea, Germany and Russia to Hainan would go down to a minimum of two persons, and they would be allowed to stay on this island for a maximum of 21 days.

Promotion of Tourism Companies

15   The government would make great efforts to push forward financial sector development in this region through cross-border yuan (renminbi) settlement. It would simplify approval procedures for new tourism firms, and eligible local tourism companies would be permitted to expand and be listed in the stock market.

Source: Compiled by the author based on the information from National Tourism Administration of the People's Republic of China, 2009. *Zhongguo Lvyou nianjian 2009* (*The Yearbook of China Tourism 2009*). Beijing: China Tourism Press.

of geographical proximity and bonded area status, the local government hopes to promote economic cooperation between Hainan and the ASEAN, and the Yangpu area, whilst Hainan as a whole may play a pioneer role in the development of China–ASEAN free trade.

As illustrated by the Statement on Accelerating Tourism Industry Development issued by the State Council of China on November 2009, the Chinese government regards the tourism sector as a strategic pillar of industry and one of the major elements of national economic growth. In fact, the Chinese government's efforts to promote Hainan's tourism can be traced back to 1996. The government has previously exhibited an intention to develop Hainan into an international tourist island. However, the government initiatives and policies were not successful; as evident in the small numbers of international tourist arrivals and low tourism income revenues. Hainan has still a long way to go if it is to become a world-renowned tourism destination. There is a lack of concerted measures for promotion of tourism. The local government of Hainan urgently needs to add substance to the state plan by providing detailed working plans in areas such as infrastructure construction, education and training.

Dilemmas of tourism development in Hainan

Historically, Hainan's economic growth was slow and lagged behind many other coastal regions. Too much focus on its real estate sector caused Hainan's bubble economy to burn and then go bust in 1993.[36] Despite the setbacks and economic difficulties, with their pristine coastline, year-round sunshine and sandy beaches, many places in Hainan (e.g. Sanya) have been transformed from poor fishing towns to prosperous cities and renowned tropical resorts equipped with modern tourism facilities.

Tourism development in Hainan has not been particularly promising over the last decade. The data shown in Table 6.7 compares the tourism development among China's 10 main tourism regions and Hainan by taking seven tourism development indicators. There were merely 0.66 million inbound visitor arrivals in Hainan in 2010, including 0.47 million foreign tourists, compared to 31.4 million visitor arrivals and 7.33 million foreign tourists in Guangdong. The share of this island in the total number of tourist arrivals in China was only 0.8 per cent in 2010. In this respect, Hainan lags a long way behind Guangdong, which received 13.5 per cent of foreign visitor arrivals in China in 2010 and was the highest ranked among China's regions. In addition, in contrast to the corresponding figures of 2.5 per cent, 2.2 per cent and 1.6 per cent in Beijing, Shanghai and Guangdong respectively, Hainan's ratio of international tourism receipts to regional GDP recorded the much lower figure of 1.3 per cent in 2008. In terms of the total number of travel agencies, total revenue of travel agencies and total revenue of star-rated hotels in 2008, the figures for Hainan were significantly lower than those of the top 10 regions in China.

Hainan has also recorded poor performance compared to other Chinese regions in foreign exchange earnings from international tourism. In 2010, it ranked No. 24 in terms of total international tourism receipts among the regions of China.

Table 6.7 Comparison of tourism development among China's regions

Region	Total Tourist Arrivals 2010 (million)	Total Inbound of Foreign Tourists 2010 (million)	International Tourism Receipts 2010 (US$ billion)	The Ratio of International Tourism Receipts in Regional GDP 2008 (%)	Total of Travel Agencies 2008 (number)	Total Revenue of Travel Agencies 2008 (billion yuan)	Total Revenue of Star-Rated Hotels 2008 (billion yuan)
Guangdong	31.40	7.33	12.38	1.6	1030	24.5	14.4
Shanghai	7.33	5.93	6.34	2.2	843	24.9	15.4
Zhejiang	6.84	4.47	3.93	0.9	1370	12.9	18.6
Jiangsu	6.53	4.73	4.78	0.8	1595	13.1	13.5
Beijing	4.90	4.21	5.04	2.5	830	28.1	26.7
Fujian	3.68	1.15	2.97	1.3	596	5.2	4.6
Shandong	3.66	2.77	2.15	0.8	1765	6.4	12.7
Liaoning	3.61	3.07	2.25	0.7	1082	5.0	6.3
Yunnan	3.29	2.31	1.32	1.1	449	6.1	4.7
Guangxi	2.50	1.41	0.80	0.3	378	2.9	3.2
Hainan	**0.66**	**0.47**	**0.32**	**1.3**	**163**	**2.4**	**3.6**

Sources:
1. National Tourism Administration of China. (2009). Zhongguo Lvyou nianjian 2009 (The Yearbook of China Tourism 2009). Beijing: China Tourism Press.
2. National Statistical Bureau of China. (2010). Zhongguo tongji nianjian 2010 (China Statistical Yearbook 2010). Beijing: China Statistics Press.
3. National Tourism Administration of China. (2011). Zhongguo Lvyou nianjian 2011 (The Yearbook of China Tourism 2011). Beijing: China Tourism Press.

In contrast to the corresponding figure of 23.9 per cent in Guangdong, in 2010, Hainan's ratio of total foreign exchange earnings from international tourism for China was only 0.2 per cent, at US$0.32 billion. In fact, Hainan has exhibited a decreasing trend in foreign exchange earnings over the last decade, down from 0.9 per cent in 1995 to 0.2 per cent in 2010. Hainan's international tourism receipts of US$1.5 billion were very low compared to those of major tourism destinations in Asia and the Pacific. The international tourism receipts for Hong Kong and Singapore were US$10.2 billion and US$5.7 billion respectively in 2005: more than six and three times higher respectively than those of Hainan (Figure 6.5).

Hainan may be a well-known tourism destination for domestic travellers, but not to foreign visitors. One of the top priorities for Hainan is to focus on foreign tourists and raise its profile worldwide. South Korea and Russia are the two most important foreign markets for Hainan's tourism industry. These countries were ranked in first and second positions in terms of numbers of foreign arrivals in Hainan by country of origin in 2007. In 2007, there were 175,200 and 151,100 visitors to Hainan from South Korea and Russia respectively, which indicates that Hainan is highly on South Korean and Russian tourists. Japan and Singapore are also crucial markets (Figure 6.6). That is quite risky, and Hainan needs to diversify its tourist markets and attract more foreign tourists from other parts of the globe.

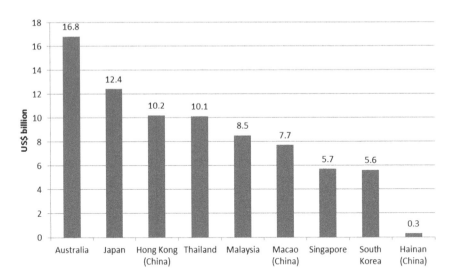

Figure 6.5 Comparison of international tourism receipts by country of Asia and the Pacific, 2005

Note: The figure for Hainan was calculated on the year of 2009.

Sources:
1. The data for other regions was collected from The United Nations World Tourism Organization. (2009). *2009 International tourism results and prospects for 2010*, 18 January 2010, Spain, pp. 1–12.
2. Hainan Statistical Bureau. (2008). *Hainan tongji nianjian 2008 (Hainan Statistical Yearbook 2008)*. Beijing: China Statistics Press.

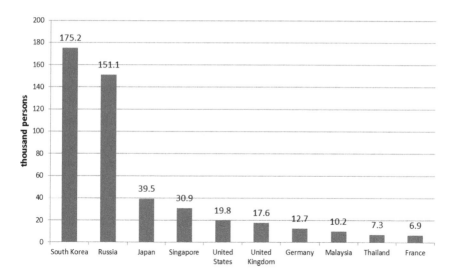

Figure 6.6 Numbers of foreign visitor arrivals in Hainan by top 10 countries, 2007

Source: Hainan Statistical Bureau. (2008). *Hainan tongji nianjian 2008 (Hainan Statistical Yearbook 2008)*. Beijing: China Statistics Press.

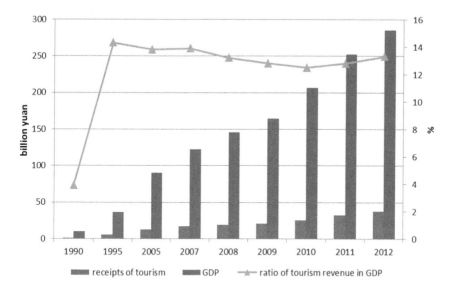

Figure 6.7 Indicators of receipts of tourism and GDP in Hainan

Sources:
1. Hainan Statistical Bureau. *Hainan tongji nianjian (Hainan Statistical Yearbook)*, (2008, 2009, 2013). Beijing: China Statistics Press
2. Hainan Statistical Bureau. "Hainan guomin jingji he shehui fazhan tongji gongbao" (Public record of economic and social development statistics of Hainan), (2008, 2009, 2010).

Hainan has been facing strong competition from other popular tourism destinations, and experiencing difficulty in attracting international visitors for a number of years. Its ratio of receipts for tourism in GDP was only around 13.3 per cent in 2012 (Figure 6.7). There is an enormous amount of work to be done before it can compete against Guangdong and Shanghai, let alone Hong Kong and Singapore. In order to pursue a pro-tourism development strategy and strengthen regional competitiveness, the government needs to make great market efforts to promote Hainan's tourism and attract more foreign vacationers. Even with the support of the Chinese central government, developing Hainan into a world-renowned international tourism destination will be a lengthy process, and such a goal is unlikely to be achieved in the near future.

Future obstacles and policy recommendations

The government's ambitious plan to build Hainan into a top-level international tourism destination by 2020 is by no means certain to succeed, as it is likely to encounter numerous obstacles at the local level. First, the lack of skilled personnel or adequate training in tourism and hospitality remains an unresolved issue. Jackson[37] argues that the development of tourism education and manpower training are the two key factors in strengthening regional competitiveness in this field. Without a skilled workforce, it has been impossible to meet the increase in tourists' demands or to manage tourist facilities and this has hampered local tourism development.[38] To be fair, the lack of education and training is not unique to Hainan; it is suggested that many tourism-oriented regions have faced a similar problem: a dilemma posed by a fast growing tourism sector hampered by poor tourism-oriented human resource development. The state-oriented tourism plans paid little attention to education and skills training among local residents. Considering the backwardness of the existing education framework, the necessary development of human resources in Hainan could take many years.

Tourism infrastructure improvement may not be a problem for the cash-rich Chinese government: the key lies in enhancing manpower training and developing comprehensive tourism education. Wang and Wall[39] suggest that the current tourism development planning in Hainan has overly emphasized the development of luxury physical infrastructure such as hotels, golf resorts and theme parks, while the well-being of the local Li minority people is largely ignored. In the absence of such training, preferential policies and capital investment may contribute little to Hainan's tourism sector. Regardless of their social and economic status, and whether their interests are powerful or weak, the stakeholder theory suggests that all affected groups should have the right to get involved in regional tourism policy-making in Hainan. In other words, in order to realize their social development goals and improve living standards, the voices of disadvantaged minority communities such as the Li people must be heard in the formulation and implementation of tourism development plans.

Due to a lack of willingness to invest in training on the part of the private sector and the scale of the investment required, the government should take a leading role in development of tourism education via universities, secondary professional schools, tourism training and research centres. Given the size of the problem, the government may need to designate and implement a long-term strategy for tourism training programs, complemented by development of cultural consciousness among the local people, especially the less-educated and vulnerable minority community. The formulation of 'tourism-oriented' education programs and training courses should be based on local people's needs and local conditions. Local community consultation is crucial to the setting up of valuable and acceptable training courses and effective local education programs. The key to the provision of such education is to rise above short-term and narrow profit-driven motives and to meet the needs of residents who wish to be involved in tourism development by gradually nurturing their capacity in a consistent and long-term manner. Only by these means will the local people evolve as tourism ambassadors to outsiders.

Second, the government may need to further put capital investment into airports and an inter-regional high-speed rail link; and above all, completely overhaul the local infrastructure. A comprehensive, efficient and advanced transportation system is a key precondition for realizing robust tourism development in Hainan. To achieve fast economic growth, it is essential to improve backward local transportation and other infrastructure facilities. The poor standard of local transportation in Hainan is evident from a comparison road density between various regions within China. In comparison to the corresponding figures of 184.1 and 130.8 per 100 square km in Shanghai and Jiangsu, the road density in Hainan was much lower, with merely 56.6 per 100 square km in 2009 (Figure 6.8). Infrastructure development requires enormous capital investment. The problem for Hainan is how to finance these infrastructure projects. Hainan simply does not have enough fiscal capacity. Local budget expenditure has been much higher than revenues over the past three decades, resulting in a huge public financial deficit (Table 6.8).

Hainan depends on external funding sources to deal with its own financial shortages. In 2008, the central government spent 5.6 billion yuan on Hainan's infrastructure, accounting for merely 8.2 per cent of total investment in fixed assets in Hainan. Hainan really needs to get more support from the central government to speed up infrastructure improvement and economic growth. In addition to state investment, foreign capital is also crucial for this region. As the existing transport network is relatively backward, modernization of the entire system would represent a massive task.

Third, the development of tourism in Hainan might not dramatically enhance the living standards of local residents or reduce their poverty to the extent anticipated by the government. In particular, the minority population, which accounts for around 20 per cent of total population in Hainan, are generally poorly educated and still largely rely on the agricultural sector for income revenue.[40] In fact, Liu and Wall[41] point out that most of the economic benefits from tourism development would be enjoyed by outsiders, and local people, due to their lack of relevant expertise, might gain very little. Hainan might become a playground and area of speculation for China's new rich: whilst the poor local and minority people could be squeezed out. One of the crucial tasks for the government is to ensure

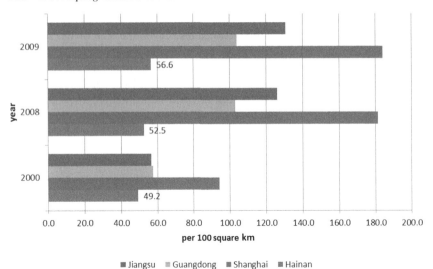

Figure 6.8 Road density comparison

Note: Compiled by the author.

Sources:
1. Guangdong Statistical Bureau. *Guangdong tongji nianjian (Guangdong Statistical Yearbook)*, (2001, 2009, 2010). Beijing: China Statistics Press.
2. Jiangsu Statistical Bureau. *Jiangsu tongji nianjian (Jiangsu Statistical Yearbook)*, (2001, 2009, 2010). Beijing: China Statistics Press.
3. Shanghai Statistical Bureau. *Shanghai tongji nianjian (Shanghai Statistical Yearbook)*, (2001, 2009, 2010). Beijing: China Statistics Press.
4. Hainan Statistical Bureau. *Hainan tongji nianjian (Hainan Statistical Yearbook)*, (2001, 2009, 2010). Beijing: China Statistics Press.

the distribution of benefits of tourism development to the poor areas and the local communities in Hainan.

Fourth, in seeking to raise the profile of local tourism, with the collaboration of private tourism agencies, the local government may need to channel efforts into promotion of Hainan's tourism worldwide. An international advertising campaign must be launched: one which recognizes that Hainan is not a copy or reproduction of Hawaii, Bali, Hong Kong or Singapore. This island needs to offer something different and new to tourists and develop its own tourism brand. Over the past few years, Hainan's tourism industry has depended too much on international tourists visiting for conference and business. One of the key promotion areas in the future will be the expansion of international tourist arrivals for leisure and duty-free shopping. Hosting major international events would be is a positive way to increase the influx of foreign visitors to Hainan. Organizing large events based on sport, festivals, movies and other celebrations could be an effective and cost-saving way to promote local tourism. The research by Dwyer, Forsyth and Spurr[42] and Getz[43] points out the motivational and promotional role played by

Table 6.8 Local budget revenue and expenditure in Hainan, 1978–2012 (billion yuan)

Year	Local Revenue	Local Expenditure	Local Budget Deficit	The Ratio of Local Expenditure in Local Revenue (%)
1978	0.14	0.17	0.03	121.4
1980	0.12	0.21	0.09	175.0
1985	0.32	0.59	0.27	184.3
1990	0.74	1.74	1.0	235.1
1995	2.85	4.24	1.39	148.7
1998	3.65	5.75	2.1	157.5
2000	4.49	7.05	2.56	157.0
2005	8.49	16.76	8.27	197.4
2007	15.25	28.71	13.46	188.2
2008	22.98	43.87	20.89	190.9
2009	29.96	60.41	30.45	201.6
2010	55.16	81.87	26.71	148.4
2011	62.75	108.13	45.38	172.3
2012	71.43	129.56	58.13	181.4

Sources:
1. Hainan Statistical Bureau. (1999). *Hainan wushi nian 1949–1999 (Hainan's Fifty Years 1949–1999)*. Beijing: China Statistics Press.
2. Hainan Statistical Bureau. *Hainan tongji nianjian (Hainan Statistical Yearbook)*, (2009, 2010, 2013). Beijing: China Statistics Press.

such events in stimulating tourism development. They serve three main goals: attracting tourists, fostering a positive image for local tourism and acting as a catalyst for urban renewal.[44]

The government should further relax entry restrictions and encourage private tourist companies' participation in Hainan's tourism. The government may want to lower market thresholds to enable private and foreign sectors to compete on an equal basis in the local tourism sector. To expand market share, the qualified local agencies in Hainan should be allowed to directly negotiate with foreign tourism agencies and set up promotional branches in countries which are a major source of tourists. By adopting means such as organizing tourism exhibitions, seminars and fairs and distributing marketing materials and flyers to potential tourists, these promotional branches and offices could help Hainan to improve public relations and achieve marketing goals. The case study of Denmark conducted by Hjalager[45] shows that the establishment of the Danish Tourist Board helped local tourism enterprises to better connect and communicate with potential tourists, and achieve scale of tourism economies. With the rapid technological development of recent times, Hainan's marketing employees also need to be creative and adopt new means to promote local tourism and attract the internet savvy young tourists, such as advertising on smartphones and using social networking websites.

Finally, achieving high service standards is important in building a reputation, gaining customer loyalty and increasing the market share for Hainan's tourism sector. By providing a personal, high quality, differentiated service to the tourists and creating a tourist-friendly atmosphere, the staff working in the hospitality industry can create a memorable experience for the inbound tourist to Hainan and enhance the international reputation of Hainan's tourist industry. Due to the labour-intensive characteristic of the tourism industry, Smith[46] argues that its service standards can generate a profound effect on tourist satisfaction and loyalty toward a tourism destination. The study by Xu[47] also stresses the importance of high service standards to the hospitality industry.

Tourism services in Hainan are currently unable to meet international standards. Illegal commission from tourism, unfair and hostile competition among tourism agencies, unethical tourism practices and conduct by the tourist guides are still widespread in Hainan. The fact that many employees lack tourism expertise and educational qualifications has exacerbated the problem of poor customer service. Luo Baoming, Governor of Hainan Province, has received persistent reports of tourists being treated badly, sold fake goods, abandoned by tour guides and generally ripped off on this island.[48] It would be impossible to transform Hainan into an international tourism resort without eradication of this abuse of tourists. The local tourism administration must address such complaints, and take tough action to combat poor service quality and unethical practices. To develop top-level international tourism, Hainan has to ensure all tourists are satisfied and willing to recommend their travel experience to others. A proper framework of rules, regulations and sanctions regarding tourism operations is badly needed. In addition, a properly functioning system for service provision evaluation should be developed to rank service offered by the employees. It would be desirable for all tourist employees to be properly trained and obtain licences before starting work.

In Hainan's long journey towards becoming a world famous tourism destination, the local government may need to understand that overall development rather than construction of tourism facilities is the fundamental goal. If handled correctly, tourism development has the potential to gradually change Hainan's economic backwardness and stimulate its socio-economic development in the future.

Conclusion

Development of Hainan as an International Tourism Destination has been upgraded to a national strategy. Natural geographic advantages and local tourist attractions have given Hainan a regional and international edge in tourism development. The boom in the Chinese economy has greatly increased the wealth and prosperity of Chinese people. The tourism sector is a key means of boosting local economic development in Hainan, and help reducing regional economic disparities between Hainan and the eastern provinces. A sound and well-planned tourism development plan for Hainan will be able to boost domestic tourism demand, and help transforming China's economic development pattern from investment and export-driven to consumption-led in the next decade.

The economic development history of Hainan has shown a typical 'up and down' style since 1978. Hainan's economic growth has been slow and lagged behind that of many other eastern regions. Is it possible for the new state blueprint of tourism to stimulate local economic growth in Hainan and eventually change its backward economic status in China? Will it lead to another round of boom-to-bust? It is still too early to tell. The plan for developing Hainan as an international tourism destination is still just a plan. It will by no means become a reality in the near future. In addition, the local governments and community in Hainan have not been given the opportunity to get involved in the policy-making process for this state plan, and therefore, local voices and interests have not been properly taken into account. This lack of local participation will impede the full implementation of the policy and the achievement of its intended goals in the long term.

Moreover, tourism development in Hainan has not been particularly promising over the last decade. This island still faces serious challenges and problems to its goal of becoming a top holiday destination in the world. Hainan has still a long way to go if it is to become a world-renowned tourism destination. A lack of skilled personnel, backward transport network and poor service standards in tourism and hospitality are some pressing issues. In addition, unless the real estate boom issue is addressed by the government, it could not only trigger another run of property bubble, but also, harm Hainan's economy by affecting its future development as an international tourism centre.

Notes

1 "Hu Jintao orders Hainan to work on construction of tourism infrastructure facilities," *China News*, 6 January 2010. http://news.xinhuanet.com/firtune/2010-01/06/con tent_12767140.htm (accessed 6 January 2010)
2 Krutwaysho, O., and Bramwell, B. (2010). "Tourism policy implementation and society", Annals of Tourism Research, 37:3, pp. 670–691; Murphy, P. E. (1988). "Community driven tourism planning", Tourism Management, 9:2, pp. 96–104.
3 Sabatier, P. (1986). "Top-down and bottom-up approaches to implementation research: a critical analysis and suggested synthesis", *Journal of Public Policy*, 6:1, pp. 21–48.
4 Krutwaysho and Bramwell, 2010.
5 Barrett, S. (2004). "Implementation studies: time for a revival? Personal reflections on 20 years of implementation studies", Public Administration, 82:2, pp. 249–62; Wang, Yang, and Wall, Geoffrey. (2007). "Administrative arrangements and displacement compensation in top-down tourism planning – A case from Hainan province, China", Tourism Management, 28, pp. 70–82.
6 Barrett, 2004.
7 Brinkerhoff, D. (1996). "Process perspectives on policy change: highlighting implementation", *World Development*, 24:9, pp. 1395–1401.
8 Byrd, E. T. (2007). "Stakeholders in sustainable tourism development and their roles: applying stakeholder theory to sustainable tourism development", *Tourism Review*, 62:2, pp. 6–13.
9 Freeman, R. E. (1984). *Strategic management: a stakeholder approach*, Massachusetts and London: Pitman.
10 Murphy, P. E. (1988). "Community driven tourism planning", *Tourism Management*, 9:2, pp. 96–104; Clarkson, M. B. E. (1995). "A stakeholder framework for analyzing and evaluating corporate social performance", *Academy of Management Review*, 20:1, pp. 92–117; Donaldson, T., and Preston, L. E. (1995). "The stakeholder theory of the corporation: concepts, evidence, and implications", *Academy of Management Review*, 20:1, pp. 65–91; Brunt, P. and Courtney, P. (1999). "Host perceptions of socio-cultural impacts", *Annals of Tourism Research*, 26, pp. 493–515; Timothy, D.

(1999). "Participatory planning: a view of tourism in Indonesia", *Annals of Tourism Research*, 26:2, pp. 371–91; Pforr, C. (2006). "Tourism policy in the making: an Australian network study", *Annals of Tourism Research*, 33:1, pp. 87–108; Stevenson, N., Airey, D., and Miller, G. (2008). "Tourism policy making: the policymakers' perspectives", *Annals of Tourism Research*, 35:3, pp. 732–50.

11 Freeman, 1984, p. 25.
12 Sautter, E.T., and Leisen, B. (1999). "Managing stakeholders: a tourism planning model", *Annals of Tourism Research*, 26:2, pp. 312–28, see p. 315.
13 Sautter and Leisen, 1999, p. 316.
14 Dwyer, L., Forsyth, P., and Spurr, R. (2006a). "Collaboration theory and community tourism planning", *Annals of Tourism Research*, 22:1, pp. 186–204.
15 Dwyer, Forsyth, and Spurr, 2006a, see p. 195.
16 Gunn, C.A. (2002). *Tourism planning: basics, concepts, cases*. New York and London: Routledge, see p. 130.
17 Brødsgaard, K.E. (2009). *Hainan—state, society, and business in a Chinese province*, London and New York: Routledge.
18 Liu, Abby, and Wall, Geoffrey. (2003). Human resources development for tourism in a peripheral island: Hainan, China. In Stefan Gössling (Ed.), *Tourism and development in tropical islands: Political ecology perspectives* (pp. 222–36), Cheltenham and Northampton: Edward Elgar.
19 National Tourism Administration of China. (2009). *Zhongguo Lvyou nianjian 2009* (*The Yearbook of China Tourism 2009*). Beijing: China Tourism Press.
20 Timothy, 1999.
21 Yeh, K.C. (1991). *The lessons of East Asian development and alternative development strategies for Hainan*. California: Rand.
22 The HYEDZ, with the strategic geographical advantage of proximity to the Association of Southeast Asian Nations (ASEAN), has a total land area of 31 square km and the benefit of a deep-water harbour.
23 The real estate market in Hainan in the early 1990s showed rocketing growth of housing price, according to official data from the yearbook on China's real estate market.
24 "Hainan fazhan dashiji" (Big development events in Hainan), *21cbh*, 26 April 2010. http://www.21cbh.com/HTML/2010-4-26/yNMDAwMDE3NDMyNA.html (accessed 28 June 2010).
25 "Officials in China at odds over food scandal," *The New York Times*, 3 March 2010. http://www.nytimes.com/2010/03/03/world/asia/03hainan.html (accessed 6 June 2010).
26 Feng, Chongyi, and Goodman, David S.G. (1997). Hainan: communal politics and the struggle for identity. In David S.G. Goodman (Ed.), *China's provinces in reform: class, community and political culture* (pp. 53–88), London and New York: Routledge.
27 Feng, Chongyi, and Goodman, David. S.G. (1995). *China's Hainan province: economic development and investment environment*. Nedlands: University of Western Australia Press.
28 Feng and Goodman, 1997; Cadario, Paul. M., Ogawa, Kazuko, and Wen, Yin-Kann. (1992). "A Chinese province as a reform experiment: the case of Hainan", *Work Bank Discussion Papers*, Washington, DC: The World Bank, pp. 1–58.
29 Hainan Statistical Bureau. (1999). *Hainan wushi nian 1949–1999* (*Hainan's fifty years 1949–1999*). Beijing: China Statistics Press.
30 "China property bubble, 1990s style," *The Wall Street Journal*, 17 March 2010. http://blogs.wsj.com/chinarealtime/2010/03/17/china-property-bubble-1990s-style/tab/article/ (accessed 5 April 2010)05-04-2010).
31 "Estate bubbles will trap Hainan in another lost decade," *Global Times*, February 2010. http://business.globaltimes.cn/comment/2010-02/507266.html (accessed 26-03-2010).
32 "China begins space center construction in Hainan," Xinhua, 14 September 2009. http://www.chinadaily.com.cn/bizchina/2009-09/14/content_8978345.htm (accessed 15 March 2010).

33 "On Hainan: Lottery, yes – Gambling, no," *The Wall Street Journal*, 6 January 2010. http://blogs.wsj.com/chinarealtime/2010/01/06/on-hainan-lotter-yes-%e2%80%93-gambling-no/ (accessed 20 March 2010).

34 "Resorts, lotteries coming to Hainan," *China Daily*, 7 January 2010, http://www.china daily.com.cn/bizchina/2010-01/07/content_9277898.htm (accessed 16 March 2010).

35 "Hainan: Not just another Hawaii", *China Daily*. 22 January2010, http://www.chinadaily. com.cn/hkedition/2010-01/22/content_9359018.htm. (accessed 22 March 2010).

36 Li, Yiping. (2003). "Development of the Nanshan cultural tourism zone in Hainan, China: Achievements made and issues to be resolved", *Tourism Geographies*, 5:4, pp. 436–45.

37 Jackson, Julie. (2006). "Developing regional tourism in china: the potential for activating business clusters in a socialist market economy", *Tourism Management*, 27, pp. 695–706.

38 Liu, Abby, and Wall, Geoffrey. (2006). "Planning tourism employment: A developing country perspective", *Tourism Management*, 27, pp. 159–70.

39 Wang and Wall, 2007.

40 Wang, Yang, and Wall, Geoffrey. (2005). Sharing the benefits of tourism: a case study in Hainan, China. http://www.entrepreneur.com/tradejournals/article/134857446_1.html (accessed 7 March 2011)

41 Liu and Wall, 2006.

42 Dwyer, L., Forsyth, P., and Spurr, R. (2006b). "Assessing the economic impacts of events: a computable general equilibrium approach", *Journal of Travel Research*, 45:1, pp. 59–66.

43 Getz, Donald. (2008). "Event tourism: definition, evolution, and research", *Tourism Management*, 29, pp. 403–28.

44 Getz, 2008.

45 Hjalager, Anne-Mette. (2007). "Stages in the economic globalization of tourism", *Annals of Tourism Research*, 34:2, pp. 437–57.

46 Smith, S.L.J. (1997). "Challenges to tourism in industrialized nations". In S. Wahab and J.J. Pigram (Eds.), *Tourism, development and growth: the challenges of sustainability* (pp. 147–163), London and New York: Routledge.

47 Xu, Jing Bill. (2010). "Perceptions of tourism products", *Tourism Management*, 31, pp. 607–610.

48 "Hainan: Not just another Hawaii", 2010.*Table 6.6* Continued

7   Development of the central region in China

Central China seeks rapid growth

During the 1980s and 1990s, many reform and opening up policies implemented by the Chinese central government favoured the coastal regions, which led to highly unbalanced regional development between the eastern, central and western regions.[1] The Chinese leaders considered it inevitable or even desirable to pursue unbalanced development, especially during the early stage of its opening up.

To take advantage of eastern China's inherent geographical advantages, the majority (over 60 per cent) of China's development zones are located along the coast (Table 7.1). For example, China's five special economic zones, namely, Shenzhen, Zhuhai, Shantou, Xiamen and Hainan, are in the south and southeast coast of China.

Due to China's development strategy and unfavourable geography, regional gaps have widened considerably, especially during the 1990s and early 2000s. The central region's economic growth has been much slower than that of the eastern region in recent decades. In 2009, per capita gross regional product (GRP) for the coastal region was around 41,570 yuan, more than double those of the central (19,828 yuan) and western regions (19,288 yuan).[2]

The central region, which covers six provinces of Hunan, Hubei, Anhui, Shanxi, Henan, and Jiangxi, had a combined land area of 1.03 million square km and a population of 356 million in 2009, accounting for 10.7 per cent and 27 per cent of the national total, respectively. The region has a comparative advantage in agriculture, energy and minerals, and is rich in coal, China's main source of energy. Its production of grain, coal, and nonferrous metals has increased rapidly in recent years.[4]

The central region is China's leading producer of grain and oil bearing crops, producing 31.3 per cent and 43.9 per cent of national total in 2009, respectively (Appendix 7.1). The region is also relatively strong in resource related industries, such as coal, steel and electricity which accounted for a respective 36 per cent, and 21 per cent, and 23 per cent of the national total.

Nonetheless, the six provinces differ considerably in some aspects, including population size and level of development. Their population ranges from 30 million in Shanxi to 84 million in Henan. Per capita GDP ranges from a relatively

Table 7.1 Locations of special zones for economic and technology development approved by China's central government, as of 2009

Type	Eastern Region	Central Region	Western Region	Total
Special Economic Zone	5	0	0	5
Economic and Technological Development Zone	27	10	10	47
High-tech Industry Development Zone	28	13	13	54
Bonded Zone[3]	15	0	0	15
Total	**75**	**23**	**23**	**121**

Sources: *China Special Economic Zone & Development Area Yearbook*, 2003 and *List of High-tech and New-tech Development Zones*, The Ministry of Science and Technology of PR China, 2009

low of 16,408 yuan in Anhui to a relatively high of 22,677 yuan in Hubei. The composition of the six provinces' GRP also differs considerably. Agriculture has a strong presence (13 per cent to 15 per cent of GDP) in all provinces, except for Shanxi (6 per cent of GDP). In 2010, the secondary sector (industry and construction) was most significant in Shanxi (56.9 per cent of GDP) and Henan (57.3 per cent of GDP), while the tertiary sector contributed nearly 40 per cent to GRP in Hunan (Table 7.2).

Rising regional inequality has been popularly singled out as a hindrance to China's sustainable development and efforts have been channelled to closing regional gaps since the late 1990s. To boost local economic growth, the Chinese central government has paid increasing attention to the development of China's inland regions since 2007 and approved the further opening up of the central and western regions (Appendix 7.2).

In 2007, the State Council approved the Setting Up of Comprehensive Testing Zone for Developing National Resource Conservation and an Environmentally Friendly Society in Changsha–Zhuzhou–Xiangtan and Wuhan City Clusters, and in September 2009, the Chinese government approved the Proposal for Economic Rejuvenation of the Central Region. Beijing is expected to formulate favourable policy measures to stimulate the overall economic growth of central China. In particular, Changsha–Zhuzhou–Xiangtan area and Wuhan city have been urged to take steps to protect the environment and to achieve high standards in resource conservation.

In the state plan for central China, industrial development will focus on steel, smelting and pressing of non-ferrous metals, petrochemicals and building materials. The Chinese central government is resolved to developing the central region into a major base for the modern equipment manufacturing industry through research, innovation, and key indigenous technology. Within the modern equipment industry, the focus would be on electricity transmission, production of mining equipment and modern medical equipment, electricity control and environmental protection (Appendix 7.3).

Table 7.2 GRP composition of six central provinces, 2010 (%)

Province	Primary Industry	Secondary			Tertiary Industry
		Sub-total	Industry	Construction	
Shanxi	6.0	56.9	50.6	6.3	37.1
Anhui	14.0	52.1	43.8	8.3	33.9
Jiangxi	12.8	54.2	45.4	8.8	33.0
Henan	14.1	57.3	51.8	5.5	28.6
Hubei	13.4	48.6	42.1	6.5	37.9
Hunan	14.5	45.8	39.3	6.5	39.7

Source: *China Statistical Yearbook*, 2011

Despite a slew of supportive measures for the economic development of the inland regions, the central region has continued to lag behind the eastern region. Economic disparity between the eastern and central regions remains conspicuous. As shown in Figure 7.1, the contribution of the eastern region to GDP in China hit 61.7 per cent in 2010 from 57.4 per cent in 1978, while that of the central region slid to 19.7 per cent in 2010, from 21.7 per cent in 1978. Despite exciting speeches by the central leaders and the announcement of development plans, there seems to be a lack of detailed policy measures and concrete working plans for China's central region. But even with concrete plans in place, they will take time to generate significant results.

Looking to the future, the eastern region will continue to be the major national economic powerhouse and the leader in industrialisation and industrial upgrading in China. Taking into account the crucial role of the eastern region in China's overall economic development, it is understandable that the government will continue to give emphasis to the eastern region. Any policy shift that is detrimental to the eastern region will have adverse consequences for the overall economic growth of China.

Nevertheless, the central region enjoys Beijing's backing for rapid future growth even though it is relatively unknown to foreign investors. Understandably, serious obstacles and challenges lay ahead. The development of China's central region is essential to achieving balanced regional development in China. China's central region has the potential of becoming increasingly attractive to foreign investors, as well as to foreign companies already operating in the eastern part of China. For example, Foxconn, a Taiwanese-owned company and one of the world's largest electronics manufacturers, has moved its production line from the coastal city of Shenzhen to a manufacturing plant in Henan.[5]

The main incentives for the foreign investment inflows to central China are in the variation in minimum wage. The minimum wage of the eastern region is considerably higher than that in the inland regions. Such cost differentials are important enough for many industries, especially labour-intensive and low technology manufacturing plants, to move their production facilities to the central and western regions. To develop local industries, the central government is encouraging the relocated industries to bring modern technology and management to the

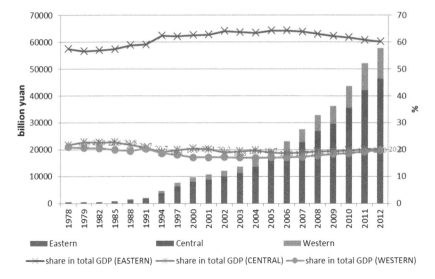

Figure 7.1 Region's share in China's total GDP, 1978–2012

western region. The improved infrastructure in China's inland regions in recent years along with the central region's generous incentives has also played a part in diverting foreign investment and foreign-owned companies from eastern China.[6]

The relative decline of the central region

China's eastern region has thrived on its strategic geographical location and Beijing's slew of favourable policies to play a crucial and dominant role in China's industrialisation and development since 1978. Over the past three decades this dominance has strengthened. The contribution of the eastern region to GDP in China had increased to 60.1 per cent in 2012 from 57.4 per cent in 1978. In contrast, the central and western regions have contributed much less. The inherent backwardness of these regions in China's overall economy has not reversed, but reinforced; the contribution of the central region to GDP in China had fallen further to 20.2 per cent in 2012, from 21.7 per cent in 1978 (Figure 7.1).

Over the past decade, with average annual growth rate of 15.1 per cent between 2000 and 2009, the central region has fared badly against both the eastern (16.0 per cent) and western (16.7 per cent) regions, although the region sits in the centre of the national transportation networks of railways, highways, and waterways. This gave rise to a phenomenon referred to as "subsidence of the central region" (*zhongbu taxian*). Although central China has achieved a decent growth rate, the region is not only falling far behind the dynamic and robust coastal region in development, but also registering a decline in its share of the nation's GDP.

This could be attributed to the favourable policies enjoyed by the western region.[7] The region enjoys the state's investment in infrastructure and tax reductions for companies,[8] thus greatly enhancing the region's growth prospects. To arrest the increasing coastal-inland gap in development, the central government has invested heavily in the western region since 1999 through its western developmental programme, and in the northeast since 2003 through the northeastern revival programme. The six provinces of central China, which are not included in either and are largely neglected, have been left behind in economic growth rate. The region is further disadvantaged by its distance from coastal harbours, generating higher transportation costs for both the central and western regions.

Due largely to China's biased regional development strategies and policies, the eastern region receives the biggest share of foreign direct investment (FDI) inflows. There were 38,752 foreign-owned enterprises (FOEs) in the eastern region by 2008, contributing a gross industrial output of 8,780 billion yuan. In contrast, the total number of FOEs and their gross industrial outputs in the central and western regions were much lower; the corresponding figures were merely 1,981 and 626.8 billion yuan in the central region in 2008.[9] These FDIs are mostly in export-oriented industries such as the manufacturing of communication equipment, computers and other electronic equipment. By 2008, the three coastal areas of the Pearl River Delta, Yangtze River Delta and Jing-Jin-Ji Economic Zone jointly accounted for three quarters of total national foreign paid-up capital.

Industrial production, in particular, is largely concentrated in the eastern region, accounting for nearly 60 per cent of the national total in 2012, while the central and western regions accounted for 21.5 per cent and 19.1 per cent respectively. The eastern region has played a crucial and dominant role in China's overall industrial development since 1978, and has shown signs of weakening only in the past three decades. The eastern region's value-added industrial output in the national total decreased to 59.4 per cent in 2012 from 66.9 per cent in 1978 (Figure 7.2).

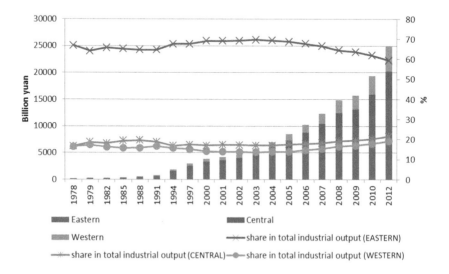

Figure 7.2 Region's share in total value-added industrial output of China, 1978–2012.

Developing China's central region to sustain growth

China's attempt to engineer the rise of central China has come in the form of regional developmental programmes to sustain growth and curtail rising regional inequality since the late 1990s. The central drive serves three key goals: First, the narrowing of the regional gap is important to regaining political loyalty from the central region. Second, a more balanced regional development is essential to social stability in the central region; in recent years, rising large-scale and violent social unrests particularly in the central region have raised the alarm for the Chinese central government to accelerate development in the region. Third, a more balanced regional development is essential to stimulating domestic consumption, which is also consistent with China's efforts to transform its economy from trade dependent to domestic demand driven.

The Chinese leaders are now committed to speeding up the development of central China, the backbone of the country in both political and geographic terms. In March 2004, Premier Wen Jiabao's declaration of a shift in regional development strategy has since fostered "the Rise of Central China" (*zhongbu jueqi*) as a priority on the central government's agenda.

In 2005, the National Development and Reform Commission (NDRC) had promulgated five policy initiatives to speed up development of central China.[10] These include (1) stepping up support for grain production; (2) assisting the development of large metropolitan areas, especially those around Wuhan, Zhengzhou and Nanchang-Jiujiang; (3) encouraging industrial restructuring of the central's main old industrial bases; (4) increasing the extent of economic opening; and (5) promoting the development of basic education.[11]

Of greater significance is the national government's announcement of the phasing out of agricultural tax in 2006. This is a move to narrow the income gap and unify the tax systems of the rural and urban areas. This move reportedly saved peasants 50 billion yuan in taxes a year.[12] As the country's largest grain production base, central China is the main beneficiary of these pro-peasant policies.

Accelerating central China's development was identified as the major task at the central government's economic work conference in December 2004. In the Government's Work Report in 2005, Premier Wen articulated the need to promptly work out plans and measures to energise central China.[13] In September 2009, the State Council approved the "Proposal for Economic Rejuvenation of the Central Region" (referred to hereafter as the Plan), an important development strategy to narrow regional development gaps in China.

Under the Plan, the central region is expected to speed up the modernisation of the equipment manufacturing industry through developing key technologies and increasing R&D spending. The goal is to transform the central region into a manufacturing base for modern equipment manufacturing and high-tech industries by the next decade. The central region also hopes to accelerate its economic development programme through the Plan (Appendix 7.3, see also Table 7.3 for key development indicators).

The central government will also introduce new policies to boost foreign and domestic private investments in industries in this region, particularly in the energy,

Table 7.3 Key development indicators for the central region

Category	Indicator	2008	2015
Economic development	Per capita GRP (yuan)	17,860	36,000
	Urbanisation rate (%)	40.3	48
	Grain output (million ton)	164	168
Environment	Energy consumption for per 10,000 yuan GDP (%)	4.4	2.5
	Water consumption for per 10,000 yuan value-added industrial output (ton)	148	105
	Forest coverage rate (%)	35.7	38

Note: 2015 figures are estimated.

Source: *Proposal for Economic Rejuvenation of the Central Region*, National Development and Reform Commission, September 2009

automobile, petrochemical, equipment manufacturing, and high-tech industries. It will increase the amounts of fiscal transfer to support the region's industrial development including interest-free loans for public infrastructure construction and flexible land use policies at the national level and high-tech industrial zones in the central region. Banks and other financial institutions have been encouraged to offer preferential bank credit and favourable loans to innovative small and medium-sized enterprises in the central region.

For Beijing, an important goal is to forge new growth poles capable of leading the development of the central region. The development of six large city-clusters with industrial agglomerates forms the major part of this strategy. The Chang–Zhu–Tan city cluster[14] and Wuhan Economic Zone are two key regions targeted by the government. Since December 2007, the two have embarked on pilot programmes towards 'double-oriented society' reform (energy conservation society and environmentally friendly society).

Central China's two city clusters will serve as a model for energy conservation and environmental protection. More specifically, while the Wuhan City Cluster is to be developed into a base for advanced manufacturing, high-tech industries and food processing, the Chang–Zhu–Tan metropolis is set to become a base for advanced equipment manufacturing and electronic information industries. In 2009, Chang–Zhu–Tan metropolis accounted for around 42 per cent (550.6 billion yuan) of regional GDP of Hunan and Wuhan City accounted for 35.7 per cent (462.1 billion yuan) of regional GDP of Hubei.[15] It is hoped that these city clusters could generate spillovers to neighbouring areas and thus speed up the overall development of the central region.

Despite media enthusiasm over the programme, national policies for central China have been selective, targeting only a few sectors and areas, including agriculture, energy production, old industrial bases, and city clusters. The hard truth is that despite renewed efforts in recent years to step up industrial development in inland regions, the central region continues to lag behind that of the eastern region, and remains generally an underdeveloped region. Government policies to reduce regional industrial development gap have thus only produced limited outcome.

State-backed efforts to reduce economic gaps have been hindered, and might have been largely offset, by the unfavourable geography and weak industrial foundation of the central region and the self-reinforcing industrial agglomeration in the eastern region. Despite exciting speeches by central leaders and the announcement of ambitious development plans, there is a lack of detailed policy measures to translate plans into reality. Even with these policy measures in place, the new plan for the central region is expected to take time to generate significant results.

Meanwhile, the coastal regions have not been relegated to the periphery. To accelerate local industrial upgrading and maintain rapid economic growth, the Chinese central government has approved the opening up of several new areas in the coastal regions and increasingly introduced preferential policies towards their development over the past few years. It is thus clear that government priorities have not shifted to the western region, as emphasis still remains largely on the coastal eastern region.

Despite Beijing's ambitious master plan, the central region still faces serious challenges to its economic development. First, compared to the prosperous eastern region, the economic foundations of the central region are still very weak. Per capita GDP for the coastal region is more than double that of the central region. Except for Shanxi province, agriculture still accounts for a fairly high proportion of GDP in all five central provinces, indicating a lack of development in the manufacturing and service-driven sectors of the economy. The lack of economic integration of its provinces also represents a serious challenge to the central region. Second, the central region is facing difficulty in attracting low-end and low value-added industries from the eastern region. The development of an industrial cluster covering both the upstream and downstream industrial sectors will take a long time to forge in the central region.

In pursuance of coordinated regional development

Central China faces challenges in achieving coordinated regional development and close regional economic cooperation. Firstly, economic integration of the six provinces of Hubei, Hunan, Henan, Shanxi, Jiangxi and Anhui provinces is far weaker than that of the cities within the Yangtze River Delta (YRD) and Pearl River Delta (PRD) regions. Although this has been an issue for many years, no concrete progress has yet been apparent.

Independence of industrial structures and the duplication of developments are the more pressing issues. All provinces within the central region seek to thrive as independent economies, and adopt different initiatives and development strategies, as evident in the individual development plans for the Chu–Zhu–Tan region, Hunan and Wuhan City Cluster in Hubei. There are currently no formal regional administrative mechanisms or regular government meetings to coordinate the development of this region.

Although the Chinese central government has previously given its backing to the Great Western Development and the Northeast Revitalisation Strategies, no such institutional arrangement exists for the central provinces. For central China, this lack of national initiatives and institutional arrangements has hindered efforts to coordinate intra-regional development, thus weakening the region's request for financial and policy support from Beijing. Moreover, there appears to be a lack of willingness on the part of the local governments to forge closer mutual collaboration.

Unlike the cities within the PRD regions, the six provinces are all centrally administrated provinces and do not regard themselves as subordinate players, making it difficult for the provinces to forge close socio-economic ties. Regional cooperation requires a leader. Nevertheless, it is hard to single out a core or dominant region. None of the six provinces is powerful enough to lead the region. Due to the administrative boundaries and underdevelopment of their inter-regional transport network, core areas or city clusters such as Chang–Zhu–Tan and Wuhan City were unable in the past to radiate large-scale agglomeration effects to the neighbouring areas. There has been little free movement of human talent, capital and information between cities. Policies on the construction of airports also reflect a lack of coordination. According to the state plan for the central region, another 14 airports[16] across the provinces will be constructed and put into operation by 2020.

Duplication of industrial structures is another unresolved problem. Regions have developed similar traditional industries[17] and central provinces with comparable industrial structures and similar economic clout continue to compete in both

Table 7.4 Competing development priorities of central provinces

Province	Advanced Manufacturing Industries	High-Tech and Emerging Industries
Hunan	Electricity-generation equipment manufacturing, rail transportation-related equipment, food, textiles and garments	Aircraft
Hubei	Electricity-generation equipment manufacturing, smelting and pressing of ferrous metals, automobile, food, textiles and garments	New energy vehicle
Anhui	Automobile, equipment manufacturing, food, home appliances and electronic products, textiles and garments	New energy vehicle
Jiangxi	Food, textiles and garments, smelting and pressing of nonferrous metals, electrical machinery and equipment	Aircraft, civil aviation-related equipment
Shanxi	Mining and washing of coal, smelting and pressing of ferrous metals, resource-exploiting equipment and industries, food	X
Henan	Food, home appliances and electronic products, textiles and garments	X

Source: *Proposal for Economic Rejuvenation of the Central Region*, National Development and Reform Commission, September 2009

new and existing industries. For example, to promote the development of advanced manufacturing, Hunan and Hubei have focussed on electricity-generation equipment manufacturing, food, and textiles and garments. Hubei and Anhui are both developing the automobile sector and have coincided in their development priorities for the high-tech new energy vehicle industry (Table 7.4).

The development of new and emerging industries requires large investments as well as government support ranging from subsidies to favourable policies, triggering intense competition among regions. The industrial linkages within the central region are loose and weak. This lack of industrial cooperation results in duplicated developments and cut-throat competition. It also limits the development of an integrated regional market.

Developing local economies, mainly through industrialisation, is often the prime objective of local leaders for several reasons. First, local economic performance is important for job performance evaluations of government officials for promotion. Second, local governments rely heavily on local businesses for government revenue. Third, local governments are responsible for providing various public goods to local residents, such as basic education, health care and welfare. These services have to be financed locally since fiscal transfers from the central to local governments are limited and insufficient. At the same time, the domestic market has become fragmented after local governments have begun to shield local industries from competition.[18]

Developing a well-functioning intra-regional transport system, avoiding excessive competition in industrial development and promoting coordination and cooperation among provinces are thus essential. In the short term, the current approach of focussing on developing urban clusters at sub-regional levels may be effective. However, for the region to sustain its development in the longer term, a coordinating body at the national level may be necessary.

Appendix 7.1 Regional shares of selected industrial and agricultural products

Regions	Year	Coal		Grain		Oil-Bearing Crop	
		Amount (billion tons)	*% of National Total*	*Amount (billion tons)*	*% of National Total*	*Amount (billion tons)*	*% of National Total*
Eastern	2005	0.29	13	0.13	26	0.09	30
Central	2009	0.28	10	0.14	26	0.08	26
	2005	0.92	42	0.15	31	0.13	41
	2009	1.06	36	0.17	31	0.14	44
Northeast	2005	0.19	8	0.07	15	0.02	5
	2009	0.20	6	0.08	16	0.01	4
Western	2005	0.81	37	0.13	28	0.08	25
	2009	1.40	48	0.14	27	0.08	26

Source: *China Statistical Yearbook*, 2006 and 2010

Appendix 7.2 A chronological list of important state decisions on regional development and opening up

Year	Important State Decision
1980	The State Council approved the establishment of Shenzhen, Zhuhai, Shantou and Xiamen Special Economic Zones (SEZs).
1984	The State Council granted the status of coastal opening city to the following fourteen cities: Shanghai, Tianjin, Beihai, Zhanjiang, Guangzhou, Fuzhou, Ningbo, Nantong, Lianyungang, Qingdao, Weihai, Yantai, Dalian and Qinhuangdao.
1985	The State Council granted the status of coastal economic opening region to Yangtze River Delta, Pearl River Delta, Minnan River Delta, Liaodong Peninsula, Shandong Peninsula and Circum-Bohai Bay Region.
1988	The State Council approved the establishment of Hainan SEZ.
1990	The State Council approved the opening up of Shanghai Pudong New District. The State Council approved the establishment of bonded zones in Futian and Shaotoujiao (Shenzhen), Waigaoqiao (Shanghai) and Ningbo (Zhejiang).
2007	The State Council approved the Setting up of Comprehensive Testing Zone for National Urban-Rural Reform in Chongqing and Chengdu, June. The State Council approved the establishment of Hainan Yangpu Bonded Area, October. The State Council approved the Setting up of Comprehensive Testing Zone for Developing National Resource Conservation and Environmentally Friendly Society in Changsha–Zhuzhou–Xiangtan and Wuhan City Clusters, December.
2008	The State Council approved the establishment of Guangxi North Bay Economic Zone, February. The State Council finally approved the Overall Plan for the Comprehensive Supporting Reform Pilot in Tianjin Binhai New Area, April. The State Council approved the establishment of Guangxi Qinzhou Bonded Zone, May. The State Council approved the "Outline of Reform and Development Plan for the Pearl River Delta Region", December.
2009	The State Council approved the "Proposal on Accelerating the Development of Modern Service and Advanced Manufacturing Industries, and Building International Financial and Shipping Centre in Shanghai", March. The State Council approved the "Development Proposal for Accelerating the Construction of Western Strait Economic Zone in Fujian", May. The State Council approved the "Development Plan for Guanzhong–Tianshui Economic Region", June. The State Council approved the "Development Proposal for Jiangsu Coastal Economic Area", June. The State Council approved the "Development Proposal for Liaoning Coastal Economic Area", July. The State Council approved the "Proposal for Economic Rejuvenation of the Central Region", September. The State Council approved the establishment of Tianjian Binhai New Area, November. According to the Chinese central government's new development plan in the "Several Opinions on Development of Hainan as an International Tourism Destination" in December, Hainan was identified as the key area for promoting tourism in China.

(*Continued*)

Appendix 7.2 (Continued)

Year	Important State Decision
2010	The State Council approved the establishment of Chongqing Liangjiang New Area, May. The central government will grant similar preferential treatments (e.g. land use, finance, taxation, investment, foreign trade and administrative system) as those granted to Shanghai Pudong New Area and Tianjin Binhai New Area for the development of this region. The State Council approved the "Regional Development Outline for the Yangtze River Delta", June.

Source: The table was compiled by the authors based on information from various sources.

Appendix 7.3 Industrial development priorities for the central region

According to the state plan, industrial development will focus on steel, smelting and pressing of non-ferrous metals, petrochemicals and building materials. The Chinese central government intends to develop the central region into a major base for modern equipment manufacturing through more research, innovation, and developing indigenous core and key technologies. Within the modern equipment industry, the focus would be on electricity transmission, mining equipment, electricity control and environmental protection, and modern medical equipment.

• For the steel industry, the government aims to strengthen competitiveness by readjusting the industrial structure and boosting the development of high-end and high value-added steel products. The government encourages the forging of large industrial giants through mergers and acquisitions, particularly Wuhan Steel and Taiyuan Steel.
• The central region intends to boost the development of the petrochemical industry and develop into a large oil refinery base by expanding production and technological upgrading of the large and medium-sized enterprises in Luoyang, Wuhan and Jiujiang.
• For the smelting and pressing of nonferrous metals industry, industrial reorganisation through merger and acquisitions (M&A) is encouraged to enhance competitiveness. The local authority will also raise minimum requirement for entry to such traditional industries and gradually eliminate industrial capacities of backward technologies.
• The central government will support the development of the automobile industry with homegrown brand names, energy-conserving, and environmentally friendly cars.
• For high-tech industries, the focus is on electronic information, biology, new energy, and new material.
• In traditional industries such as food, textiles and garments, technological upgrading is encouraged to improve product quality and strengthen competitiveness.

However, the lack of coordination has led to many duplications and fierce competition since the regions have quite similar industrial structures and aim to develop similar industries. For example, many regions focus on developing industries such as steel, automobile, and electronic information, which are considered significant in quickly generating local GDP growth and employment, and leading to hostile cut-throat competition among regions. The competition directly leads to low overall efficiency due to unproductive resource allocation, lack of economy of scale, and poor financial performance.

Nevertheless, central China could still benefit from the industrial developmental programme for several reasons. First, facing decreasing returns in the more developed coastal regions, capital shall flow increasingly to the adjacent central China. Central China will also benefit from the "pull" effects of its own development. As the income level of local residents rises, it pays for producers to set up factories in central China, reducing transport costs in delivering products to consumers in central China. Second, as labour and other production costs in the coastal region have risen considerably in recent years, pressure is rising for low value-added industries to move to the central region which has not witnessed major increases in labour costs. For example, Wahaha, one of the largest producers of potable drinking water, has opened a sales office in Hubei.

As a large economy, China has the advantage of further exploiting its size and diversity by promoting national market integration and regional production specialisation. As labour and land costs rise, especially in the coastal region, low-skilled labour-intensive industries will be squeezed out of the coastal regions to set up shop in the relatively underdeveloped inland regions. Coastal regions would then be forced to develop industries of higher technology-intensity. With different endowment of natural and human resources and through competition, regions can gradually explore their different comparative advantages.

Source: "Plan to Boost the Rise of Central Region", The State Council of the People's Republic of China.

Notes

1 The eastern region covers Beijing, Tianjin, Hebei, Liaoning, Shanghai, Jiangsu, Zhejiang, Fujian, Shandong, Guangdong, Hainan, Heilongjiang and Jilin; the central region includes Shanxi, Anhui, Jiangxi, Henan, Hubei and Hunan; and the western region covers Guangxi, Chongqing, Sichuan, Guizhou, Yunnan, Xizang, Shaanxi, Gansu, Qinghai, Ningxia, Xinjiang and Inner Mongolia.

2 *China Statistical Yearbook 2010*

3 Bonded zone (保税区): A bonded zone is an area in which dutiable goods may be stored, manipulated or undergone manufacturing operations without payment of duty. In China, the bonded zones are under the direct supervision and regulation of its customs. It allows certain export-related activities and applies preferential policies such as export VAT refund.

4 Lai Hongyi, *"Developing Central China: Background and Objectives (I)", EAI Background Brief No. 288*, Singapore: EAI, National University of Singapore, 15 June 2006.

5 "New Foxconn factory in central China begins production with hope of peace, prosperity", *Xinhua News*, http://news.xinhuanet.com/english2010/china/2010-08/02/c_134 26617.htm

6 *China's National and Regional Industrial Development*, a report for the Ministry of Trade and Industry, Singapore, prepared by the East Asian Institute, National University of Singapore, March 2011.

7 The key documents outlined the specific preferential policies for the western region and include the following: (1) *Industrial Dictionary for Foreign Investment in the Central and Western Regions*, issued in 1999 and revised in 2004; (2) *The Preferential Treatment Notice Issued by the State Administration of Taxation* in 1999; and (3) *Several Opinions on the Implementation of State Policies in the Western Region*, released in 2001. (Yu Hong. (2010). "The Rationale, Prospects, and Challenges of China's Western Economic Triangle in Light of Global Economic Crisis," *Asian Politics & Policy*, 2:3, pp. 437–461)

8 In contrast to national terms by which the existing favourable taxation policies expire after a three-year period, a reduction of 15 per cent of the income tax rate would continue to be granted to FOEs located in the western region and in preferred industrial sectors designated by the state, such as postal services, transportation, and energy. (Source: Ministry of Finance People's Republic of China, State Administration of Taxation, & General Administration of Administration of Customs of the People's Republic of China (2001, December 30) *Notice of preferential tax treatment for the western development* [Electronic version], accessed 4 March 2010, from http://www. mof.gov.cn/mof/zhengwuxinxi/caizhengwengao/caizhengbuwengao2002/caizhengbu wengao20024/200805/t20080519_21081.html

9 *China Industry Economy Statistical Yearbook 2009*

10 Other ministries have also put forward measures to assist central China's development. In 2004, the Ministry of Finance increased fiscal transfer to central China by 15.7 billion *yuan*. The People's Bank of China, China's central bank, is considering pilot experiments of providing agricultural insurance and financial services to the non-state sector to support central China's agriculture. The State Grain Bureau pledges to increase fiscal transfers to subsidise central provinces, such as Henan, to sell grain to other provinces. The State Environmental Protection Bureau will assist the region in ecological protection, including cleaning up the Huai River Valley and reducing acid rain in the cities ("A Focus on the Two Sessions: Decoding the Rise of Central China" [*Lianghui jujiao: "Zhongbu jueqi" poti le*], posted at http://ha.people.com.cn on 7 March 2005.)

11 "*Guojia fagaiwei chubu zhiding wuda zhengce zhichi zhongbu jueqi*" (The State Development and Reform Commission Tentatively Formulates Five Policies to Support the Rise of Central China), *Changsha Wanbao (Changsha Evening Post)*, 7 March 2005.

12 "NPC moves to abolish agricultural tax", *China Daily*, 26 December 2005, http:// www.chinadaily.com.cn/english/doc/2005-12/26/content_506534.htm

13 "Relief for Depressed Central Region," *Beijing Review*, 21 April 2005, pp. 22–24.

14 To promote accessibility, the "Blueprint for Changsha–Zhuzhou–Xiangtan Circle City Expressway" was approved by the NDRC in 2009. According to the "Blueprint for Changsha–Zhuzhou–Xiangtan Circle City Expressway", express rail lines linking seven cities with a combined length of 760 km are in the pipeline. Travel time between the seven cities will fall below 60 minutes once the network is completed. The express rail lines between Changsha, Zhuzhou and Xiangtan are due to open in 2015. As a result, travel time between Changsha, Zhuzhou and Xiangtan will be less than 25 minutes.

15 *Hunan Yearbook 2010*; *Hubei Statistical Yearbook 2010*

16 These 14 airports include Lvliang and Wutaishan airports in Shanxi, Jiuhuashan, Bangbu and Wuhu airports in Anhui, Yichun and Gandong airports in Jiangxi, Xinyang

and Shangqiu airports in Henan, Shennongjia airport in Hubei, Hengyang, Yueyang, Wugang and Shaodong airports in Hunan.

17 The six provinces within central China have similar production structures and have such main industries as smelting and processing of ferrous and non-ferrous metals, manufacturing of non-metallic mineral products, coal mining, and food processing.

18 *China's National and Regional Industrial Development*, a report for the Ministry of Trade and Industry, Singapore, prepared by the East Asian Institute, National University of Singapore, March 2011.

8 China's western development strategy

Ten years on*

Widening regional inequality continues

China's vast western region accounted for nearly 60 per cent of national land area but only contributed around 27 per cent of its total population and 18.7 per cent of its gross domestic product (GDP) in 2010. Compared to the eastern and central regions, the western region[1] is the least economically developed region. Over the last three decades, the western region has yet to equal the economic development of the more prosperous eastern and central regions (Figure 8.1).

This phenomenon could be traced back to the 1980s and 1990s when the Chinese government implemented policies that favoured the coastal regions. Since the late 1990s, the Chinese leaders have been increasingly concerned with the huge gap between the wealthy eastern and poor western regions and the deteriorating developmental trend. Severe spatial disparity has become a major challenge to the Chinese government's attempts to maintain balanced economic development, social justice and political stability. To narrow the widening development gap, the central government adopted the Great Western Development (GWD) strategy (*xibu da kaifa*) in 1999.

With the GWD strategy, preferential policies in terms of taxation rates, land use rights and favourable bank loans, as well huge fiscal transfers, have been extended to the western region. The government has also invested heavily on improving transportation and other infrastructure in the region.

In terms of reversing the declining trend in the relative importance of the western region in the national economy as compared to the pre-2000 period, the GWD strategy had made modest contributions. The share of western region in total GDP of China increased to 18.7per cent by 2010 from 17.1 per cent in 2000, while the contribution of the eastern region to GDP in China decreased slightly to 61.6 per cent in 2010 from 62.5 per cent in 2000 (Figure 8.2). The GWD strategy has provided some badly needed assistance to western China, especially in infrastructure investment, and has been instrumental in creating a more positive investment environment and strengthening development foundations for this region.

However, in the assessment of the effectiveness of the GWD strategy since the 1978 reform, the western development strategy has failed to achieve its aims. The contribution of the western region to GDP in China had in fact dipped to 18.4 per cent in

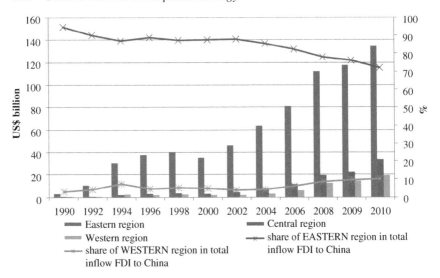

Figure 8.1 Regional distribution of FDI inflow to China, 1990–2010

Source: China Data Online

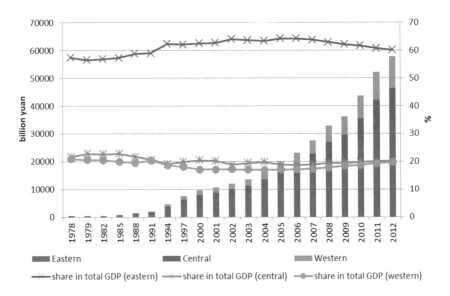

Figure 8.2 Region's share in China's total GDP, 1978–2012

Source: *China Statistical Yearbook*, various years

2009, from 20.9 per cent in 1978. This indicates that the government's efforts since the late 1990s to achieve more balanced regional development have yet to bear much fruit.

Despite the various shortcomings of the GWD strategy, Beijing has vowed to continue with this strategy and to renew its efforts to develop the western region for the next decade. To-date, the Chinese central government has yet to announce new policies and measures to deal with the widening regional inequality for the next 10 years.

Although the local governments in the western region are overwhelmingly optimistic about future development, the likelihood of this region replacing the eastern growth engines in the near future and narrowing the regional gap seem remote. What accounts for this phenomenon is possibly its geography. The western region is restricted by its poor accessibility. The western region is far from both the sea and ocean-navigable rivers. This setback has been aggravated by the biased government policies implemented since the 1980s and 1990s. The government has been careful to keep such disparity at a relatively low level to ward off threats of social stability and to work toward sustainable national development.

Uneven regional development

Unequal economic development between the eastern, central and western regions has been a cause for concern for the Chinese leadership for the last three over decades. Unbalanced regional development was a strategy of the 1980s and 1990s. In order to accelerate national economic growth and catch up with the developed nations, the Chinese leaders had prioritized the eastern region over the western and central regions. From the government's perspective then, unbalanced regional development was unavoidable and might even be desirable in its pursuit of economic growth. As a result of the government's coast-biased regional development strategy, the majority (over 60 per cent) of China's development zones are located in the eastern region (Table 8.1).

The favourable strategies and policies China has implemented in the coastal region have led to a concentration of foreign direct investment (FDI) in the east. The region also enjoys close geographic proximity to foreign investors and markets, as well as an efficient transport system and other supporting infrastructure. In the 1990s, around 85 per cent of total FDI to China went to the eastern region,

Table 8.1 Location of special zones for economic and technology development approved by China's central government

Type	Eastern Region	Central Region	Western Region	Total
Special Economic Zone	5	0	0	5
Economic and Technological Development Zone	27	10	10	47
High-Tech Industry Development Zone	28	13	13	54
Bonded Zone[2]	15	0	0	15
Total	75	23	23	121

Note: The data are for the years up to 2009.

Source: The Ministry of Science and Technology of PR China, 2009[3]

while central and western China attracted roughly 10 per cent and 5 per cent, respectively.[4]

Although the share of the western region in total FDI inflow to China had increased to 10.2 per cent in 2010 from 3 per cent in 1990, the eastern region still dominated FDI inflow to China, with 72 per cent in 2010 (Figure 8.1). The eastern region's increasing dominance of China's trade is even more remarkable. Its share in total value of exports from China was over 87 per cent in 2010, while the western region made up roughly 4.5 per cent of the total.[5]

Although the western region has achieved decent economic development over the past three decades, it is still unable to keep up with the growth of the coastal eastern region. The widening inequality among regional economies has aroused the concerns of the Chinese academia and the policy makers. Severe spatial disparity has posed a major challenge to the Chinese government's attempts to maintain balanced economic development, social justice and political stability. Rising regional inequality has not only affected long-term economic development of China, but also hampered the development of social welfare in the poor western region.

Since the late 1990s, the widening income gap has become a serious concern of the Chinese leaders. In 1999, a policy shift was witnessed with the adoption of the GWD strategy initiated by Jiang Zemin, former Chinese president. The GWD strategy was to maintain national stability, boost domestic demand and eliminate discontent within the western region.[6]

The State Council's Leading Group for Western Development (LGWD) was set up in early 2000 and the State Council announced its "Notice on Implementing Policy Measures to Western Development" in late 2000. [7] The formation of the LGWD under the State Council is reflective of Beijing's resolve to boost the development of China's poor and backward western region. The state has also backed GWD policies to deal with the increasing pollution problems in the western region brought about by the rapid economic development of China. [8]

Compared to the pre-2000 period, the GWD strategy has slightly reversed the declining trend of western region's development vis-à-vis the eastern and central regions of China. The share of western region in total GDP increased to 19.7 per cent in 2012 from 17.1 per cent in 2000, while the contribution of the eastern region to GDP in China had decreased slightly from 62.5 per cent in 2000 to 60.1 per cent in 2012 (Figure 8.2). In terms of total value-added industrial output, the contribution of the western region had also nudged up a few percentage points to 17.7 per cent in 2010 from 13.8 per cent in 2000 (Figure 8.3). Annual GDP growth and annual growth of industrial output value in the western region were about 18 per cent and 24.3 per cent respectively during the period 2000–2010, slightly higher than the corresponding figures of 16.2 per cent and 16.8 per cent respectively for the period 1989–1999 (Table 8.2). These data indicate that the western region's industrial and economic growth has accelerated over the past 10 years as a result of the state's western development strategy.

However, from a broader post-1978 time perspective, economic disparity between the eastern and the western regions has still been huge and regional

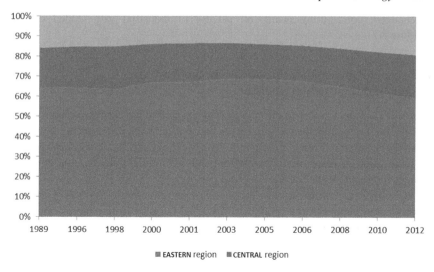

Figure 8.3 Regional distribution of value-added industrial output in China, 1989–2012

Source: Compiled by the author.

Table 8.2 Key performance indicators before and after the implementation of the GWD strategy (percentage)

Indicator	1978–1988	1989–1999	2000–2010
Annual GDP growth	14.6	16.2	18
Annual growth of exports	n.a	7[a]	19.5
Annual growth of industrial output value	12.9	16.8	24.3[b]

Note: [a] The data are for 1993–1999; [b] the data are for 2000–2009

Source: Compiled by the author based on *China Statistical Yearbook*.

inequality trend has widened continually over the past three decades. The contribution of the eastern region to GDP in China increased to 61.6 per cent in 2010 from 57.4 per cent in 1978, while the contribution of the western region to GDP in China dipped to 18.7 per cent in 2010, from 20.9 per cent in 1978 (Figure 8.2). This indicates that there has been little improvement in the inferior position of the inland western region in terms of China's overall economy despite efforts made by the government since the late 1990s.

Industries located in the central and western regions have for many years suffered from the weak industrial clustering, excessive exploitation of resources and lack of technological investment; as a result, industrial growth of the regions has been slow compared to that of their eastern counterpart. By 2012, the importance of China's eastern region in terms of the country's industries had remained unchanged, contributing nearly 60 percent of industrial value-added output (Figure 8.3).

The central government's policies on the western region and their achievements

The GWD strategy is key to efforts made by the central government to boost economic development in the western region and to narrow the widening regional disparity. The strategy is also important to local governments in the western regions in their quest for more capital investment and preferential policies from the central government. With better economic performance, the western region hopes to strengthen its bargaining power with the central authority, influence central policymaking and eventually improve its inferior status in the current regional development of China.

To a limited extent, the GWD strategy and related government policies have been useful in generating various economic benefits for the underdeveloped western region. First, huge fiscal transfer of various kinds, amounting to 3,000 billion yuan, had been provided to the western region between 2000 and 2010.[9] This was possible due to the growing economic strength of the central government, following the fiscal reform in 1994.

Second, between 2000 and 2010, the central government provided 2,200 billion yuan of capital investment on key infrastructure projects in the western region.[10] In particular, 13,900 km of highway and 8,000 km of railway have been newly established in this region since 2000.[11] Some of the well-known projects brought in by the western development program include Qinghai–Xizang (Tibet) railway (completed in 2006) (Table 8.3).

The development of an advanced cross-provincial borders transportation system and other infrastructure facilities is necessary for the western region to hasten inter-regional economic cooperation and achieve economic take-off. Infrastructure investment will remain a key area in regional development. In fact, 10 new key western infrastructure projects funded by the state kicked off in 2008, including

Table 8.3 Key transportation construction projects completed during the 11th Five-year Program for the Western Region

1. Expressway	The western parts of Beijing–Kunming; Baotou–Maoming; Shanghai–Xi'an; Shanghai–Chongqing; Shanghai–Kunming; Fuzhou–Yinchuan; and Guangzhou–Kunming
2. Railway	Taiyuan–Yinchuan; Lanzhou–Chongqing; Guiyang–Guangzhou; Xi'an–Pingliang; Chongqing–Lichuan; Dali–Ruili; and the Expansion Line of Qinghai–Tibet railway
3. Airport	Upgrading and further expansion of airports in Chengdu, Xi'an, Urumqi, Xining, Chongqing, Guiyang and Lanzhou

Source: The 11th Five-year Program for the Great Western Development, the State Council of China

the Guiyang–Guangzhou, Lanzhou–Chongqing railway and airport expansion in Chengdu, Chongqing and Xi'an. In total, 436.1 billion yuan is expected to be invested by the central government.[12] The completion of these infrastructure projects is expected to further improve local transportation conditions and the investment environment in the western region.

Third, the central government has adopted various preferential policies to attract foreign investment so as to boost industrial development in western China.[13] Foreign-owned companies in preferred industrial sectors designated by the state, such as postal services, transportation and energy in the western region, enjoy a favourable corporate tax rate. These companies also enjoy tax exemption for imported equipment.[14] Other policy measures include providing more central fiscal transfer and preferential bank loans to the western region, granting favourable land use rights, and offering more capital investment on improving transportation and other infrastructure facilities.[15]

Local governments in the western region are also offering additional incentives to foreign investors and businesses. For example, in Chongqing, tax reductions are granted on a company's operating profit (for the first six years of operation, corporations are exempted from local taxes, while from the seventh to the tenth years, there is 50 per cent relief from local taxes on operating profit).[16] These preferential policies have attracted more foreign investors to the western region and contributed to growth in inward FDI. The share of FDI inflow to China's western region increased to 10.2 per cent in 2010 from 4.9 per cent in 2000 (Figure 8.1).

Such measures have enhanced the region's competitiveness and helped in its industrial development. Rising land rent and labour wages, and strict environmental protection regulations practiced in the eastern region have pushed low-end and labour-intensive manufacturing industries (e.g. shoe making, plastic and toy manufacturing) to relocate to the western region. Although values and share proportions are still low, the ratio of investment in the western region to total foreign investment in China has been increasing over the past ten years.

Fourth, efforts to reduce poverty and raise living standards have also been strengthened. In addition to spending around 58.1 billion yuan on anti-poverty projects in the western region since the late 1990s,[17] Beijing has been implementing anti-poverty projects by promoting partnership schemes between the wealthy eastern and poor western regions. From the government's standpoint, through mutual tie-in, the coastal region can help strengthen the western region's development capability by providing capital and advanced technology, and skilled labour.[18] For example, Guangdong has provided nearly 1.2 billion yuan and sent teachers to Guangxi to fight poverty and promote local education. The total number of people living in poverty in Guangxi dived to 0.52 million in 2008 from 4.86 million in 1996.[19]

The Chinese leaders have also taken steps to boost industrial growth in the western region over the past few years. As shown in Appendix 8.1, there are significant variations across regions in terms of minimum wage, with wages in eastern region being considerably higher than those in inland regions. Such cost differentials, as well as initiatives of the central state, have provided considerable incentives for labour-intensive and low-end manufacturing companies to shift their production facilities to the central and western regions. The government is hoping to bring modern technology and management to the west with this shift.

Overall, the GWD strategy has provided some badly needed assistance to western China, and it has been creating a more positive investment environment and strengthening development foundations for this region.

Implementation of the GWD strategy: Challenges and prospects

From the perspectives of achieving balanced regional growth and developing the western region into a growth engine for sustainable national development, the GWD strategy has not been very successful. The regional inequality between the eastern and western regions is still huge. The western region has continued to lag behind the eastern region and it remains an underdeveloped region.

The western region is home to China's main supplies of natural resources (Appendix 8.2). For example, Shaanxi's coal and petroleum accounted for around 8 per cent and 7.6 per cent respectively of China's production, and the share of Sichuan in national ensured reserves of iron ore was about 13.6 per cent in 2010.[20] Over the last three decades, based on its rich resource reserves, the western region has been the key supplier of natural resources and raw materials for the country's burgeoning economic development in the coastal eastern region. Nevertheless, the resource-oriented development strategy implemented by the local governments has yet to benefit the western region. For years, the domestic commodity prices of natural resources such as coal, gas and oil were deliberately kept at a very low level to facilitate eastern development. The resource-exploited western region has thus little to gain in this distorted price structure.[21]

In the past few years, the Chinese leadership led by President Hu Jintao and Premier Wen Jiabao have come to acknowledge that rising regional inequality works in contrary to the development of a harmonious society and that pursuing balanced regional development is in the national interest. First, facing enormous regional gaps, the Chinese leaders have found that it is getting harder to justify uneven regional development to the western region. Second, achieving balanced regional development is essential to social stability in the western region especially in areas inhabited by sizable ethnic minorities. China's western region is home to many ethnic minorities. The central government is deeply concerned about the issues of large-scale and violent social protests, particularly in Tibet in 2008 and Xinjiang in 2009 in western China. The widening regional income gap is an important factor contributing to social unrest.[22] Third, boosting domestic demand and investment by developing the western region is essential for sustaining economic growth in China.

The Chinese leadership seems to be taking a proactive but unchanging stance on implementing the GWD strategy. Past policies of pursuing more balanced regional development will most likely be continued. During the high level meeting of the LGWD, Wen Jiabao vowed that China would continue to offer state preferential policies to the western region and put more effort into boosting industrial and economic growth in the light of the global economic crisis.[23]

Despite the strong commitment by Chinese leaders to address regional inequality, the central government has yet to find an effective solution to, or announce many new policies and measures to deal with the issue. Beijing's emphasis for this region is on infrastructure improvement, environmental protection and social development in the coming 10 years.[24] In fact, these new initiatives have been incorporated in China's 12th Five-year Program (12th FYP) for National Social and Economic Development (2011–2015). This Program emphasises adopting a more balanced development approach.[25]

Achieving balanced regional development is not an easy task for the government. The general economic power of the western region is still relatively weak. It seems an almost impossible task for the region to transform itself into growth engines like in the eastern coastal regions given the scale and degree of the underdevelopment of the western region. Instead of making hollow speeches or chanting hollow slogans, the central government will have to do more in terms of adopting long-term strategic policies and taking concrete actions for the region.

Geographical conditions will remain as one the biggest challenges faced by the central government. The western region is restricted by its poor accessibility and distance from both the sea and ocean-navigable rivers. These regions suffer from extreme geographical features and high inter-regional transportation costs. More comprehensive infrastructural and transportational network is needed to provide that all important link.

Another serious challenge is the lack of economic scale, weak industrial agglomeration, excessive exploitation of resources and generally low technological levels. The industrial linkages within the western region are loose and weak. This lack of industrial cooperation results in duplicated developments and cut-throat competition. It also limits the development of an integrated regional market.

However, the development potential of China's west cannot be overlooked. Chongqing, in particular, has enjoyed strong state support. In December 2008, the central government gave the green light to establish a bonded area in Chongqing. This is the first free trade zone located in the western region and represents the central government's attempt to boost the economic growth and opening up of this inland municipality.[26] Chongqing's growth has been remarkable over the last decade, registering an average annual growth rate of 17 per cent between 2000 and 2009, outpacing Shanghai's 14.2 per cent and the national average's 13.4 per cent.[27]

The Development Plan for Chengdu–Chongqing Economic Zone (Cheng–Yu Economic Zone) issued by the State Council of China in March 2011 was an indication that the Chinese central government is developing Chongqing into an economic centre and an important production base for modern manufacturing industries in the western region. Though key cities and provinces like Chongqing have great development potential, their economic foundations alone are insufficient for them to become growth engines and generate strong effects on the western region.

Appendix 8.1 Minimum monthly wages for regions in China (yuan)

Region	Province	Minimum Monthly Wage (yuan)
Eastern region	Guangdong	850–1,320 (from May 2011)
	Shanghai	1,450 (from April 2012)
	Jiangsu	800–1,140 (from February 2011)
	Zhejiang	950–1,310 (from April 2011)
	Beijing	1,260 (from January 2012)
	Tianjin	1,310 (from April 2012)
	Liaoning	780–1,100 (from July 2011)
	Fujian	750–1,100 (from March 2011)
	Shandong	950–1,240 (from March 2012)
	Hebei	860–1,100 (from July 2011)
Central region	Shanxi	740–980 (from April 2011)
	Henan	820–1,080 (from October 2011)
	Anhui	680–1,010 (from July 2011)
	Hubei	750–1,100 (from December 2011)
	Hunan	770–1,020 (from July 2011)
	Jiangxi	610–870 (from January 2012)
Western region	Shaanxi	790–1,000 (from January 2012)
	Chongqing	710–870 (from April 2011)
	Sichuan	800–1,050 (from January 2012)
	Ningxia	950–1,100 (from April 2012)
	Guizhou	740–930 (from September 2011)

Source: Compiled by the author based on various information.

Appendix 8.2 Key energy bases in the western region of China

1	Coal Production	Shaanxi, Ningxia, Inner Mongolia, Guizhou, Yunnan, Xinjiang and Gansu
2	Oil and natural gas exploitation	Xinjiang, Sichuan, Chongqing, Shaanxi, Qinghai, Inner Mongolia and Guangxi
3	Coal and petroleum processing	Shaanxi, Inner Mongolia, Ningxia, Guizhou
4	Recycle and renewable energy	Xinjiang, Inner Mongolia, Ningxia, Gansu, Tibet (wing and solar power), Guangxi, Yunnan, Sichuan and Chongqing
5	National oil reserve base	Gansu

Source: The 11th Five-year Program for the Great Western Development, the State Council of China

Notes

* This chapter draws reference to a journal article written by the author, "The rationale, prospects, and challenges of China's western economic triangle in light of global economic crisis", *Asian Politics & Policy*, 2:3, 2010, pp. 437–461.
1 The eastern region covers Beijing, Tianjin, Hebei, Liaoning, Shanghai, Jiangsu, Zhejiang, Fujian, Shandong, Guangdong, Hainan, Heilongjiang and Jilin; the central region includes Shanxi, Anhui, Jiangxi, Henan, Hubei and Hunan; and the western region

covers Guangxi, Chongqing, Sichuan, Guizhou, Yunnan, Xizang, Shaanxi, Gansu, Qinghai, Ningxia, Xinjiang and Inner Mongolia.

2 Bonded zone: A bonded zone is an area in which dutiable goods may be stored, manipulated or have undergone manufacturing operations without payment of duty. In China, the bonded zones are under the direct supervision and regulation of its custom authorities. It allows certain export-related activities and applies preferential policies such as export VAT refund.

3 *China Special Economic Zone & Development Area Yearbook 2003* and "List of high-tech and new-tech development zones"

4 China Data Online

5 *China Statistical Abstract 2011*

6 Lai Hongyi, Harry. (2002). "China's Western Development Program: Its Rationale, Implementation, and Prospects". *Modern China*, 28, pp. 432–466.

7 *China's National and Regional Industrial Development*, a report for the Ministry of Trade and Industry, Singapore, prepared by the East Asian Institute, National University of Singapore, March 2011.

8 Tian Xiaowen. "China's drive to develop its western region (I): why turn to this region now?" *EAI Background Brief No. 71*, East Asian Institute, National University of Singapore, 28 September 2000.

9 Office for Western Development, National Development and Reform Commission, China, http://xbkfs.ndrc.gov.cn/mzfz/t20100706_359360.htm (accessed 17 April 2012)

10 Ibid.

11 Office for Western Development, National Development and Reform Commission, China, http://xbkfs.ndrc.gov.cn/mzfz/t20100706_359389.htm (accessed 17 April 2012)

12 National Development and Reform Commission. (2008, 20 June). "10 new key projects to be constructed in the light of great western development in 2008", http://www.chinawest.gov.cn/web/NewsInfo.asp?NewsId=46622 (accessed 17 April 2012)

13 The key documents outlined the specific preferential policies for the western region and included (1) *Industrial Dictionary for Foreign Investment in the Central and Western Regions*, issued in 1999, and further revised in 2004 to develop industries with comparative advantages in the western region; (2) The Preferential Treatment Notice issued by the State Administration of Taxation in 1999; and (3) Several Opinions on the Implementation of State Policies in the Western Region released by the Western China Development Office of State Council in 2001.

14 "*Guanyu xibu dakaifa ruogan zhengce cuoshi de shishi yijian*" (Implementation opinions for several state polices on the western region), issued by the National Development and Reform Commission, China, in August 2001.

15 Sources: (1) "*Xibu dakaifa shiyiwu guihua*" (the 11th Five-Year Program for the Great Western Development), issued by the State Council of China in March 2011; (2) "*Zhongxibu diqu waishang touzi youshi chanye mulv*" (2008 revised) (List of priority industries for foreign investment in the central and western regions of China) issued by the Ministry of Commerce, 2008; (3) "*Zhongguo xishou waizi zhengce*" (Policies to attract foreign investment) issued by the Ministry of Commerce, February 2001; (4) "*Guanyu xibu dakaifa ruogan zhengce cuoshi de shishi yijian*" (Implementation opinions for several state policies on the western region), issued by the National Development and Reform Commission, China in August 2001.

16 Ibid.

17 Office for Western Development, National Development and Reform Commission, China, available at http://xbkfs.ndrc.gov.cn/mzfz/t20100706_359360.htm (assessed 17 April 2012)

18 Yu, Hong. "The Rationale, Prospects, and Challenges of China's Western Economic Triangle in Light of Global Economic Crisis", *Asian Politics & Policy*, 2:3, 2010, pp. 437–461

19 "The cooperation between Guangdong and Guangxi moves toward comprehensive level from traditional development assistance", *People's Daily*, 21 May 2009, http://www.chinawest.gov.cn/ web/NewsInfo.asp?NewsId=52967 (accessed 17 April 2012)

20 *China Statistical Yearbook*

21 Tian Xiaowen "China's drive to develop its western region (II): priorities in development?" *EAI Background Brief No. 72*, East Asian Institute, National University of Singapore, 28 September 2000.

22 Yu, Hong. "The Rationale, Prospects, and Challenges of China's Western Economic Triangle in Light of Global Economic Crisis", *Asian Politics & Policy*, 2:3, 2010, pp. 437–461

23 "China urges efforts to boost economy in western regions", *China Daily*, 21 August 2009, http://www.chinadaily.com.cn/bizchina/2009-08/21/content_8600110.htm (assessed 7 October 2011)

24 *"Hu Jitao zhuchi zhengzhiju huiyi: yanjiu shenru shishi xibu dakafa zhanlue"*, (Hu Jintao chairs Political Bureau meeting to analyze western development strategy), International Department, Central Committee of the Communist Party of China, 28 May 2010, http://www.idcpc.org.cn/ zhonggong/100528.htm (assessed 7 October 2011)

25 This is detailed in a research report submitted by the East Asian Institute to the Ministry of Trade and Industry of Singapore titled "China's National and Regional Industrial Development". The author appreciates the contribution made by other members of the research team, including Prof. John Wong, Dr. Sarah Tong, Dr. Yang Mu, Ms. Jessica Loon, Ms. Catherine Chong Siew Keng, Ms. Pan Rongfang, and Ms. Yao Jielu.

26 "China approves first inland bonded area", *Xinhua*, 16 December 2008, http://www.china daily.com.cn/china/2008-12/16/content_7311361.htm (accessed 23 September 2011)

27 *China Statistical Yearbook 2010* and *China Statistical Yearbook 2001*

9   Chengdu
A rising economic star in western China

Chengdu: an energetic growing city and the site of Fortune Global Forum 2013

The landlocked western region has, despite its abundant land area and natural resources, historically been an underdeveloped area of China. Nevertheless, the western region has outperformed the eastern coastal areas on economic growth for the past several years. The internal regional dynamics are helping China to sustain fast economic growth.

During a keynote speech at the Fortune Global Forum 2013, Zhang Gaoli, the executive vice premier of China, stated that the initiation of a new wave of development and opening up in the western region would give greater vitality to the Chinese economy.[1] Against the backdrop of sluggish global economic growth, China is now becoming the world's key growth engine of economic recovery.

Chengdu, the provincial capital of Sichuan, is a star of the western region and has been one of the world's fastest-growing cities over the recent years. The remarkable economic growth has put this city in the world spotlight. The gross regional product (GRP) had risen to 813.9 billion yuan by 2012 from 115.6 billion yuan in 2000, with an average annual growth rate of over 17 per cent during this period. The multinational corporations (MNCs) have shown a growing interest in pursuing business opportunities in Chengdu. The inflow of foreign direct investment (FDI) to Chengdu was 8.6 billion US$ in 2012.

By March 2013, 238 of the Fortune Global 500 companies had operations in this city as compared to 40 in 2003, making it one of the most popular foreign investment destinations in western China.[2] The MNCs have invested in various industries in Chengdu, covering electronics, information technology, automobile, machinery, new energy, as well as financial sectors. Currently, Singapore is the second largest foreign investor in Chengdu, with total investments of 0.93 billion US$ in 2011,[3] and 299 Singapore companies have set up operations in this city.[4]

The Singapore–Sichuan Hi-Tech Innovation Park (SSHIP) was set up in the city of Chengdu in 2012. This is the fourth large cooperation project between the Singapore and Chinese governments, after the Suzhou Industrial Park, Tianjin Eco-city and Guangzhou Knowledge City. The SSHIP is the first development project between Singapore and a location in western China. It is an indication of

Singapore's confidence in Chengdu's future development, and the Singapore government's support for the Chinese government's western development strategy.

Liu Qibao, a Politburo Bureau member and head of the Propaganda Department of the Chinese Communist Party, stated that the SSHIP is a "milestone" project for Singapore in China's western region.[5] The SSHIP focuses on attracting investment in the electronics and information technology, outsourcing, biomedicines, digital media and environmental service industries.

Against this backdrop, the city of Chengdu was chosen as the site of Fortune Global Forum 2013 under the theme "China's New Future". This forum is one of the world's most important business summits and is organized by *Fortune Magazine*, which is published by the US-based Time Warner Inc. The forum was held in Chengdu from 6th to 8th June and was attended by leaders of the world's largest companies, government officials and thinkers. The Chengdu government is keen to boost local economic growth and raise its international profile by capitalizing on this event.

The Chinese companies have developed rapidly and emerged as global players over the past few years. The number of Chinese companies listed in the Fortune Global 500, which is an influential index that annually ranks world companies on the basis of sales revenue and profits, had increased dramatically to 73 by 2012, making China second only to the United States, which had 132 companies on the list. Only five private Chinese companies appear on the Fortune Global 500 list, whilst the others are state-owned enterprises with monopolies in the relevant domestic sectors.

Although the Fortune Global Forum was held in Shanghai, Hong Kong and Beijing in 1999, 2001 and 2005 respectively, and hence Chengdu the fourth-Chinese city to host the forum, it is the first western city to do so. This is symbolic. According to *Fortune Magazine*, Chengdu is emerging as a leading global business city.[6] This observation not only reflects the rising international profile of Chengdu and the growing economic importance of the western region, but also signals that the juggernaut that is the Chinese economy is advancing towards the western region after 30 years of reform and opening up.

Chengdu's development is backed by strong central government support. Chengdu is one of the main beneficiaries of the state-driven western development initiative launched in 1999. Along with Chongqing, Chengdu was granted approval to become a National Comprehensive Coordinated Urban-Rural Development Experimental Zone (CURDEZ) (全国统筹城乡综合配套改革试验区) by the Chinese central government in June 2007. In March 2011, the State Council of China approved the Development Plan for Chengdu-Chongqing Economic Zone (成渝经济区区域规划). Inclusion in these zones is instrumental in promoting the development of Chengdu by means of the accompanying new policy measures and initiatives introduced by the Chinese authority.

The Chengdu authority anticipates that the city of Chengdu will become as important a regional centre as Shanghai over the next decade. The Chengdu government leaders understand that the only way for Chengdu to achieve a fast-growing economy and catch up with the eastern cities is to open up to the world and attract foreign investment. This is the lesson they learned from the development stories of China's eastern cities.

Economic development of Chengdu

Chengdu has undergone tremendous economic transformation over the last decade, with an economic growth rate of 17.6 per cent during the past 10 years; GRP increased from 115.6 billion yuan in 2000 to 813.9 billion yuan in 2012 (Figure 9.1). The value-added industrial output of Chengdu increased from 32.8 billion yuan in 2000 to 314.9 billion yuan in 2012, while the value-added output of tertiary industry rose to 400.0 billion yuan in 2012 from 61.8 billion yuan in 2000, with average annual growth of 16.8 percent during this period (Figure 9.2).

All of this development was achieved in just a decade and was a consequence of the state-led western development. The growth in Chengdu's economy has been remarkable, especially in light of its relatively small starting point. Chengdu is the key engine of this state strategy and now has one of the largest economies in the western region. Along with its vibrancy and rich background, this has made Chengdu one of the most influential western cities.

Mao Zedong, the then Chinese leader, moved many heavy industries to western region locations such as Chengdu back in the 1950s, in an attempt to protect these industries from outside attacks. This policy had a great impact on the local industrial make-up and laid out the industrial foundation for Chengdu. Chengdu, an old industrial base and second tier city, has now been transformed into an economic hub of the western region, the centre of logistics and transport in western China. Among China's western cities, Chengdu has the largest presence of Fortune Global 500 companies, foreign banks and foreign consulates.

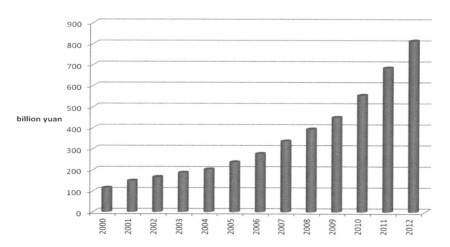

Figure 9.1 Gross regional product of Chengdu

Source: *Chengdu Yearbook*, relevant years

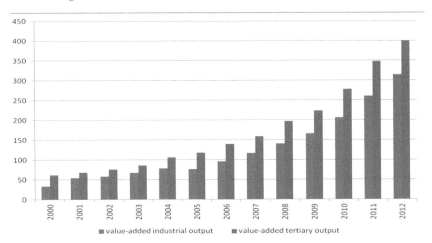

Figure 9.2 Value-added industrial and tertiary output of Chengdu

Source: *Chengdu Yearbook*, relevant years

Because of their high dependence on foreign trade and export-oriented manufacturing industries, China's eastern cities are vulnerable to global economic downturn, and the effects of a sluggish global economy are reflected in the decline in their economic growth since 2008. However, in contrast, Chengdu's economy is driven by strong domestic investment and consumption demand, and local industrial development created by inter-regional industrial transfer within the nation.

Whilst in China as a whole growth has slowed, Chengdu is still enjoying rapid economic growth. Chengdu's model of economic development, based on domestic consumption is one that the new Chinese leadership of Xi Jinping, China's president and Li Keqiang, China's premier, is determined to achieve for the nation. In that sense, Chengdu is a showcase for a new Chinese development model that represents a shift from over dependence on export and investment to greater reliance on domestic consumption.

Chengdu's industrial strength lies in its six pillar sectors, ranging from electronics and information technology, food, beverage and tobacco, automobiles, petroleum and chemicals, to building materials and medicines, which in 2012 achieved total value-added output of 211.8 billion yuan. Respectively they accounted for 20.1 per cent, 15.4 per cent, 17.7 per cent, 6.9 per cent, 9.1 per cent and 4.7 per cent of the total value-added output of Chengdu's industries in 2011 (Figure 9.3).

The electronic and information industry is the primary mainstay sector for this city; around two thirds of the iPads and half of the laptop microchips produced globally are made in Chengdu.[7] The global leading electronic and information companies have set up plants in Chengdu, including Intel, Dell, Foxconn, Compal and Lenovo. For example, Intel, the world's largest manufacturer of computer chips, already has two assembly factories in Chengdu. Dell, the world's leading

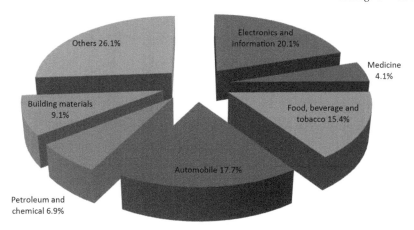

Figure 9.3 Percentage shares of the six pillar sectors in total value-added industrial output of Chengdu

Source: *Chengdu Yearbook 2012*, p. 553

manufacturer of personal computers, has established a new factory in Chengdu with a production capacity of seven million desktops a year in June 2013.[8]

Chengdu is also the base for some of China's key electronic research and development (R&D) institutes. A cluster of electronic and IT sectors linking both the upstream and downstream industries has been forged in Chengdu, providing impetus for further development of its electronics industry. The Chengdu government is keen to support the development of the high-end and high value-added manufacturing and modern service industries and anticipates that these industries will establish the foundation for sustainable long-term economic growth in Chengdu.

The total amount of actually utilized FDI to Chengdu rocketed from 0.2 billion US$ in 2000 to 8.6 billion US$ in 2012, with average annual growth of 37 per cent during this period. The growth of inward FDI to Chengdu has been particularly impressive over the last five years. Chengdu's contribution to China's total inward FDI had increased to 6.5 per cent by 2011 from 0.3 percent in 2000 (Figure 9.4). Alongside Chongqing, Chengdu is becoming one of the most attractive cities in western China for business investment.

To achieve Chengdu's economic take-off, the Chengdu government has made massive capital investments in the expressways, railways and other infrastructure projects over the last decade. In addition, the Chinese central government has invested heavily in capital expenditure on transportation and other infrastructure improvements in western China. Chengdu has benefited significantly from this state infrastructure spending. The infrastructure investment in Chengdu increased to 226.7 billion yuan in 2011 from merely 22.8 billion yuan in 2000, with average annual growth of 23 per cent between 2000 and 2011. The growth since 2008 has been particularly impressive (Figure 9.5).

138   *Chengdu*

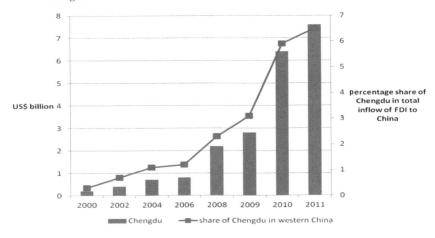

Figure 9.4 Inward foreign direct investment to Chengdu

Source: *Chengdu Yearbook*, relevant years

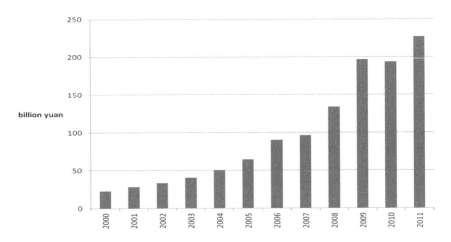

Figure 9.5 State infrastructure investment in Chengdu

Source: *Chengdu Yearbook*, relevant years

A preliminary comprehensive transportation network has been built up around Chengdu. Metro One (running north-south and connecting the North Train Station and convention centre) and Metro Two (running east-west and connecting the west and southeast regions of Chengdu) were put into operation in 2010 and 2012 respectively. The Chengdu–Chongqing high-speed rail line has already come into service and has cut the travel time between these two cities to less than one hour.

Chengdu Shuangliu International Airport recorded throughput of up to 31.6 million passengers and 0.5 million tons of cargo in 2012, an increase from 11.7 million passengers and 0.2 million tons of cargo in 2004, making it the nation's fourth largest air hub after Beijing, Shanghai and Guangzhou. Chengdu is connected to the international airway network with direct flights to nearly 40 cities across Asia, Europe, Middle East and North America.

"Go west, go Chengdu" and Chengdu's competitive advantages

Shanghai, Tianjin, Guangzhou and other eastern coastal cities in China have benefited greatly from the integration of China into global economy that has led to the development of export-oriented industries in China over the past 30 years. As an inland and western city far away from the sea, Chengdu's economic development has historically lagged behind that of China's coastal cities.

Nevertheless, Chengdu has achieved remarkable economic growth and caught up to some extent with the eastern cities thanks to the state initiatives for western development and its geographical location as a linkage between the eastern, central and western regions of China. Chengdu's history, unique culture, historical sites and the presence of rare animals such as the giant panda have also made it one of the most popular tourism destinations in the nation. The founding of Chengdu city can be traced back over 2,000 years to the Three-Kingdom period.

The first and foremost competitive advantage for Chengdu lies in its favourable geographical location as the gateway to the western region. Chengdu is located at the heart of the western region of China and has easy access to other western places. In that sense, Chengdu's market extends throughout the six provincial-level regions of Sichuan, Yunnan, Chongqing, Guizhou, Qinghai and Tibet, with a total population of 200 million people. It is a huge and highly lucrative business market.

Another key advantage comes in the form of government support. In 1999, to boost western growth and pursue balanced regional development, the Chinese central government initiated the western development strategy. Chengdu has been transformed by this 'go west' campaign and the preferential state policies implemented over the last decade. This western development campaign has boosted the development of large-scale infrastructure in Chengdu.[9]

Beijing's policies to boost western economic development include granting preferential tax rates,[10] land use rights, and provision of infrastructure construction investment. These initiatives have encouraged many foreign companies to set up business operations and factories in Chengdu to ride on this policy wave. During his speech to the opening ceremony of the 2012 China (Ningxia) International Investment and Trade Fair and the 3rd China–Arab States Economic and Trade Forum in September 2012, Li Keqiang stressed that China is establishing bridgeheads for opening up the western region.[11] Chengdu could be the ideal location for such development.

In addition, the rising production and labour costs in the eastern region and the global economic turmoil have pushed many foreign-invested manufacturing factories to relocate to the western region in search for cheap labour and land. As a consequence of the lure of home, an increasing number of migrant workers have left the eastern cities and returned to their hometowns for work.

According to *The Economist*, the number of migrant workers from Sichuan who worked in other provinces, estimated at 20 million, had dropped to 52 per cent in 2011 from 58 per cent in 2008, and this shift in migrant worker patterns is continuing.[12] Chengdu is desperate to grasp this development opportunity of industrial transfer by attracting more foreign investors to set up business operations in the city.

In addition, Chengdu and Chongqing were granted approval as new National Comprehensive Coordinated Urban-Rural Development Experimental Zones by the Chinese central government in June 2007. The CURD policy measures aim to tackle the disparity between urban and rural region in China on multiple fronts, ranging from social, physical to economic aspects.[13]

The coordinated urban-rural development strategy aims to promote rural-urban integration through supporting industrial and infrastructure development, and forging unified urban planning and public service provision by means of unified rural-urban management system. The CURD is a branch of the Chinese authority's efforts to promote economic growth and reduce regional development inequality between eastern and western China.

As an experimental zone and under the CURD framework, Chengdu has been given the autonomy to take 'one-step-ahead' on reform in fields such as rural land management, *hukou* system and rural health care. The Chengdu government has announced that the rural *hukou* holders in the countryside within the city limits can move into Chengdu's urban areas. They will be able to enjoy the same public services and social welfare benefits as the urban citizens of Chengdu without losing their land entitlements.[14]

The CURD policy initiatives and other innovative approaches taken by the Chengdu government have boosted rural consumption demand and local economic growth in the city and have accelerated the process of rural-urban integration within Chengdu as well as its industrialization and urbanization.

In addition, Chengdu's competitive strength has been boosted by its huge consumer market and abundant supply of low cost talent. These advantages can help Chengdu to become one of China's most important economic growth engines in the coming decade. The city of Chengdu is called "a land of abundance", having jurisdiction over nine districts, four cities and six counties and a total of 14 million residents. The vast western consumer market and the fast increasing middle class with strong spending capacity are decisive competitive advantages for Chengdu.

The increasingly wealthy local people demand more consumption choices and high quality goods. In contrast to their goals in the eastern regions, the MNCs have set up factories in Chengdu to produce goods targeting local consumers and to meet local demand, rather than for exports.

Chengdu has an abundant pool of relatively low cost labour. The city of Chengdu has the largest number of higher educational and scientific research institutions among China's western cities, with more than 30 universities and colleges located in this area, including some of the nation's best universities – Southwest Jiaotong University and Southwestern University of Finance and Economics.

Around 100,000 university graduates annually provide fresh blood for local manufacturing and service industries and scientific research. Many of them are qualified engineers and wages are comparatively low. In addition, the Chengdu government has been making efforts to streamline the bureaucratic structure, boost administrative efficiency and reduce red tape by such measures as simplifying administrative approval procedures.

Challenges for Chengdu in the face of fierce regional competition

Despite its remarkable development, Chengdu is still confronting serious challenges. First, compared to other developed cities in China, Chengdu's economy is still relatively small. Chengdu's GRP was 685.4 billion yuan in 2011, compared to the corresponding figures of 1625.1 billion yuan, 1919.5 billion yuan and 1242.3 billion yuan for Beijing, Shanghai and Guangzhou, respectively. In terms of per capita GRP, Chengdu achieved barely half that of Guangzhou (Table 9.1).

This economic background renders it difficult for Chengdu to generate the spillover effects to the neighbouring regions that would enable it to become the western region's growth engine. Chengdu accounted for around 7 per cent of the total GRP of western China in 2012; and the figure remained largely unchanged between 2000 and 2012. Chengdu still has a long way to go before it can become a leading Chinese city with global influence.

Another serious challenge facing Chengdu is the fierce regional competition, both domestically and internationally. In domestic terms, the city of Chongqing, another rising star in western China, is a particularly fierce competitor to Chengdu and the two cities have long had a relationship based on rivalry. The separation of Chongqing from Sichuan Province and the formation of Chongqing Municipality did not end this rivalry; in fact, it has evolved this long-term intra-provincial rivalry into an inter-provincial rivalry. In terms of GRP, Chengdu was substantially lower than that of Chongqing, with 685.4 billion yuan and 1001.1 billion yuan in 2011, respectively. In addition, the inward FDI to Chongqing was higher than that of Chengdu in 2011 (Table 9.1).

The industries of Chengdu and Chongqing are quite similar, as exemplified by the involvement of both in the electronics, information technology, automobile, and financial sectors. A cut-throat style of industrial competition and duplication has emerged in these two cities due to self-interest, administrative boundaries and their individual industrial strategies.[15]

Chongqing and Chengdu are competing fiercely with each other to attract foreign investment. As their tenure is short-term and they are intent on promotion, the government leaders in Chengdu and Chongqing tend to focus on local GDP growth, government tax revenue and employment, while neglecting inter-regional cooperation and collaboration.

Chengdu does not have clear-cut advantages or superiority over Chongqing in terms of developing high value-added manufacturing industries or becoming the region's major financial centre. Although a close collaboration between Chengdu and Chongqing on traditional industrial development and nurturing new industrial sectors, based on their mutual complementary advantages, would enhance the competitiveness of both places, the two cities are finding it difficult to forge

Table 9.1 Comparison of economic development among selected cities in China

City	Total Permanent Residential Population (million persons)	Gross Regional Product (GRP) (billion yuan)	Per Capita GRP (yuan)	Value-Added Manufacturing Industry (billion yuan)	Value-Added Tertiary Industry (billion yuan)	Total Value of Import and Export (US$ billion)	Actually Utilized FDI (US$ billion)
Beijing	20.18	1,625.1	80,394	303.9	1211.9	389.5	7.0
Shanghai	23.47	1,919.5	82,560	723.1	1111.1	437.4	12.6
Guangzhou	12.75	1,242.3	97,588	409.6	756.7	116.1	4.3
Shenzhen	10.46	1,150.5	110,387	499.5	615.3	414.1	4.6
Tianjin	13.54	1,130.7	84,337	538.1	515.4	103.4	13.1
Chengdu	**14.07**	**685.4**	**49,438**	**261.1**	**347.9**	**37.9**	**6.5**
Chongqing	29.19	1,001.1	34,500	469.1	362.4	29.2	10.5
Wuhan	10.02	676.2	68,226	270.9	330.3	22.7	3.7
Changsha	7.09	561.9	79,530	266.2	222.4	7.5	2.6
Xi'an	8.51	386.4	45,495	118.9	199.4	12.5	2.0
Jinan	6.88	440.6	64,311	150.8	233.9	10.4	1.1
Dalian	6.78	615.1	91,287	281.6	255.0	60.0	11.0
Nanchang	5.08	268.8	53,023	122.3	97.4	7.8	2.3
Kunming	6.48	250.9	38,831	84.8	121.4	12.0	1.2
Guiyang	4.39	138.3	31,712	45.5	73.3	3.7	0.3

Sources:
1. *China Statistical Yearbook, 2012*
2. *Chengdu Yearbook, 2012*

cooperative economic alliance as their respective governments lack the motivation to promote inter-city economic cooperation.

From the international perspective, Chengdu is confronting competition from countries such as Vietnam and Bangladesh. Based on their relative advantages of lower labour costs and favourable coastal location, these emerging nations are potentially strong competitors for Chengdu in attracting foreign investment. In fact, the combined production and transport costs of goods imported to China from these countries may even be lower than the cost of production alone in Chengdu.

Third, the need for industrial upgrading and restructuring is a pressing challenge. Although the Chengdu government is keen to transform Chengdu's economic focus from low-end and labour-intensive industries to high-end industries, the development of high value-added industrial sectors has been sluggish.

Chengdu's industrial growth depends on the low-end and labour-intensive manufacturing industries and local industrial upgrading will take time. The foreign investors are mainly inflowing to the low-end and labour-intensive industries in search of cheap labour, with little inflow to high-end sectors and research and development activities. Nevertheless, this industrial upgrading challenge is common to other major cities in China as well as other world's emerging economies.

Another challenge concerning Chengdu is the urgent need to tackle traffic congestion. Transportation infrastructure improvement are not progressing rapidly enough to cater for the fast growing volume of traffic and meet the travel demands of both passengers and freight. The schemes for road and bridge building have been unable to keep up with the increase in traffic. There are around 3.5 million privately owned vehicles in Chengdu, a number exceeded only by Beijing and Guangzhou.[16]

The serious issue of traffic gridlock not only has an adverse effect on the daily quality of life for Chengdu's citizens, but also increases business costs and raise concerns for foreign investors, thereby reflecting a negative image of Chengdu that may affect companies' long-term investment decisions.

Notes

1 "Full text of Chinese vice premier Zhang Gaoli's address at opening dinner of 2013 fortune global forum", *Xinhua News*, 7 June 2013, http://news.xinhuanet.com/english/china/2013-06/07/c_124824012.htm (accessed 7 June 2013)
2 "*Chengdu yanfa chengxian xin liangdian*" (The new spotlight for the research and development activities in Chengdu), *Lianhezaobao*, 6 June 2013, p. 23.
3 *Chengdu Statistical Yearbook 2012*
4 "Singapore investments in Chengdu reach $3.9 billion", *The Straits Times*, 15 May 2013, http://business.asiaone.com/news/singapore-investments-chengdu-reach-39-billion#sthash.spKvk2E5.dpuf (accessed 18 June 2013)
5 "PM assures support to investments in Sichuan", Singapore-Sichuan Hi-Tech Innovation Park, http://www.ssipcd.com/zh/News/news_content.htm?m_id=201209210007&lx_dm=en0402 (accessed 18 June 2013)
6 "Chengdu aspires to be nation's expo capital", *China Daily*, 28 March 2012, http://www.chinadaily.com.cn/regional/2012-03/28/content_15006469.htm (accessed 3 June 2013)
7 "Finding China's new future", *China Daily*, 6 June 2013, p. 25.

144 Chengdu

8 "Dell looks beyond the big Chinese cities for PC push", *South China Moring Post*, 7 June 2013, http://www.scmp.com/business/companies/article/1255169/dell-looks-beyond-big-chinese-cities-pc-push (accessed 7 June 2013)

9 McNally, Christopher A. (2004). "Sichuan: driving capitalist development westward", *The China Quarterly*, 178, pp. 426–447.

10 Please refer to the Notice on Preferential Tax Policy for Further Implementation of Western Development Strategy jointly issued by the Ministry of Finance, General Administration of Customs and State Administration of Taxation in July 2011.

11 "Vice Premier Li Keqiang attends the opening ceremony of the 2012 China (Ningxia) International Investment and Trade Fair and the 3rd China-Arab States Economic and Trade Forum and delivers a speech", http://www.fmprc.gov.cn/eng/zxxx/t971512.htm (accessed 3 June 2013)

12 "Changing migration patterns", *The Economist*, 25 February 2012, http://www.economist.com/node/21548273 (accessed 17 June 2013)

13 Zhong Sheng. (2011). "Towards China's urban-rural integration: issues and options", *International Journal of China Studies*, 2:2, pp. 345–367.

14 "Urbanization: where do you live?" *The Economist*, 23 June 2011, http://www.economist.com/node/18832092 (accessed 17 June 2013)

15 Chen Shu, *et al.* (2007). Analysis and Prediction of Economic and Social Situation of Chongqing from 2006 to 2007. In Jianhua Yang (Ed.), *Report on Development of Provinces in China 2007* (pp. 429–454), Beijing: Social Science Academic Press.

16 "Chengdu paying a heavy price for rapid growth", *China Daily*, 10 February 2012, http://www.chinadailyapac.com/article/chengdu-paying-heavy-price-rapid-growth (accessed 21 June 2013)

10 The Guangxi Beibu Gulf economic zone

Pursuing an active role in expanding China–ASEAN cooperation

The Beibu Gulf Economic Zone (BGEZ) (广西北部湾经济区) in Guangxi, China consists of six prefecture-level cities: Nanning, Beihai, Qinzhou, Fangchenggang, Chongzhuo and Yulin. It is one of the most prosperous areas in Guangxi, accounting for around 45 per cent of the region's gross domestic product (GDP). During an inspection trip to Guangxi in July 2013, Chinese Premier Li Keqiang (李克强) expressed the government's intention to develop Guangxi into a focal point for the opening up of the western region to economic development.

The development of Beibu Gulf region is receiving strong backing from the central government, and since 2008 the BGEZ has enjoyed multi-level preferential central policies on developing the western, coastal and border areas. Since 2006, the contribution of BGEZ to GDP surged from 87.8 billion yuan in 2000 to 590.1 billion yuan in 2012, or an average growth rate of 17.2 per cent during this period (Table 10.1), outstripping the average growth of Guangxi as a whole.

Bilateral trade between China and the Association of Southeast Asian Nations (ASEAN) had grown over the last 20 years from US$7 billion in 1990 to US$400 billion in 2012, a 57-fold increase.[1] China has proposed to upgrade the China–ASEAN Free Trade Area, and achieve bilateral trade worth up to US$1 trillion by 2020 to enhance the already burgeoning economic integration between China and ASEAN.[2] ASEAN has been Guangxi's largest trade partner for 13 consecutive years and in the first half of 2013 trade volume hit US$6.14 billion, accounting for 44.5 per cent of the region's total foreign trade and a 29.1 per cent year-on-year growth, according to the Statistics Bureau of Guangxi.

Guangxi is perceived as the gateway to China–ASEAN cooperation. The Guangxi government is very active in initiating proposals to promote bilateral cooperation between China and ASEAN member states. It is hence eager to tap on the "maritime silk road of the 21st century" (MSR 21世纪海上丝绸之路) initiative announced by the Chinese central government in 2013. The Guangxi government attempts to make Guangxi an important part of this maritime silk road. In particular, China's MSR initiatives could add new dynamics for boosting

Table 10.1 Regional GDP of the Beibu Gulf Economic Zone and Guangxi (unit: billion yuan)

Year	China	Guangxi		Beibu Gulf Economic Zone						Total (Six Cities' GDP)	
				Nanning	Beihai	Yulin	Fangcheng-gang	Qinzhou	Chongzuo		
	GDP	GDP	/China	GDP	GDP	GDP	GDP	GDP	GDP	GDP	/Guangxi
1990	1,871.8	44.9	2.40%	7.1	1.7	4.1	0.7	2.3		16.0	35.75%
1991	2,182.6	51.8	2.38%	7.9	2.1	5.0	0.8	2.8		18.8	36.19%
1992	2,693.7	64.7	2.40%	9.2	3.2	6.5	1.2	3.8		23.9	37.09%
1993	3,526.0	87.1	2.47%	13.5	5.4	9.7	1.7	5.2		35.7	40.96%
1994	4,810.8	119.8	2.49%	18.7	7.5	13.4	2.5	7.0		49.2	41.09%
1995	5,981.1	149.7	2.50%	23.6	8.8	15.6	2.9	8.6		59.6	39.82%
1996	7,014.2	169.8	2.42%	26.7	9.2	16.8	3.7	9.7		66.1	38.97%
1997	7,806.1	181.7	2.33%	30.4	9.5	17.3	4.5	10.9		72.7	40.04%
1998	8,302.4	191.1	2.30%	33.9	10.2	18.7	4.9	11.8		79.7	41.69%
1999	8,847.9	197.1	2.23%	35.7	10.8	19.1	5.2	12.2		83.1	42.14%
2000	9,800.0	208.0	2.12%	37.8	11.4	19.9	5.5	13.1		87.8	42.19%
2001	10,806.8	227.9	2.11%	41.8	12.3	21.3	6.0	14.2		95.8	42.03%
2002	11,909.5	252.4	2.12%	46.3	13.4	23.1	6.7	14.8		104.4	41.36%
2003	13,497.7	282.1	2.09%	52.2	14.0	25.8	7.2	15.2	10.4	125.0	44.31%
2004	15,945.4	343.4	2.15%	61.9	15.6	31.2	8.3	17.1	12.6	146.7	42.74%
2005	18,361.7	398.4	2.17%	72.8	16.5	35.2	9.9	18.8	15.1	168.3	42.25%
2006	21,590.4	474.6	2.20%	88.0	17.9	41.0	12.3	23.5	19.4	202.3	42.63%
2007	26,642.2	582.3	2.19%	108.9	22.6	50.1	16.3	28.6	23.2	249.8	42.89%
2008	31,603.0	702.1	2.22%	132.0	27.6	60.2	21.3	34.5	27.3	303.2	43.18%
2009	34,032.0	775.9	2.28%	152.5	32.1	68.3	25.1	39.6	30.4	348.1	44.86%
2010	39,975.9	956.9	2.39%	180.0	40.1	84.0	32.0	52.0	39.2	427.5	44.68%
2011	46,856.2	1,172.1	2.50%	221.1	49.7	101.9	41.4	64.6	49.2	528.0	45.05%
2012	51,628.2	1,303.5	2.52%	250.3	63.0	110.2	44.4	69.1	53.1	590.1	45.27%

Source: Statistical Bureau of Guangxi

the development of the Beibu Gulf Zone. As Heipu county in Guangxi was one of the birthplaces of the maritime silk road route in ancient times, this maritime initiative could link China's vast inland central and western regions such as Guangxi to global maritime trade through the South China Sea, Indian Ocean and East China Sea.

However, many other Chinese regions are making the same claim to historical links with the maritime silk road. China's regional governments have been lobbying for preferential policies and financial support from the central government since the MSR initiatives were announced in 2013.

Guangxi's proposed "Pan-Beibu Gulf Economic Zone" and "Nanning–Singapore Economic Corridors" have played a very active role in promoting cross-border maritime and economic cooperation between China and Southeast Asian countries since the early 2000s and have now become part of Guangxi's political lexicon. Guangxi seeks to further expand its economic ties and trade linkages with ASEAN countries based on existing bilateral platforms such as the China–ASEAN Expo,[3] the China–Malaysia Qinzhou Industrial Park and Pan-Beibu Gulf Economic Cooperation Forum.[4] It also aims to become a regional hub for port development by pushing for close inter-regional maritime trade and port cooperation with Southeast Asia, thereby connecting the vast western provinces with ASEAN countries.

Guangxi officials travel frequently to ASEAN countries to promote bilateral trade, investment and economic cooperation (see Appendix 10.1). The Guangxi government aims to develop Guangxi into a trade and logistics hub for China–ASEAN cooperation and a genuine growth pole for western development.

In October 2013, the Chinese government announced its plan to establish the Asian Infrastructure Investment Bank (AIIB) (亚洲基础设施投资银行) to finance inter-regional connectivity-related infrastructure construction within Asia together with the existing China–ASEAN maritime cooperation fund it had set up in 2010. This proposed bank is a new arm for China's outward investment, and it will prioritize ASEAN connectivity-related infrastructure projects. The Guangxi government has been lobbying the central government to set up one of its bank branches in Guangxi. If successful, the financial and economic status of Guangxi could be improved through China–ASEAN relations.

China is keen to aid ASEAN countries in modernizing their infrastructure and is hence supportive of Chinese companies' participation in ASEAN infrastructure development projects. China sees participation in the construction of ports and other related facilities in this region as important to boosting its manufacturing investment and economic growth. Guangxi is taking the lead in this respect and Guangxi Beibu International Port Corporation has invested $1 billion in expanding local port capacity in Kuantan, Malaysia.[5]

Beibu Gulf region's competitive advantage

The State Council of China approved the Development Plan for the Guangxi Beibu Gulf Economic Area (广西北部湾经济区发展规划 referred to as the Plan hereafter) in 2008. The development of BGEZ has been upgraded to a national strategy since then; the Plan constitutes an important part of the western development strategy that has been implemented by the Chinese government since the early 2000s. The approval of the Plan and the preferential policies introduced for the Beibu Gulf region are reflective of the central government's commitment to pursue more balanced regional development.

These detailed policies cover taxation reduction, preferential land use, and finance for industrial development and infrastructure construction. Lin Nianxiu, the newly promoted vice minister of the National Development and Reform Commission of China (NDRC) in 2014, is in charge of implementing the regional development policy. As the former vice governor of Guangxi, he is likely to use his power and influence to promote the development of Guangxi by granting more favourable preferential policies to it in the coming years.

In terms of resources, Guangxi is rich in mineral reserves, such as manganese, aluminium, copper and nickel, which are among the most important in the nation. In comparison to the eastern region, Guangxi has an ample supply of relatively cheap land and labour and a growing domestic consumption market, which could provide the basis for developing labour-intensive manufacturing sectors and a modern service industry.

Since 2006, the BGEZ has achieved fast economic growth. The region's GDP increased from 87.8 billion yuan in 2000 to 590.1 billion yuan in 2012. In particular, the manufacturing industry, an important force for the development of Beibu Gulf region, registered stupendous growth for its value-added industrial output from 19.3 billion yuan in 2000 to 199.7 billion yuan in 2012. The BGEZ accounted for 34.3 of total value-added industrial output of Guangxi in 2012 (Table 10.2).

Guangxi is perceived as the gateway to China–ASEAN cooperation as it is the only province in China which has both land and sea access to the ASEAN countries and the only western province with a sea gateway. Qinzhou Port, Fangchenggang Port and Beihai Port jointly formed the regional port network of the BGEA in 2007. These three ports are now under the supervision and management of Guangxi Beibu International Port Corporation, one of the major local state-owned companies in Guangxi.

However, due to historical reasons, the Beibu Gulf area has been lagging behind for many years with a weak foundation and low starting point. The Beibu Gulf area has been marginalized for many years and its economic development is still backward in comparison with other coastal areas of China.

Beibu Gulf area does not have a leading city that meets world or regional standards. Nor is there a strong, sizable and competitive industrial cluster with pillar industries. The level of urbanization and industrialization is still quite low, while its modern service industry has yet to keep pace with that of other regions in China.

The economic hinterland of the Beibu Gulf, mainly southwest China (an area that includes Yunnan, Guizhou, Chongqing and Sichuan) and the northern part of the Indochina Peninsula (the north area of Vietnam, Laos and Thailand), consists

Table ... Value Added Industrial Output (VAIO) of the Beibu Gulf Economic Zone and Guangxi (unit: billion yuan)

Year	China	Guangxi		Beibu Gulf Economic Zone						Total (Six Cities' VAIO)	
				Nanning	Beihai	Yulin	Fangcheng-gang	Qinzhou	Chongzuo		
	Industry	Industry	/China	Industry	Industry	Industry	Industry	Industry	Industry	Industry	/Guangxi
1990	685.8	10.4	1.53%	2.3	0.4	0.6	0.08	0.3		3.8	36.37%
1991	808.7	12.4	1.53%	2.5	0.5	0.9	0.1	0.4		4.5	36.71%
1992	1,028.4	16.1	1.57%	2.7	0.7	1.7	0.1	0.5		5.8	36.45%
1993	1,418.8	27.3	1.92%	4.4	1.2	3.3	0.3	0.9		10.2	37.56%
1994	1,948.0	40.5	2.08%	5.8	2.1	4.5	0.5	1.2		14.2	35.15%
1995	2,495.0	46.1	1.85%	6.5	2.1	4.6	0.6	1.3		15.2	32.87%
1996	2,944.8	50.3	1.71%	6.7	1.8	4.7	0.8	1.4		15.4	30.62%
1997	3,292.1	52.4	1.59%	7.1	2.2	4.7	0.9	1.6		16.6	31.65%
1998	3,401.8	56.1	1.65%	7.7	2.4	5.2	1.0	1.7		18.2	32.36%
1999	3,586.2	57.1	1.59%	7.7	2.5	5.2	1.1	1.7		18.3	32.11%
2000	4,003.4	61.2	1.53%	7.9	2.7	5.5	1.2	1.9		19.2	31.47%
2001	4,358.0	63.9	1.47%	8.5	2.9	5.5	1.3	2.1		20.4	31.96%
2002	4,743.1	69.9	1.47%	9.3	3.1	6.5	1.7	2.2	1.9	23.0	32.79%
2003	5,494.5	81.4	1.48%	10.9	3.3	7.7	1.8	2.8	2.5	28.6	32.92%
2004	6521.0	104.5	1.60%	13.8	4.4	8.8	2.2	3.6	3.6	35.3	31.44%
2005	7,723.1	126.5	1.64%	16.5	4.2	10.4	2.9	4.2	5.8	41.9	30.25%
2006	9,131.1	159.2	1.74%	22.1	5.0	12.9	4.1	6.8	6.8	56.9	32.11%
2007	11,053.5	209.0	1.89%	28.4	6.1	16.5	6.4	8.6	8.9	72.9	31.61%
2008	13,026.0	262.7	2.02%	35.2	8.2	20.2	8.8	10.7	9.1	92.0	31.66%
2009	13,523.9	286.4	2.12%	39.6	10.0	24.1	10.9	11.8	12.7	105.6	33.71%
2010	16,072.2	386.0	2.40%	48.4	14.5	32.4	13.8	18.8	16.9	140.6	33.13%
2011	18,847.0	485.1	2.57%	61.3	17.6	39.5	18.7	25.3	18.4	179.4	33.48%
2012	19,967.1	527.9	2.64%	70.6	26.8	40.4	19.8	23.7		199.7	34.34%

Note: Chongzuo was granted the status of prefectural-level city in 2003. Prior to that, it was a part of Nanning city.

Source: Statistical Bureau of Guangxi

of economically underdeveloped areas where industrialization is still at an initial stage. The transportation infrastructure in Guangxi is developed to a certain extent but its business, management and services are still lagging behind. The transportation charges of coastal railroads are also very high.[6]

Nanning, the capital city of Guangxi, is like one big construction site. Many new large-scale projects are being built, ranging from metro lines, expressways, stadiums, museums, housing, and shopping malls to other infrastructure projects. One senior official said the development of Guangxi had stagnated for a very long time due to a lack of supportive policies from the central government, which had compounded its historically weak economic foundations; it thus needs to outperform other regions in terms of economic growth to make up for the lost ground.[7]

However, due to relative late development, the Beibu Gulf area faces challenges of capital and human resource outflow, in contrast to eastern China which is more economically developed and offers more job opportunities.

The Chinese central government needs to back up this region more strongly, especially in funding, projects arrangement, introduction of talents and opening policies to build capacity and lay a good foundation for sub-regional economic development. At the national level, the issue of insufficient coordination and cooperation among different sectors and mechanisms remains unresolved.

For Beibu Gulf area, it has an additional concern. The border it shares with Vietnam is both a boon and a bane. In times of conflict, as with the China–Vietnam Border War in 1979, the economy of the area would suffer a downturn. In times of peace, much economic benefit can be reaped with wider opening up. The current conflict between the two sides remains a serious test for bilateral ties as well as China–ASEAN relations in the coming years.

The China–Malaysia Qinzhou Industrial Park

The China–Malaysia Qinzhou Industrial Park (CMQIP) (中马钦州工业园), which was approved by the Chinese authority and officially opened in 2012, is the third government-to-government project between Chinese and foreign governments, after the China–Singapore Suzhou Industrial Park and China–Singapore Tianjin Eco City. In 2013, the Chinese and Malaysian governments also set up the Malaysia–China Kuantan Industrial Park in Pahang, Malaysia based on the so-called Two Countries, Two Industrial Parks model.

The Chinese and Malaysian governments aim to develop the CMQIP into an advanced manufacturing base and a flagship project for cooperation that could even enhance China–ASEAN relations as a whole. During Xi's visit to Malaysia in October 2013, an agreement had been reached to elevate bilateral China–Malaysia cooperation to a comprehensive strategic partnership.[8]

CMQIP is expected to boost local industrial take-off. After the completion of basic transportation and other infrastructure construction, the Qinzhou Industrial Park has now become operational and is starting to attract foreign and domestic private investment in new manufacturing plants.

Currently, three companies are investing in the industrial park. The two factories, which are currently being built and scheduled for operation by the end of

2014, have Chinese investors: (1) the Guangxi Beibu International Port Corporation, which will be engaged in the storage and production of palm oil and cooking oil: and (2) a relocated plant from the city of Qinzhou, which will manufacture anti-cancer related drugs and other medical products. The third company is a Malaysian firm which will produce Halal food; the construction of the plant is expected to start in late 2014.

The success of the CMQIP model for joint industrial development has led the Malaysian government to call for a second cooperation project, namely, the Malaysia–China Kuantan Industrial Park in Pahang. The basic transportation and other infrastructure construction projects are currently being built and Chinese companies are playing an important role in the improvement of Kuantan port and other local infrastructure.[9]

The funding for local infrastructure improvements in the CMQIP comes mainly from the Chinese central and Guangxi governments. The Chinese government has already invested heavily in transportation and other critical infrastructure improvement to this park over the past few years and is committed to spending another 800 million yuan annually on these projects for the next three years. China and Malaysia have set up a jointly funded investment corporation for future park infrastructure construction. However, the Malaysian side has yet to contribute its share to the company due to problems in sourcing funds.[10]

Similarly, both the Chinese central and Guangxi governments have made huge investments in infrastructure improvement in the Qinzhou Bonded Port Zone, which was approved by the State Council of China in May 2008. Thirteen new berths for accommodating large vessels of up to 100,000 dwt have been put into operation, while two high-quality expressways have been built to connect the CMQIP and the Qinzhou Port to the Nanning city.

Obstacles and challenges for the development of the Beibu Gulf economic area

Although Guangxi has achieved fast economic growth since 2006, it remains one of the poorest and most underdeveloped regions in China. Guangxi accounted for merely 2.6 per cent (1,303.5 billion yuan) of China's GDP in 2012. Guangxi's contribution to the total value of China's GDP has changed little since 1990 (see Table 10.1); it is outstripped by not only the eastern provinces, but also Sichuan, Chongqing, Shaanxi and some other western provinces.

The regional economic disparities between Guangxi and other developed Chinese provinces as measured by gross regional product (GRP) per capita are striking. In 2012, the GRP per capita of Guangxi (27,952 yuan) was less than one-third of Shanghai's 85,373 yuan and Beijing's 87,475 yuan. Guangxi's GRP per capita was also substantially lower than those of many other western provinces in 2012, including Chongqing, Sichuan and Shaanxi. (Figure 10.1)

Multinational firms have shown little interest in Guangxi. In 2013 Guangxi attracted only US$700 million in foreign investment. In 2010, the 10 ASEAN countries invested just US$124 million, while the value of trade between Guangxi and ASEAN was US$12.05 billion in 2012, accounting for roughly 3 per cent of

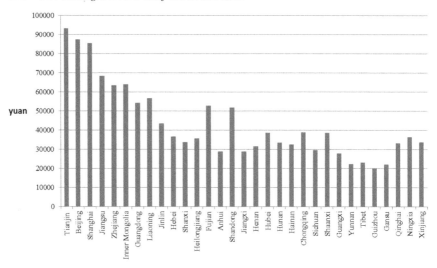

Figure 10.1 Per capita gross regional products by region in China, 2012

Source: *China Statistical Yearbook*, 2013

total value of bilateral trade between China and ASEAN countries.[11] Guangxi thus needs to improve its investment environment by cutting red tape and increasing administrative efficiency.

One of the main challenges faced by Guangxi BGEZ region is the underdevelopment of its ports and harbours. A regional network of ports has been formed, but ports located in Guangxi have yet to achieve efficiency and cost effectiveness in the shipment of cargo. None of Guangxi's ports was even on the 2012 list of top 20 container ports in the world, half of which were Chinese ports, as measured by throughput (Table 10.3). In 2012, Shanghai ranked as the largest exporter of containerized goods worldwide, recording a volume of 32.53 million TEUs. In comparison, the Beibu Gulf ports of Qinzhou, Fangchenggang and Beihai handled a total of only 0.82 million TEUs in that year (Figure 10.2).

To improve operational efficiency and achieve coordinated development of Qingzhou, Beihai and Fangchenggang ports, the Guangxi government has established the Guangxi Beibu International Port Corporation (GBIPC). All the three ports now come under the supervision of GBIPC, which is responsible for all port and harbour-related activities in Guangxi. However, the government's efforts have yet to bear much fruit in terms of improving operational efficiency and profit-making capability of Guangxi's ports.

Despite recentralizing port supervision institutions, the three Beibu Gulf ports are still in hostile competition for container cargo and freight transport. This has impeded the development of a coordinated and efficient regional port network in the Beibu Gulf region.

Although the Guangxi government has made huge investment in port upgrading projects in Qinzhou, Beihai and Fangchenggang, none of the ports has handled as

Table 10.3 Top 20 world container ports by 2012 throughput

Ranking	Port, Country	Volume 2012 (million TEUs)
1	Shanghai, China	32.53
2	Singapore, Singapore	31.65
3	Hong Kong, China	23.10
4	Shenzhen, China	22.94
5	Busan, South Korea	17.04
6	Ningbo-Zhoushan, China	16.83
7	Guangzhou Harbour, China	14.74
8	Qingdao, China	14.50
9	Jebel Ali, Dubai, United Arab Emirates	13.30
10	Tianjin, China	12.30
11	Rotterdam, the Netherlands	11.87
12	Port Kelang, Malaysia	10.00
13	Kaohsiung, Taiwan, China	9.78
14	Hamburg, Germany	8.86
15	Antwerp, Belgium	8.64
16	Los Angeles, the United States	8.08
17	Dalian, China	8.06
18	Keihin ports, Japan	7.85
19	Tanjung Pelepas, Malaysia	7.70
20	Xiamen, China	7.20

Source: World Shipping Council, 2014

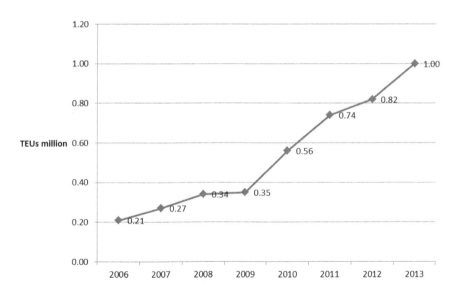

Figure 10.2 The Beibu Gulf container ports by 2013 throughput

Source: Data provided by the Planning and Construction Commission of Guangxi Beibu Gulf Economic Area, the Guangxi government.

much passenger and freight transport as hoped. An indicator is the extremely low traffic along the two expressways connecting Qinzhou Port, the QIP and Nanning. The author spent 15 minutes during the peak hour in the morning recording the number of trucks passing along the Nanning–Qinzhou Port expressway; only four cargo vehicles plied the expressway.

As transport costs at Qinzhou Port are much higher and operational efficiency is lower than at the ports in Hong Kong, Shenzhen and Guangzhou, many companies located in Guangxi and other inland western provinces prefer to use the Hong Kong and Shenzhen ports. The plant set up by Foxconn in Nanning, a Taiwan-owned company and the world's largest electronics contract manufacturer, has transported 90 per cent of its manufactured electronics goods to Shenzhen for export by sea, and not via the Beibu Gulf ports for cargo shipping.[12]

In terms of foreign trade, Guangxi and the other inland western provinces have little involvement. Beibu Gulf region recorded only US$25.6 billion in foreign trade in 2013 (Figure 10.3).

Although the percentage of Guangxi's foreign trade in the national total has increased since the early 2000s, it has still accounted for less than 1 per cent since 1996 (Table 10.4). Local companies in Guangxi produce few manufactured goods for maritime export due to its economic backwardness and lack of openness to the world, a reason for the low usage of Qinzhou port and the lack of large cargo vehicles along its expressways.

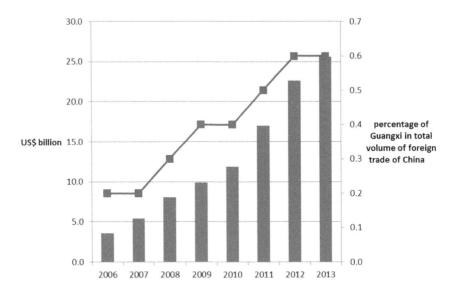

Figure 10.3 Foreign exports and imports of the BGEZ, 2006–2013

Note: Foreign trade consists of total value of imports and exports.

Source: Planning and Construction Commission of Guangxi Beibu Gulf Economic Area, the Guangxi government

Table 10.4 Foreign trade of Guangxi and the nation (unit: billion yuan)

Year	China			Guangxi			Guangxi/China
	Exports (X)	Imports (M)	Total = X + M	Exports (X)	Imports (M)	Total = X + M	
1990	298.5	257.4	556.0	3.4	0.8	4.3	0.772%
1991	382.7	339.9	722.6	4.4	1.0	5.4	0.754%
1992	467.6	444.3	911.9	6.1	2.9	9.0	0.991%
1993	528.5	598.6	1,127.1	7.6	4.3	11.9	1.062%
1994	1,042.2	996.0	2,038.2	13.8	7.4	21.2	1.040%
1995	1,245.2	1,104.8	2,349.9	18.8	8.1	26.9	1.144%
1996	1,257.6	1,155.7	2,413.4	15.9	7.6	23.5	0.974%
1997	1,516.1	1,180.6	2,696.7	19.7	5.7	25.4	0.943%
1998	1,522.4	1,162.6	2,684.9	20.0	4.7	24.7	0.920%
1999	1,615.9	1,373.6	2,989.6	10.3	4.2	14.5	0.485%
2000	2,063.4	1,863.9	3,927.3	12.4	4.5	16.9	0.430%
2001	2,202.4	2,015.9	4,218.4	10.2	4.6	14.9	0.353%
2002	2,694.8	2,443.0	5,137.8	12.4	7.6	20.1	0.392%
2003	3,628.8	3,419.6	7,048.4	16.3	10.1	26.4	0.375%
2004	4,910.3	4,643.6	9,553.9	19.8	15.7	35.5	0.372%
2005	6,264.8	5,427.4	11,692.2	23.2	18.6	41.8	0.358%
2006	7,759.7	6,337.7	14,097.4	28.4	24.2	52.6	0.373%
2007	9,356.4	7,330.0	16,686.4	38.1	31.0	69.2	0.414%
2008	10,039.5	7,952.6	17,992.1	50.2	40.2	90.4	0.503%
2009	8,202.9	6,861.8	15,064.8	57.2	39.8	96.9	0.644%
2010	10,702.3	9,469.9	20,172.2	64.1	53.9	118.0	0.585%
2011	12,324.1	11,316.1	23,640.2	79.1	69.1	148.2	0.627%
2012	12,935.9	11,480.1	24,416.0	97.2	88.0	185.3	0.759%

Source: Statistical Bureau of Guangxi

Similarly, the Nanning Bonded Logistics Centre has attracted little take-up for its bonded logistics facilities. Many of the potential maritime infrastructure projects in Guangxi are government driven rather than industry driven. Economic returns of this newly built infrastructure could take a very long time to be realized, if ever.

What aggravates the situation further is the fierce inter-regional competition from other western provinces. For example, Chengdu is a rising economic star in the development of the western region and has attracted many multinational companies and much foreign investment over the past 10 years.[13]

In the meantime, the preferential policy treatment given by the Chinese central government to Guangxi and other western regions is converging and becoming quite homogeneous. Guangxi will have to reduce its dependence on central policy support and find new ways to boost local economic development by tapping on its geographical advantages and resource abundance.

Externally, relations between China and some ASEAN member states have soured after the South China Sea disputes and this has impacted Guangxi economically. With the Philippines, the Philippine Department of Foreign Affairs had lodged a protest against China over its "reclamation" of Johnson South Reef. The dispute over Johnson South Reef coincided with anti-Chinese riots in southern Vietnam, after a state-owned Chinese oil company set up a $1 billion oil drilling rig off the coast of southern Vietnam and near another disputed coral atoll, Triton Island. Commercial ties between Guangxi and Vietnam have since been negatively impacted.

Guangxi's proposal to expand bilateral maritime trade and economic cooperation with ASEAN countries has now been stalled given the uncertainties. The future of this economic zone is dependent on the overall security situation in the South China Sea, a development which is beyond the control of the Guangxi government.

Appendix 10.1 A chronology of Guangxi–ASEAN cooperative activities

Year	Cooperation	Country
2006	The Nanning-Singapore Economic Corridor to extend the range of cooperation in the Great Mekong Sub-Region	Singapore
2008	The Cross-Border Economic Cooperation Zones (CBEZs) at the China–Vietnam Border to develop "Two corridors, One circle" of economic growth	Vietnam
2010	China–ASEAN Free Trade Area (CAFTA) took effect	ASEAN
2010	Asia Pulp & Paper Co., Ltd., which comes under Indonesia's Sinar Mas Group, invested 79 billion yuan to build the largest Asia–Pacific wood-pulp-paper integration base in Qinzhou, Guangxi	Indonesia
2012	China–Malaysia Qinzhou, Kuantan Industrial Park focuses on six major industries including equipment manufacturing, IT, food processing, new materials, biotechnologies and modern services	Malaysia

(Continued)

Appendix 10.1 (Continued)

Year	Cooperation	Country
2013	The China–Indonesia Economic and Trade Cooperation Zone extends across 500 hectares of land in Bekasi's industrial sub district of Cikarang	Indonesia
2013	China initiated the $50 billion Asian Infrastructure Investment Bank to invest in major infrastructure projects across the region	ASEAN
2013	Maritime Silk Road Project proposed by President Xi	ASEAN
2014	The 8th Forum on Pan-Beibu Gulf Economic Zone was held in Nanning, Guangxi	ASEAN

Source: Compiled by the author.

Notes

1 Source: "The impact of ACFTA on People's Republic of China–ASEAN trade," *ADB Working Paper Series on Regional Economic Integration* No. 99, July 2012, Asian Development Bank.
2 "President Xi gives speech to Indonesia's parliament," *China Daily*, 2 October 2013, http://www.chinadaily.com.cn/china/2013xiapec/2013-10/02/content_17007915_3.htm (accessed 4 December 2013)
3 The China–ASEAN Expo, co-sponsored and jointly organized by the Chinese and 10 ASEAN governments and the ASEAN Secretariat, is an international trade promotion event. The China–ASEAN Expo is held annually in Nanning, Guangxi.
4 Local informant.
5 "Down the maritime silk road," *The Australian*, 6 December 2013, http://www.theaustralian.com.au/business/in-depth/down-the-maritime-silk-road/story-fnjy4qn5-1226776242929 (accessed 19 February 2014)
6 Huang Xiaoqing. (2007). "Pan Beibu Gulf Cooperation Core-The Rise of Guangxi Beibu Gulf Economic Zone", in *Pan Beibu Gulf Cooperation Development Report*, edited by Gu Xiaosong, Beijing, Social Science Academic Press.
7 Local informant.
8 "Malaysia-China set to achieve bilateral trade of US$160 billion by 2017," *The Sun Daily*, 4 October 2013, http://www.thesundaily.my/news/847500 (accessed 20 February 2014)
9 Local informant.
10 Local informant.
11 Data source: *China Statistical Yearbook 2013* and *Guangxi Statistical Yearbook 2013*.
12 Local informant.
13 Yu Hong, "Chengdu: a rising economic star in western China," *EAI Background Brief* No. 843, National University of Singapore, 22 August 2013.

11 Inter-regional industrial transfer in China

Inter-regional industrial transfer: pursuit of more balanced regional industrial growth

China's huge land mass has given rise to differing levels of development across the country. Since the early 1980s, China's coastal eastern region has pioneered China's industrial development during the reform and opening up period. Many of China's manufacturing industries are concentrated in the coastal region. Industrial activities in the inland regions pale in comparison. China's inland region covers both the central and western regions.

The hinterland region in China concentrates on the exploitation and export of its primary commodities, raw and mineral resources and has fewer developed manufacturing industries.[1] Most of the major industrial cities are located in China's coastal eastern region, the country's main industrial powerhouse. The eastern region accounted for 66.3 per cent of gross national industrial output in 2010, while the central and western regions accounted for 33.7 per cent (Figure 11.1). China's uneven regional industrial development in favour of the eastern region is evident.

The Chinese central government has boosted industrial development of the eastern region by granting various preferential policies, including favourable land use policies and land rental fees, tax concessions and tariff exemption for foreign investors (e.g. value-added tax and import tax), and high retention ratios of foreign exchange earned. In contrast, preferential policies have not been granted to the western region until a much later period,[2] a reason for the widening regional inequality in China.[3]

The development experience of China's coastal region and the developed nations shows that vibrant and prosperous manufacturing industries are the foundation for broad-based economic development. Inter-regional industrial transfer[4] (IRIT) is thus crucial to enhancing the industrial and economic competitiveness of China's central and western regions.

The labour-intensive industries in coastal China, from the textile, garments, toy, shoe making, clothing to other sectors, have been shifted to the inland regions since the early 2000s, a process that has further gained momentum since 2008.

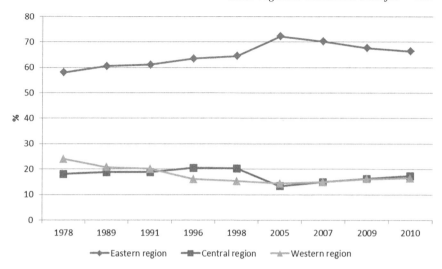

Figure 11.1 Percentage of gross regional industrial output in the nation, 1978–2010.

Source: *China's Industrial Development Report*, 2009 and 2011

According to a survey conducted by the *Journal for Asia on Textile & Apparel*, 70 per cent of the surveyed textile companies have relocated their plants to the inland regions, accelerating the industrial growth in these regions.[5]

As the coastal region has lost its competitive edge as the world's low-cost manufacturing factory, IRIT could thus herald a golden period of rapid industrial growth for the inland central and western regions and fundamentally shape the nation's industrial distribution and development in the future. China's inland regions have competitive advantages in terms of their sizeable domestic market and rich reserves of resources. IRIT would have to accommodate local conditions and comparative advantages and let the private sector, not the state, be the dominant force in IRIT.

State rationale for pushing inter-regional industrial transfer

The inland western region has many important industrial cities, with a concentration of military and heavy steel industries. These industries were the legacy of the Third Front Construction period which established the industrial foundation for the western region in the 1960s. During this period, Mao instructed many heavy industries to relocate to the remote west as so-called third front construction projects for the purpose of national security and defence.[6]

Nevertheless, the western region was also known for its unbalanced industrial structure, with a low share of light industry and high concentration of heavy and military-related industries. These problems have made it difficult for the western region to meet the changing demands of the international market or produce up-to-date products.[7]Consequently, many local industries in the inland region have gradually withered over the past 30 years.

This development has led to the polarization of China's industrial development in the past three decades. The fast industrial development in the eastern region did not eventually boost industrial activities in the inland region and promote its industrial growth through generating inter-regional spillover effect on a significant scale as assumed.

The interior central and western regions have long lobbied the Chinese central government and local governments in the coastal region to facilitate IRIT from the coastal region to the inland region to boost inland industrial development. IRIT formed an important part of the "coordinated regional development strategy" announced by the Chinese central government in the early 2000s. As an endorsement and support for IRIT, the central government successively released an amended version of *Guiding Catalogue of Priority and Encouraged Industries for Foreign Investment in Central and Western Regions of China* in 2008 and the *Guideline on Undertaking Inter-Regional Industrial Transfer for the Central and Western Region* in August 2010.

IRIT indicates a reorientation of national industrial development strategy for China: a shift from an eastern region-focused to a more balanced regional industrial growth. The state's endeavours to promote IRIT have raised awareness of preferential policies available in the inland region, and increased the interest of foreign investors in China's inland region.

The central government has encouraged the coastal and inland regions to forge partnerships so that the former could help the latter develop local industries through relocation of labour-intensive and manufacturing assembling industries to the interior. By doing this, the coastal region can actively pursue industrial restructuring and upgrading through moving up the production value chain.

The Chinese government also seeks to forge a complementary network of regional industrial production within the nation, doing away with the need to transfer labour-intensive industries overseas and retaining these industries on Chinese soil. The Chinese leadership intends to form an internal "flying geese model" to speed up regional industrialization within China. The term *flying geese model* was first proposed by the Japanese scholars. It refers to an industrial hierarchy of Asian countries led by Japan. According to this model, the production of industrial products will continually shift from the more advanced industrial countries to the less advanced industrial countries based on comparative advantage and stages of development. Facing the pressure of rising labor costs, the more advanced countries will move up the industrial value chain and produce the capital and technology-intensive industries goods, while relocating their labour-intensive production to the other less advanced countries.

Wanjiang Economic Zone in Anhui province is the first national zone in the inland region approved by the Chinese central government in January 2010 to boost IRIT.[8] In all, the Chinese government had approved the establishment of five economic zones for undertaking IRIT by 2011, including Wanjiang Economic Zone, Anhui; Guidong Economic Zone, Guangxi; Coastal Economic Zone,

Chongqing; Xiangnan Economic Zone, Hunan and Jingzhou Economic Zone, Hubei (Table 11.1).

China leaders view IRIT as a way to reduce regional industrial gaps and regional economic disparity, and achieve a more balanced regional development. It is hoped that IRIT will help ease social and ethnic tension, maintain social harmony and political stability in the inland region, boost local tax revenue and greatly expand employment opportunities of China's central and western regions. However, detailed policy measures and specific policy goals are lacking, greatly undermining its effectiveness.

Table 11.1 List of economic zones approved by the Chinese government for Inter-Regional Industrial Transfer

Zone	Administrative Coverage	Inter-Regional Industrial Transfer Targeted	Approval Date
Wanjiang Economic Zone, Anhui (皖江经济带)	Hefei, Wuhu, Ma'anshan, Chaohu, Chuzhou, Xuancheng, Tongling, Anqing, Chizhou and Liu'an (10 cities)	Equipment manufacturing, textile and garments, raw materials	January 2010
Guidong Economic Zone, Guangxi (桂东产业转移示范区)	Wuzhou, Guigang, Hezhou and Yulin (four cities)	Equipment manufacturing, textile and garments, raw materials	October 2010
Coastal Economic Zone, Chongqing (重庆沿江产业转移示范区)	Peiling, Banan, Jiulongpo, Bishan, Yongchuan, Shuangqiao, and Rongchang (seven cities and counties)	Advanced equipment manufacturing, electronic information, new materials, biology, chemistry, and modern service industries	February 2011
Xiangnan Economic Zone, Hunan (湘南产业转移示范区)	Hengyang, Chengzhou and Yongzhou (three cities)	Electronic information, new materials, new energy, auto part, chemical, and equipment manufacturing	October 2011
Jingzhou Economic Zone, Hubei (荆州产业转移示范区)	Jingzhou city	Labor-intensive industries, process for agricultural products, chemical, and equipment manufacturing	December 2011

Source: *China's Industrial Development Report 2012*

The status of inter-regional industrial transfer

As IRIT within China has only taken place in the past few years, it is still too premature to assess its overall effectiveness and performance. Manufactured value-added output (MVAO) and per capita MVAO are important indicators of industrial production capacity, extent of local industrialization and competitive industrial performance of a region. Compared to the coastal eastern region, the central and western regions have much lower MVAO and MVAO per capita.

Although regional disparity in industrial development is substantial, the gap is narrowing. The ratios of per capita MVAO in the eastern region to corresponding figures in the central and western regions had decreased to a respective 2.04:1 and 2.30:1 in 2009 from 2.54:1 and 2.91:1 in 2003; these ratios had fallen further to 1.66:1 and 2.04:1 in 2012 (Table 11.2). The statistical indicators show that IRIT within China has taken a gradual path.

According to the Chinese Academy of Social Sciences data, in terms of the output of the nation's labour-intensive intensive industries, the eastern region's share had contracted to 70.4 per cent in 2010 from 77.6 per cent in 2003, while gains were registered for the central region (17.9 per cent in 2010 from 12.4 per cent in 2003) and the western region (10.1 per cent in 2003 to 11.8 per cent in 2010) (Table 11.3). This indicates that IRIT took place at a faster pace in central China than in western China.

Table 11.2 Comparison of per capita value-added industrial output by China's regions

Region	Manufacturing Value-Added Output (MVAO) (billion yuan)			Per Capita MVAO (yuan)		
	2003	*2009*	*2012*	*2003*	*2009*	*2012*
Eastern Region	3,572.9	9,331.8	13,702.6	7,274.3	17,598.9	24,930.5
Central Region	1,022.8	3,068.1	5,376.6	2,861.3	8,617.5	14,965.3
Western Region	1,081.7	3,348.6	5,356.8	2,496.6	7,642.5	12,202.5

Source: Compiled by the author based on *China Statistical Yearbook*, 2004 and *China Statistical Yearbook*, 2013.

Table 11.3 Percentage of regional industrial output in the nation by various industrial sectors

Region	Labour-intensive industries		Capital-intensive industries		Technology-intensive industries	
	2003	*2010*	*2003*	*2010*	*2003*	*2010*
Eastern Region	77.6	70.4	74.6	69.7	87.3	82.8
Central Region	12.4	17.9	14.4	17.4	6.5	10.3
Western Region	10.1	11.8	11.0	13.0	6.3	6.9

Source: *China's Industrial Development Report*, 2012, the Chinese Academy of Social Sciences

As shown in Table 11.4, for certain labour-intensive and low technology sectors, as well as the manufacture of primary plastic, metal-cutting machine tools and micro-computer equipment, the percentages of the inland region's output to national industrial output had increased during the 2003–2012 period. This is especially true of the manufacture of micro-computer equipment, with the inland region accounting for 25.9 per cent of the industry's national output in 2012, compared to merely 1.4 per cent in 2003, a remarkable growth rate.

In the case of Shanghai, a large proportion of its assembling manufacturing industries have been transferred to areas with lower production costs along the Yangtze River Delta region, while Shanghai has gradually been transformed into a national centre for shipping, finance and other service industries over the past several years.[9]

However, the relocation of labour-intensive industries from the eastern to the central and western regions has been limited and the results on IRIT become less encouraging on closer examination. The shares of the inland region in national industrial output of several labour-intensive industries including cloth, plate glass and crude steel, fell between the years of 2003 and 2012. For example, cloth produced in the inland region accounted for 19.6 per cent of national output in 2012, compared to 25.7 per cent in 2003.

Although local governments in the inland region have established various industrial transfer demonstration parks and industrial development zones to boost and accommodate the industrial shift, the state-backed IRIT move has yet to yield concrete outcomes and China has not reached the stage of large-scale transfer.

China's inland region is not a default choice for IRIT. Some American-invested companies with manufacturing factories in China's coastal region have relocated their manufacturing work to the United States due to rising labor wages in coastal China and the narrowing wage gap between China and the United States. According to a survey by *The Wall Street Journal*, many American companies are considering this option and nearly 60 percent of surveyed companies regard labor costs as the most important factor when deciding on the location of factories.[10]

Likewise, the percentage of Japanese-affiliated companies intending to expand business and increase investment in China had dropped by 14.5 per cent to 52.3 per cent in 2012, compared to that a year before mainly due to wage increase, and under-performance and low quality of local employees. Japanese companies have stronger intention to increase outward investment in Indonesia, Bangladesh, Myanmar, India and Laos.[11]

Although the central and western regions have achieved decent industrial and economic growth over the past decade, the industrial and economic gaps are still striking; the trend of widening regional disparity has not been effectively reversed in China. In fact, based on indicators such as gross regional product, fiscal revenue, foreign direct investment (FDI) and foreign trade, regional inequalities in socioeconomic development between the western and eastern regions of China have widened significantly between the 1990s and 2000s.[12]

IRIT is largely driven by the industries, with some support from the government. Central policy measures that are pro-IRIT face serious internal and external

Table 11.4 Percentage of contribution of selected regional industrial products to national output by the inland regions

Inland Region	Cloth		Primary Plastic		Plate Glass		Crude Steel		Metal-Cutting Machine Tools		Micro-Computer Equipment	
	2003	2012	2003	2012	2003	2012	2003	2012	2003	2012	2003	2012
Shanxi	0.9	0.1	0.3	1.0	1.1	2.6	4.5	5.4	0.6	0.1	0	0
Inner Mongolia	0.1	0.05	0.6	5.3	3.1	0.7	2.6	2.4	0	0	0.2	0
Jilin	0.3	0.05	3.1	1.5	1.2	0.5	1.7	1.6	0.1	0.3	0	0
Heilongjiang	0.4	0.01	5.0	2.2	0.9	0.5	0.7	1.0	1.2	0.6	0.1	0.01
Anhui	1.9	1.2	0.8	1.1	1.5	3.2	3.1	3.0	3.9	7.0	0.5	0.9
Jiangxi	0.9	1.1	0.8	0.2	2.1	0.9	2.7	3.0	1.3	0.6	0.3	0.06
Henan	5.1	4.2	3.5	4.2	11.3	1.6	3.9	3.1	1.0	0.7	0.02	0
Hubei	5.7	8.5	1.8	1.6	3.9	9.8	5.6	4.0	1.1	0.3	0.06	0.6
Hunan	1.0	0.4	1.6	1.2	2.8	2.4	2.7	2.3	0.3	0.4	0	0.2
Guangxi	0.1	0.07	0.3	0.4	1.6	0.8	0.9	1.9	1.4	0.5	0	0
Chongqing	3.8	1.4	0.02	0.07	0.5	1.1	1.0	0.8	1.0	0.5	0.03	11.7
Sichuan	1.8	1.7	2.4	2.0	3.3	5.5	3.3	2.3	1.9	0.6	0.08	12.4
Guizhou	0.1	0	0	0.2	0.3	0.3	0.9	0.7	0.2	0.1	0	0
Yunnan	0.1	0	0.08	0.5	1.2	1.2	1.3	2.1	1.4	7.6	0	0
Shaanxi	3.0	0.8	0.3	1.7	3.1	2.0	0.8	1.1	2.4	2.5	0.07	0
Gansu	0.1	0	2.0	2.3	1.0	0.7	1.0	1.1	0.3	0.5	0	0
Qinghai	0	0	0	0.5	0.3	0.3	0.2	0.2	0.2	0.8	0	0
Ningxia	0	0	0.06	1.8	0.06	0	0.06	0.03	0.7	0.4	0	0
Xinjiang	0.4	0.08	2.9	7.4	0.2	0.5	0.9	1.6	0		0	0
Percentage of the inland region in the nation	25.7	19.60	25.60	35.20	39.50	34.6	37.90	37.60	19.0	23.5	1.40	25.90

Note: Tibet was excluded in this table.

Source: China Statistical Yearbook, 2013

challenges, and resistance from the coast. For private investors, considerations include the potential profits and costs, availability of comprehensive and efficient infrastructure, supply of skilled and cheap labor, land use fee, quality of institutional systems, local investment environment and backward and forward linkages.

Problems and challenges

Despite much fanfare, numerous barriers to the success of the IRIT prevail. The remote and mountainous geography, the self-reinforced agglomeration effect generated in the eastern region, the backward infrastructure, the underdeveloped educational system and international competition could all pose formidable problems to the success and sustainability of IRIT in the future.

First is geography. The remoteness and mountainous geography of the interior naturally implies higher intra- and inter-regional transport costs, effectively offsetting the low labour and land costs and benefits from state preferential policy measures. The central and western regions also lag behind the coastal region in terms of modern infrastructure as shown in indicators such as popularization rates for mobile phones and the internet (Table 11.5).

According to United Nations Industrial Development Organization's estimations (2005), transportation costs for road and airfreight for the inland western region are twice as high as those in the eastern region, taking a big chip off the gains derived from cheap labor costs. As indicated by one informant in Shunde,[13] high inter-regional transportation costs and the relatively long distance and long time delivery for their suppliers have deterred both local and private investors.

Competition from its neighbours is another factor. It is reported that the cost of goods manufactured in Vietnam, Indonesia, Cambodia and Bangladesh might be even lower than that for similar goods produced in China's inland region.[14] Compared to the corresponding figures for the countries including Indonesia, Vietnam, Laos, Sri Lanka, India, Cambodia, Bangladesh and Myanmar, the monthly labor wage for manufacturing industries in China was substantially higher at US$328 in 2012 (Table 11.6).

According to the surveyed data provided by JETRO (Japan External Trade Organization), Japanese-affiliated firms in Vietnam, Sri Lanka, Bangladesh and

Table 11.5 Comparison of infrastructure development among China's regions, 2012

Indicator		Length of Railway in Operation per 10,000 Persons (km)	Popularization Rate of Mobile Phone (sets/100 persons)	Popularization Rate of Internet (%)
Region	Eastern region	0.49	107.5	56.4
	Central region	0.62	66.6	34.6
	Western region	1.10	79.0	36.7

Source: Compiled by the author.

Table 11.6 Comparison of manufacturing workers' wages in selected countries (US$), 2012

Country	Monthly Labour Wage in Manufacturing Industries	Annual Total Pay Burden of Workers in Manufacturing Industries
Singapore	1,230	23,772
China	328	6,734
Thailand	345	6,704
Malaysia	344	5,942
India	290	4,577
Philippines	253	4,581
Indonesia	229	4,551
Pakistan	173	3,141
Vietnam	145	2,602
Laos	132	2,261
Sri Lanka	118	2,455
Cambodia	74	1,424
Bangladesh	74	1,478
Myanmar	53	1,100

Source: JETRO, 2012.

Laos export their manufactured products for foreign consumption rather than local consumption. In 2012, according to official data, the inflow of FDI to China dropped by 3.7 per cent to US$111.7 billion, the first decline since the outbreak of the global economic crisis in 2009.[15]

Second is the agglomeration effect in the coastal region. Compared to the inland region, China's coastal region offers a more well-established production and supply network. Without support from upstream and downstream industries that form industrial agglomeration, IRIT is hard to achieve. New economic geographers have long argued the significance of agglomeration effects to local industrial development and regional economic disparities.[16] The manufacturing industries are usually clustered in a few areas so as to benefit from the economy of scale and technological spillover.

Local protectionism is another major administrative barrier for IRIT in China. The coastal provinces are not enthusiastic about relocating their highly lucrative value-added industrial sectors to the inland region as they need local tax revenue and to provide employment.

Coastal provinces prefer to retain high value-added and technology-intensive sectors such as product design and marketing, product quality control, market research and research and development (R&D) activities, leaving low-end and labour-intensive assembling and processing activities to the inland region which would gain little from undertaking IRIT. As shown in the case of Guangdong, the coastal provinces are more interested in intra-provincial industrial transfer than cross-provincial industrial transfer. Some polluting industries have been relocated to the western region due to strict environmental regulations issued by local governments in the eastern region. The environment of western China is thus at risk.

An example is in the establishment of silicon and oil refining factories in Sichuan, which pose serious pollution risks to the local environment and human health.[17]

Third is the poor education level and the lack of quality labor force. Total expenditure on education and expenditure on education per capita in the central and western regions are substantially lower than that in the eastern region (Table 11.7). More funding from the central government on education is thus essential.

The exodus of migrant workers to the eastern region since China's opening up has caused a shortage of semi-skilled and skilled workers in the inland region which has to devise more attractive employment schemes to attract the return of its migrant skilled workers.

Fourth is the hostile inter-regional industrial competition and duplication of industries. Local governments of the inland region have adopted various means to attract industries in order to gain personal promotion, boost local tax revenue and protect the local market.

There is also a lack of coordinated regional industrial development leading to duplication of industries (Table 11.8). For example, seven provincial governments, Anhui, Chongqing, Guangxi, Sichuan, Guizhou, Hubei and Jiangxi are seeking to develop automobile and auto parts industries. Hostile competition and regional industrial duplication have adversely impacted industrial resource distribution among regions, diminished the benefits of industrial transfer for local industrial growth, and exacerbated industrial production overcapacity in China.

The interior is also plagued by serious social/ethnic tensions. The social instability and unpredictable local investment environment have deterred private investors from setting up businesses in the interior areas, particularly those with large ethnic minority population. An example is the case of Urumqi, Xinjiang. The July 2009 clash between Han Chinese and Uyghurs had left more than 300 shops burnt or destroyed by rioters.[18] Although Xinjiang possesses huge reserves of crucial mineral and energy resources to power local industrial development, its industrial growth potential has been curtailed as a result.

Fifth is the decentralization of regional industrial development to the local governments. The Decision on the 3rd Plenum of the 18th Chinese Communist Party

Table 11.7 Comparison of educational development among China's Regions, 2012

Indicator		Number of Students Enrolled in Higher Education per 10,000 persons	Number of Student Enrolled in Secondary Vocational School per 10,000 persons	Total Regional Education Expenditure (billion yuan)	Total Expenditure on Education per capita (yuan)
Region	Eastern region	186.5	118.2	1,017.5	1,851.2
	Central region	182.0	131.5	466.2	1,297.6
	Western region	162.2	129.3	669.5	1,525.1

Source: Compiled by the author.

Table 11.8 Industries encouraged and prioritized for foreign investment in China's central and western provinces

Industry	Region
Intensive processing of agricultural products	Gansu, Guizhou, Hainan, Inner Mongolia, Ningxia, Qinghai, Xinjiang, Sichuan and Chongqing
Automobile and auto parts	Anhui, Chongqing, Guangxi, Sichuan, Guizhou, Hubei and Jiangxi
Machinery	Henan, Shanxi, Hubei and Hunan
Processing of mineral and other natural resources	Guizhou, Xinjiang, Inner Mongolia, Shaanxi, Shanxi, Henan, Gansu, Jiangxim Qinghai and Sichuan
Pharmaceutical and Chinese medicine	Henan, Jiangxi, Anhui, Tibet, Chongqing, Guangxi, Guizhou and Yunnan
Manufacturing of environmental protection equipment	Chongqing, Guangxi, Inner Mongolia, Shaanxi, Shanxi, Sichuan, Xinjiang, Guizhou and Yunnan
New energy	Chongqing, Gansu, Ningxia and Xinjiang

Source: The National Reform and Development Commission, 2008

Central Committee in November 2013 outlines the further relaxation of economic control and bold decentralization of economic power over the next 10 years. In addition, the Decision calls for the further marketization of the Chinese economy by relaxing state control over local industrial activities.

Some studies however suggest that the investment environment in the inland region is quite unfavourable due to rampant corruption, administrative malpractice and disrespect for the rule of law and market economy.[19]

Some local interviewees in the Shunde and Dongguan cities pointed out that as the preferential treatment granted to the inland region is not much more favourable than that already offered by local authorities in the coastal region, there is little incentive for investors to shift inland. Some interviewees have sought to increase labor productivity and invest in automation and efficient machinery than to relocate their plants to the interior.

With these challenges, state-backed IRIT will be difficult to come to fruition. Unaddressed, large-scale industrial transfer from the coastal region to the inland region will be difficult to take place, not to mention becoming successful in the long run.

Notes

1 United Nations Industrial Development Organization (UNIDO). (2005). *Western China: Enhancing Industrial Competitiveness and Employment*, pp. 1–203.
2 Lin Wuu-Long, and Chen, Thomas P. (2004). "China's widening economic disparities and its 'go west program'", *Journal of Contemporary China*, 13:41, pp. 663–686.
3 Wei, Yehua Dennis. (2002). "Multiscale and multimechanisms of regional inequality in China: implications for regional policy", *Journal of Contemporary China*, 11:30, pp. 109–124.

4 The Coastal – Inland region and Eastern – Central – Western region are the two most conventional bases for drawing regional comparison studies of China. In this background brief, inter-regional industrial transfer within China is a term referring to labor-intensive industrial sectors relocated from the coastal region to inland regions, or from the eastern region to the central and western regions.

5 Staff Report, "Central and western China undertake industrial transition with new approach", *Journal for Asia on Textile & Apparel*, 1 August 2013, available at http://www.adsaleata.com/Publicity/ Mobile/ePub/lang-eng/article-67006872/asid-73/Article.aspx (accessed 5 February 2014)

6 McNally, Christopher A. (2004). "Sichuan: driving capitalist development westward", *The China Quarterly*, 178, pp. 426–447.

7 Lin Wuu-Long, and Chen, Thomas P. (2004). "China's widening economic disparities and its 'go west program'", *Journal of Contemporary China*, 13:41, pp. 663–686.

8 "Anhui area set to embrace new industry: party chief", *China Daily*, 24 May 2010, available at http://www.chinadaily.com.cn/china/2010-05/24/content_9882432.htm (accessed 27 January 2014)

9 Taube, Markus, and Ögütçü, Mehmet. (2002). *"Main issues on foreign investment in China's regional development: prospects and policy challenges"*, Organization for Economic Co-operation and Development (OECD) publication, pp. 1–37.

10 "Once made in China: jobs trickle back to U.S. plants", *The Wall Street Journal*, 21 May 2012, available at http://online.wsj.com/news/articles/SB10001424052702304587704577333482423070376 (accessed 3 February 2014)

11 JETRO, *"Survey of Japanese-Affiliated Companies in Asia and Oceania"*, December 2012, pp. 1–65.

12 Grewal, Bhajan S. and Ahmed, Abdullahi D. (2011). "Is China's western region development strategy on track? An assessment", *Journal of Contemporary China*, 20:69, pp. 161–181; Holbig, Heike. (2004). "The emergence of the campaign to open up the west: ideological formation, central decision-making and the role of the provinces", *The China Quarterly*, 178, pp. 335–357.

13 To gain first-hand data and better understanding of the status of local industrial upgrading and IRIT in China, the author conducted two fieldwork studies in the cities of Dongguan and Shunde, Guangdong in 2009 and 2012. The author interviewed a few chief executives or senior managers of local companies engaged in labour-intensive industries, including manufacturing of wine cellars, furniture and equipment of electronic information. These companies have been facing both external and internal pressure to move up the value chain, and to consider relocating their manufacturing plants to other regions with lower costs in labour wages and land use.

14 "China begins to lose edge as world's factory floor", *The Wall Street Journal*, 16 January 2013, available at http://online.wsj.com/news/articles/SB10001424127887323783704578245241751969774 (accessed 27 January 2014)

15 *China Statistical Yearbook*, 2013.

16 For example, please refer to Krugman, P. (1991). "Increasing returns and economic geography", *The Journal of Political Economy*, 99:3, pp. 483–499; Krugman, P. and Venables, A.J. (1995). "Globalization and the inequality of nations", *The Quarterly Journal of Economics*, 110:4, pp. 857–880; Fujita, M. and Mori, T. (1996). "The role of ports in the making of major cities: self-agglomeration and hub-effect", *Journal of Development Economics*, 49, pp. 93–120; Fujita, M., Krugman, P. and Venables, A.J. (1999). *The Spatial Economy: Cities, Regions, and International Trade*, MA Cambridge: MIT Press; Fujita, Masahisa and Krugman, P. (2004). "The new economic geography: past, present and the future", *Regional Science*, 83, pp. 139–164; Fujita, Masahisa and Thisse, J. (1996). "Economics of agglomeration", *Journal of the Japanese and International Economies*, 10, pp. 339–378; Fujita, Masahisa and Thisse, J. (2002). *Economic of Agglomeration: Cities, Industrial Location, and Regional Growth*, Cambridge: Cambridge University Press.

17 *"Xibu kaifa shinian zhijian"* (The difficulty of ten-year implementation of western development strategy), *Outlook Magazine*, 27 December 2010, available at http://xbkfs. ndrc.gov.cn/zjsj/t20101227_387750.htm (in Chinese) (accessed 3 February 2014); Lai Hongyi. (2002). "China's western development program: its rationale, implementation, and prospects", *Modern China*, 28:4, pp. 432–466.
18 Hao Yufan and Liu Weihua. (2012). "Xinjiang: increasing pain in the heart of China's borderland", *Journal of Contemporary China*, 21:74, pp. 205–225.
19 For example, please see Tian Qunjian (2007) "China develops its west: motivation, strategy and prospect," *Journal of Contemporary China*, 13:41, pp: 611–636.

12 China's ghost cities

Ordos, China's largest ghost city

Ordos, a coal-rich city in Inner Mongolia, is well known for its huge but empty skyscrapers, housing and office buildings, particularly in the newly built Kangbashi area. With a population of only 30,000, it is a far cry from the one million residents planned for Kangbashi by 2010. Ordos is known as a ghost town/city (*guicheng* 鬼城) for good reasons. Ninety per cent of its buildings are empty. Some have been sold but remain unoccupied, while others are unsold or are uncompleted. The Ordos experience is a case of a housing bubble burst. Reports indicate that 70 per cent of construction projects in the downtown area have been halted.[1]

Ordos is however not a solitary case in China; several Chinese cities are experiencing similar housing bubbles, a collapse of the real estate market, a spiralling government debt crisis and a weakening economy due to the slowdown of the domestic economy. The overreliance on its mining industry when it could have diversified its local economy and developed the manufacturing and service industries to create more job opportunities is a contributing factor. Limited employment opportunities outside the coal mining industry and poor public services have discouraged migration to Ordos.

Ordos experienced fast economic growth in the past due to the strong domestic demand for coal. As Ordos holds one-sixth of the nation's coal reserves, China's rapid industrialization process had boosted Ordos' coal mining industry and helped to create a local economic boom before 2011. Ordos was even ranked one of the richest cities in China in terms of per capita GRP then.

Many ghost cities have since emerged in China, including, reportedly, at least 12 within Inner Mongolia, Henan, Liaoning, Jiangsu, Hubei and Yunnan. According to official and non-official sources, the ghost cities of China include Ordos, Qingshuihe, Bayannur and Erenhot located in Inner Mongolia, Zhengdong New Area; some parts of Xinyang and Hebi in Henan; Yingkou in Liaoning; Changzhou and Dantu in Jiangsu; Shiyan in Hubei and Chenggong in Yunnan and a few others. These fully built urban areas have very few residents and are littered with unoccupied newly built residential properties and uncompleted construction projects.

Ghost cities and land-centred urbanization

China's rapid urbanization started in the late 1970s after the reform and open-door policies. This process has accelerated over the past three decades due to various social, political and economic factors, including agricultural productivity growth and surplus rural labor force,[2] excessive flow of rural migrants to cities, rapid industrialization and the economic boom of the eastern coastal areas. The Chinese government has also a part to play when it expanded the administrative boundaries of its cities. China's urbanization rate increased to 52.6 per cent in 2012 from 17.9 per cent in 1978 (Figure 12.1). In 2011, China's urban population exceeded its rural population for the first time.

Urbanization has boosted China's industrial development and economic growth over the past three decades. The new Chinese leadership of President Xi Jinping and Premier Li Keqiang has identified urbanization as the key national strategy to drive economic growth and reduce economic disparity between rural and urban areas. Li Keqiang has reiterated the importance of urbanization to China. Urbanization is regarded as a new engine for unleashing the benefits of reform by raising income levels of the massive rural population and achieving economic rebalancing through domestic consumption.

According to a study by the Development Research Center of the State Council of China, an annual increase of 0.2 per cent in the urbanization level will contribute to an increase of 0.13 per cent in GDP growth in China over the next 20 years.[3] The Chinese leaders envisage that urbanization will increase investment demand

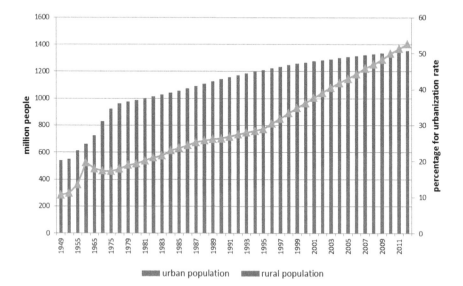

Figure 12.1 Rate of urbanization in China, 1949–2012

Source: *China Statistical Yearbook 2013*, p. 95

for urban infrastructure and social services and promote the development of the service industries.

To the local governments, the acceleration of the urbanization process means more investment in infrastructure and housing construction. Prompted by the state's urbanization push, the local authorities have rushed to invest in building new cities and towns. The state's reliance on the development of the real estate sector to boost economic growth inevitably leads to excessive housing supply. According to the IMF's (International Monetary Fund) estimations in 2013, real estate investment made up 12.5 per cent of GDP in China in 2012.[4]

In China, the overemphasis on urban infrastructure investment comes at the expense of basic social services provision (e.g. health care and education), job opportunities and decent living conditions. China's urbanization literally became an inter-regional competition and campaign for city and town building (造城运动竞赛). This flawed approach to urban planning resulted in an excessive supply of infrastructure and housing and the consequent ghost city phenomenon.

The *hukou* registration system has restricted rural migration to the urban areas. As the floating population makes up a large portion of the urban population, they could profoundly shape the process of China's urbanization. According to estimation by China's National Statistics Bureau, China had a total floating population of 261 million by 2010.[5]

However, the local governments have been far too slow to act on abolishing discriminative administrative policies on rural migration to cities. They are more concerned about obtaining more land for sale (*quandi*) to increase budget revenue and boost GDP growth. The equally important task of integrating rural migrants with the urban population is often overlooked.

The local governments' major source of income for financing infrastructure and social spending is through land transfer revenue. As a result, there was a surge in land allocation for urban construction by 2.5 times between 1990 and 2011.[6] Land acquisition is often associated with power abuse, official corruption, and forced eviction and demolition by government and property developers.

The ghost cities are the by-products of the Great Leap-style of urbanization in China. Their emergence is rooted in China's land-centred urbanization. The rural-to-urban conversion of land has proceeded much faster than the urbanization of people.

China's has a total number of 230 million migrant population, and these people have left their rural hometowns and worked in the cities they lived in, but they have not properly integrated into the cities and completely urbanized. Although the migrant workers have made enormous contribution to national industrialization and fast economic growth, they are denied the equal social welfare benefits and public services as the urban population, and treated as the second-class citizens in China. If the massive floating population is taken into account, the real urbanization rate could be much lower than the nominal rate indicated by the Chinese authority.

Land-centred urbanization has also pushed up urban housing prices and created the problem of the *chengzhongcun* (城中村) phenomenon in mega Chinese cities such as Beijing, Guangzhou and Shenzhen. These *chengzhongcun* are low cost, illegal urban settlements for large-scale migrant workers and university graduates who live there temporarily or permanently due to soaring housing prices. Such settlements have become the de facto slums in China.

Land-centred urbanization is rooted in local GDPism, which in turn results in aggressive developmentalism and excessive investment among local governments as officials' promotion is linked to local GDP growth. Key local government officials such as mayors have strong incentives to boost GDP growth figures during their tenure in the given locality. GDPism is deeply rooted in their mentality. City building and massive infrastructure construction are important means to achieving this. So is investment in real estate projects. Investment in urban real estate development in China rose to 7,180.4 billion yuan in 2012 from 634.4 billion yuan in 2001, an average annual growth rate of 24.7 per cent between 2001 and 2012. Urban real estate investment has increased particularly sharply since 2008 (Table 12.1).

During the global financial crisis, the urban real estate and infrastructure sectors accounted for nearly half of the four trillion yuan stimulus package announced by the central government (Table 12.2). Since 2009, urban investment has been used as a key means to boost domestic economic activities and offset the negative impact of global economic downturn.

Table 12.1 Fixed asset investment in urban real estate development in China, 1997–2011

Year	Urban Real Estate Development (billion yuan)	Total Investment in Fixed Assets (billion yuan)	Real Estate as Percentage of Total Fixed Assets Investment (%)
1997	317.8	2,494.1	12.7
1998	361.4	2,840.6	12.7
1999	410.3	2,985.5	13.7
2000	498.4	3,291.8	15.1
2001	634.4	3,721.4	17.0
2002	779.1	4,350.0	17.9
2003	1,015.4	5,556.7	18.3
2004	1,315.8	7,047.7	18.3
2005	1,590.9	8,877.4	17.9
2006	1,942.3	10,999.8	17.7
2007	2,528.9	13,732.4	18.4
2008	3,120.3	17,282.8	18.1
2009	3,624.2	22,459.9	16.1
2010	4,825.9	25,168.4	19.2
2011	6,179.7	31,148.5	19.8
2012	7,180.4	37,469.5	19.2

Source: China Statistical Yearbook 2013

Note: The data are taken at the national level.

Table 12.2 Breakdown of the state's four trillion yuan stimulus package by sector

Sector	Investment (billion yuan)	As a Percentage of Total 4-Trillion Yuan Stimulus Package (%)
Affordable and low-rental housing and other real estate construction	400	10.0
Urban infrastructure (e.g. railways, airports, roads, power grids and plants)	1,500	37.5
Rural infrastructure	370	9.2
Health care, education and cultural facilities	150	3.7
Ecological and environmental protection	210	5.2
Innovation, economic restructuring and industrial upgrading	370	9.2
Reconstruction of areas hit by the Wenchuan earthquake in Sichuan province	1,000	25.2
Total	4,000	100

Source: National Development and Reform Commission of China, 2009[7]

Local governments' huge debt burden

Urban infrastructure and housing construction is costly and requires huge investment from the state. The huge spending is mostly derived from borrowed money. In many cities, the debt situation has already spun out of control. What is lacking is a proper debt risk monitoring system. Borrowing from either banks or private channels to pay off old debt has become a common phenomenon. For example, Ordos is believed to be shouldering a 300 billion yuan debt, while its annual fiscal revenue is merely 80 billion yuan.

The IMF has warned that the heavy reliance on credit and investment is eroding local governments' fiscal strength. According to an IMF estimation in 2013, the "augmented" local government debt reached over 45 per cent of GDP in 2012.[8] As shown in Figure 12.2, China's public sector debt was around 46 per cent of GDP in 2012.

Local government debt has risen sharply since 2008. Under the 1994 fiscal law, the local governments are not allowed to directly borrow money from banks or issue bonds. Many local government circumvent this restriction by setting up local government-run financing vehicles (LGFVs, 地方政府融资平台) to fund local infrastructure projects, including roads, bridges, power plants, railways, and government-subsidized and low rental housing construction. Local governments so far have set up more than 10,000 LGFVs. These investment companies use land and small initial capital as collaterals to secure bank loans or issue bonds to directly finance local infrastructure construction. Many of these projects are unplanned for and linked to official corruption and other malpractices. If the issue of local government debt is not properly addressed, it could present a systemic risk to China.

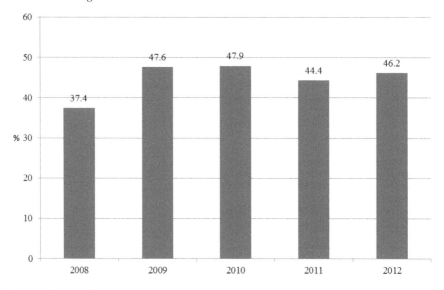

Figure 12.2 Public sector debt as a percentage of GDP in China
Source: IMF, 2013

In July 2013, the central government instructed the National Audit Office (NAO) to start a nationwide audit on local government debt. This unusual move by Beijing reflects the severity of the problem and the urgent need for solutions. The NAO report in June 2013 provided a rare glimpse of the real size of the local government liability. The NAO audited 36 provincial and municipal governments, covering 903 government departments and affiliated organizations, and 223 LGFVs. Debts of 36 local governments were in excess of 3.8 trillion yuan by 2012, up by 13 per cent from that in 2010. As shown in Figure 12.3, 78.1 per cent of this debt was in the form of bank loans, while 12.1 percent consisted of bonds.

This local government debt includes direct and indirect liabilities, and guaranteed debt. If guaranteed loans are taken into account, 16 local governments have a ratio of outstanding debt to individual annual fiscal revenue of above 100 per cent. Meanwhile, 20 local governments registered a ratio of required repayments of principal and interest payments against individual annual fiscal income of above 20 per cent. Of 223 LGFVs, the income of 151 fell short of the debt repayment requirement in 2012.[9] This implies that nearly 70 per cent of state-run finance vehicles do not have the capacity to pay off their debt, which is an ominous statistic for China.

In spite of this deficiency, local governments such as Ordos are still expected to pay off their debt when their government revenue from land sales increases. This shows the overreliance on off-budget revenue as a source of income.

A booming property market and high land premiums are thus important to local government revenue. So is the construction of infrastructure projects which local governments believe could help generate cash flow to service their debt. However, the economic viability of many newly built infrastructure projects is still an issue.

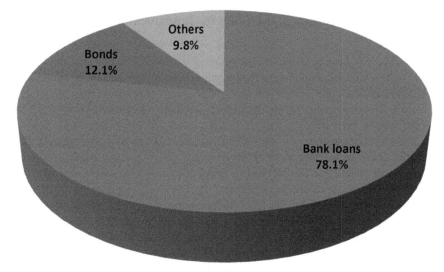

Figure 12.3 Breakdown of local government debt by source (per cent)
Source: NAO, 2013

What worsens the situation was when China's economic growth slows, the demand for undeveloped land is likely to fall as well. Land sales revenue for local governments has also plummeted after the central government has implemented policies to curtail housing speculation and tighten control over housing prices in 2011.

Compared to the same period of 2011, the land transfer revenue for 300 Chinese cities dropped nearly 40 per cent to 652 billion yuan in the first half of 2012.[10] The falling housing prices and land sales revenue will potentially trigger a debt crisis for the local governments.

The central government is apparently aware of the mounting hidden local government debt and has singled it out as one of the main challenges to the sustenance of national economic growth. However, officially, the central authority has insisted that the local government debt situation is still under control and that the cities are unlikely to default. Shang Fulin, president of China's Banking Regulatory Commission, said the overall risk of local government debt is manageable and the repayment of most debts is guaranteed with assets.[11]

In theory, China can transfer state-owned assets to deal with local government debt and the central government can allow local governments to refinance their debts by issuing bonds through the capital market. In general, China's balance sheet is still healthy; the debt-to-GDP ratio is roughly 65 per cent and it can cover all public debt and contingent liabilities. The central government's relatively strong fiscal position, reflected in the fiscal revenue increase of 25 per cent to 10.4 trillion yuan in 2011,[12] is due to prudent fiscal management.

Soaring local government debt calls for fundamental fiscal reform

Evidently, the ghost cities are on the brink of bankruptcy. Given that the banks may tighten credit and not extend repayment deadlines for credit ratings that have been downgraded, these cities will face a serious capital crunch. Fitch, one of the world's top three credit rating companies, cut China's long-term local currency debt rating in April 2013.[13]

There is concern about the ability of local authorities to pay off their debt liabilities. Some cash-strapped local governments will eventually default on debt repayments unless the central government bails them out, which will place a heavy burden on the central government.

There is thus a need for the local governments to exercise control over land sales and clamp down on loan borrowing through its self-run finance vehicles and for the central government to regulate local governments and make them responsible for mitigating debt risk and improving their fiscal management. This however poses a dilemma. Less borrowing implies less investment and eventually slower economic growth at the national level.

To solve its local government debt problems, China may have to replace its outdated system of tax and revenue sharing between central and local governments with a system that guarantees that local governments have sufficient financial resources to carry out infrastructure construction and provide social services.

Local governments would have to align expenditure with revenue. Table 12.3 shows a serious mismatch between local governments' revenue and expenditure. The problem has worsened since the implementation of the new fiscal law in 1994. The revenue of the central government had risen dramatically from 95.8 billion yuan in 1993 to 5,617.5 billion yuan in 2012. The ratio of central government revenue to the national total had gone on an upward swing to 49.4 per cent by 2011 from 22 per cent in 1993. The percentage for local governments on the other hand had dwindled from 78 per cent in 1993 to 50.6 per cent in 2011.

The 1994 fiscal reform has centralized fiscal power in favour of the central government by allocating it with the majority of tax revenue (e.g. VAT), substantially increasing central government's share of the national total. While the reform has enriched the coffers of the central government, it has made local governments a pauper, leaving them with no choice but to rely on off-budgetary revenue such as land transfer premiums as a main source of local revenue.

What worsens the matter was the ill-defined division of expenditure responsibilities between central and local governments. The sharp decline in local government revenue was associated with a dramatic increase in local government expenditure. The ratio of local government expenditure increased to 85.1 per cent by 2012 from 71.7 per cent in 1993, while the percentage of central government expenditure decreased to 14.9 per cent from 28.3 per cent during the same period.

The fall in local government revenue however does not align with a fall in mandated local government expenditure. The central government has continued to assign more expenditure responsibilities to local governments; for example, since

Table 12.3 Revenue and expenditure of central and local governments and as a percentage of national government revenue

Year	Revenue				Expenditure			
	Central Government (billion yuan)	Local Governments (billion yuan)	Ratio of Central Government Revenue to National Government Revenue (%)	Ratio of Local Governments' Revenue to National Government Revenue (%)	Central Government (billion yuan)	Local Governments (billion yuan)	Ratio of Central Government Expenditure to National Government Expenditure (%)	Ratio of Local Governments' Expenditure to National Government Expenditure (%)
1990	99.2	194.5	33.8	66.2	100.4	207.9	32.6	67.4
1991	93.8	221.1	29.8	70.2	109.1	229.6	32.2	67.8
1992	98.0	250.4	28.1	71.9	117.0	257.2	31.3	68.7
1993	95.8	339.1	22.0	78.0	131.2	333.0	28.3	71.7
1994	290.7	231.2	55.7	44.3	175.4	403.8	30.3	69.7
1995	325.7	298.6	52.2	47.8	199.5	482.8	29.2	70.8
1996	366.1	374.7	49.4	50.6	215.1	578.6	27.1	72.9
1997	422.7	442.4	48.9	51.1	253.3	670.1	27.4	72.6
1998	489.2	498.4	49.5	50.5	312.6	767.3	28.9	71.1
1999	584.9	559.5	51.1	48.9	415.2	903.5	31.5	68.5
2000	698.9	640.6	52.2	47.8	552.0	1,036.7	34.7	65.3
2001	858.3	780.3	52.4	47.6	576.8	1,313.5	30.5	69.5
2002	1,038.9	851.5	55.0	45.0	677.2	1,528.1	30.7	69.3
2003	1,186.5	985.0	54.6	45.4	742.0	1,723.0	30.1	69.9
2004	1,450.3	1,189.3	54.9	45.1	789.4	2,059.3	27.7	72.3
2005	1,654.9	1,510.1	52.3	47.7	877.6	2,515.4	25.9	74.1
2006	2,045.7	1,830.4	52.8	47.2	999.1	3,043.1	24.7	75.3
2007	2,774.9	2,357.3	54.1	45.9	1,144.2	3,833.9	23.0	77.0
2008	3,268.1	2,865.0	53.3	46.7	1,334.4	4,924.8	21.3	78.7
2009	3,591.6	3,260.3	52.4	47.6	1,525.6	6,104.4	20.0	80.0

(Continued)

Table 12.3 (Continued)

Year	Revenue				Expenditure			
	Central Government (billion yuan)	Local Governments (billion yuan)	Ratio of Central Government Revenue to National Government Revenue (%)	Ratio of Local Governments' Revenue to National Government Revenue (%)	Central Government (billion yuan)	Local Governments (billion yuan)	Ratio of Central Government Expenditure to National Government Expenditure (%)	Ratio of Local Governments' Expenditure to National Government Expenditure (%)
2010	4,248.8	4,061.3	51.1	48.9	1,599.0	7,388.4	17.8	82.2
2011	5,132.7	5,254.7	49.4	50.6	1,651.4	9,273.4	15.1	84.9
2012	5,617.5	6,107.8	47.9	52.1	1,876.5	1,071.9	14.9	85.1

Source: China Statistical Yearbook 2013, p. 328

Note: The expenditure of central and local governments refers to the expenditure disbursed by the central government and local governments only.

1994, local governments have to take responsibility for public security, public housing, urban and rural community affairs, compulsory education, social security and health care and other general public service provision.[14] This mismatch between local government revenue and expenditure is unsustainable.

The Chinese government has to reorientate its urbanization model, currently characterized by rural-to-urban converted land, and city and town buildings. It could perhaps look at urbanizing rural people by establishing a unified and equal system of social service provision across both rural and urban areas. Rural-urban integration could also be facilitated by reforming the *hukou* system. Besides ensuring the growth of towns and cities, the urbanization of people through rural migration to urban areas would also be necessary. The experience of Chengdu in this endeavour could be drawn upon by other regions.

Notes

1 "Tall order in Ordos: giving a ghost city life", *Caixin*, 30 August 2012, http://english. caixin.com/2012-08-30/100430825_all.html (accessed 25 September 2013)
2 Zhou Zhihua. (7 February 2013). "Rural land development in China: practices and problems", *EAI Background Brief*, No. 790, National University of Singapore.
3 Li Shantong. (2013). "Urbanization as China's new engine of future growth", paper presented at the International Conference "Urbanization in China: Challenges and Prospects", organized by the East Asian Institute, National University of Singapore, Singapore, 5–6 September 2013.
4 International Monetary Fund. (2013). "People's Republic of China: 2013 Article IV Consultation", *IMF Country Report No. 13/211*, Washington, DC, pp. 1–57.
5 NBS. (2011). Available online at http://www.stats.gov.cn/tjfx/jdfx/t20110428_402722 238.htm (accessed 27 September 2013)
6 *China Statistical Yearbook 2012*; construction of some of the sites earmarked for urban construction may not have started.
7 Available online at http://www.ndrc.gov.cn/xwzx/xwtt/t20090521_280383.htm (accessed 30 September 2013)
8 International Monetary Fund (2013).
9 *"36 ge difangzhengfu benji zhengfuxing zhaiwu shenji jieguo"* (The 2013 NAO audit report on 36 local government debt), National Audit Office of China, 10 June 2013, http://www.audit.gov.cn/n1992130/n1992150/n1992500/3291665.html (accessed 27 September 2013)
10 "Fiscal crunch time in the nation's capitals", *Caixin*, 28 August 2012, http://english.cai xin.com/2012-08-28/100429795.html?p3 (accessed 26 September 2013)
11 "China's Ordos struggles to repay debt: Xinhua magazine", *Bloomberg News*, 9 July 2013, http://www.bloomberg.com/news/2013-07-08/china-s-ordos-struggles-to-repay-debt-xinhua-magazine.html (accessed 26 September 2013)
12 "Is China next to suffer a debt crisis?" *Forbes*, 28 January 2013, http://www.forbes.com/ sites/kenrapoza/2013/01/28/is-china-next-to-suffer-a-debt-crisis/ (accessed 27 September 2013)
13 "China orders government-debt audit as growth risks rise", *Bloomberg News*, 29 July 2013, http://www.bloomberg.com/news/2013-07-28/china-to-audit-government-borrow ings-as-risks-to-growth-increase.html (accessed 25 September 2013)
14 Qian Jiwei. "Reforming intergovernmental fiscal system in China", *EAI Background Brief No. 808*, National University of Singapore, 11 April 2013.

Index